P9-DWG-227

"There are certainly ample moments of adrenaline and suspense and descriptions of breathtaking natural beauty in his voyages, but it's his thirst for the unknown—the blank spots—that resonated."

THE NEW YORK REVIEW OF BOOKS

"[An] engaging, hazard-strewn account."

NATURE

"It's a wonderful book."

CTV NEWS

PRAISE FOR *ALONE AGAINST THE NORTH*

"Rare insight into the heart and mind of an explorer, and the insatiable hunger for the unknown that both inspires and drives one to the edge. Adam Shoalts, twenty-first-century explorer, calmly describes the things he has endured that would drive most people to despair, or even madness."

COL. CHRIS HADFIELD, astronaut, International Space Station commander

"As gripping to read as it must've been exciting to live!"

LES STROUD, Survivorman

"Adam Shoalts's remarkable solo foray . . . is the kind of incredible effort that fosters legends."

WINNIPEG FREE PRESS

"Shoalts's love of nature, cool professionalism, and almost archaically romantic spirit draw us into his adventures . . . Shoalts is a knowledgeable and observant guide."

QUILL AND QUIRE

"Anyone who thinks exploration is dead should read this book."
JOHN GEIGER, author, CEO of the Royal Canadian
Geographical Society

"The more layers you peel away, the more you begin to see the quick
mind and quiet intensity that helps propel Adam Shoalts."
BRIAN BANKS, *Canadian Geographic*

"It is a story of brutal perseverance and stamina,
which few adventurers could equal."
JOE PATSTONE, *Life in Quebec Magazine*

"Shoalts is a fearless adventurer . . .
Alone Against the North is a rip-roaring yarn."
THE GREAT CANADIAN BUCKET LIST

"While the book is a nail-biting chronicle of polar-bear encounters,
brutal swarms of black flies, and surprise tumbles down waterfalls,
Shoalts also vividly describes an area of the country
most of us will never witness."
METRO (Toronto)

PRAISE FOR *A HISTORY OF CANADA IN TEN MAPS*

"It's an epic journey . . . Shoalts has done an elegant job of . . . reminding
us of the vast and brooding influence of geography on our history."
GLOBE AND MAIL

"Shoalts analyzes early maps in order to paint a picture of the land
that would become a nation, bringing its earliest stories, voices,
and battles to life. Combining geography, cartography, history, and
anthropology, Shoalts leaves no stone unturned."
CBC

"A brilliant book."

"[A] marvel . . . If you like maps, you'll like this book; if you like both maps and crisply recounted Canadian history, you'll love it. Shoalts . . . takes you inside [explorers'] heads as they face fear, doubt, and despair in tandem with cold, starvation, and rebellious wanting-to-turn-back companions . . . Canadian history writ well."

"A masterful approach to mapping Canada."

"[O]ne fine book perfectly written for the armchair adventurer."

BEYOND THE TREES

ALSO BY ADAM SHOALTS

A History of Canada in Ten Maps
Alone Against the North

BEYOND THE TREES

A JOURNEY ALONE
ACROSS CANADA'S ARCTIC

ADAM SHOALTS

PENGUIN

an imprint of Penguin Canada, a division of Penguin Random House Canada Limited

Penguin Canada
320 Front Street West, Suite 1400, Toronto, Ontario M5V 3B6, Canada

Originally published in hardcover by Allen Lane, an imprint of Penguin Random
House Canada Limited, in 2019.

Published in this edition, 2020

1 2 3 4 5 6 7 8 9 10

LIBRARY AND ARCHIVES CANADA CATALOGUING IN PUBLICATION
Title: Beyond the trees : alone across Canada's Arctic / Adam Shoalts.
Names: Shoalts, Adam, 1986- author.
Description: Includes index.
Identifiers: Canadiana 20190104759 | ISBN 9780735236851 (softcover)
Subjects: LCSH: Shoalts, Adam, 1986—Travel—Canada, Northern. | LCSH: Canada,
    Northern—Description
    and travel.
Classification: LCC FC3205.5 .S56 2020 | DDC 917.1904/7—dc23

Cover and interior design: Jennifer Griffiths
Cover photographs: (landscape) Chuck Brill; (clouds) Matthew Smith / Unsplash

Printed and bound in the United States of America

www.penguinrandomhouse.ca

 Penguin
Random House
PENGUIN CANADA

To Aleksia

CONTENTS

Preface 1

1 PLANS *5*

2 LAND OF THE MIDNIGHT SUN *19*

3 THROUGH THE MOUNTAINS *29*

4 UP THE MACKENZIE *41*

5 EASTWARD BOUND *57*

6 INTO THE SWAMP *68*

7 ACROSS AN INLAND SEA *87*

8 THE ICE LABYRINTH *99*

9 GHOSTS OF THE PAST *115*

10 CROSSING THE DIVIDE *128*

11 THROUGH THE DISMAL LAKES *144*

12 THE SERPENT'S COIL *156*

13 GIFTS FROM ABOVE *167*

14 LAKES BEYOND COUNT *181*

15 ON ROCKY SHORES *192*

16 OF WIND AND WAVES *200*

17 IN THE LAND OF THE MUSKOX *213*

18 CANYON COUNTRY *220*

19 DOWN THE THELON *235*

20 THE STORMS OF SEPTEMBER *247*

21 JOURNEY'S END *256*

Afterword 267

Acknowledgments 269

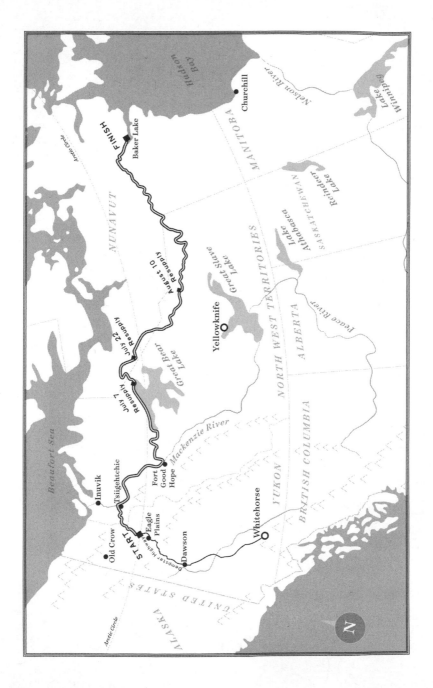

PREFACE

Have ever you stood where the silences brood,
And vast the horizons begin,
At the dawn of the day to behold far away
The goal you would strive for and win?
ROBERT SERVICE, "The Land of Beyond"

The rock was ancient, old as time, the oldest rock on the planet. Not a patch of soil could be seen among the vast heaps of boulders that lay scattered far inland from the lake's frigid shore. Only that desolate grey rock, cold, primordial, unwelcoming to the traveller. Its unyielding surface, blasted with the frosts of a hundred million winters and covered in slow-growing lichens, would not permit a tent to be staked down—and with the arctic gales no tent could last long unanchored. Despairingly, I swung my paddle again into the icy water, the fierce wind driving me into the landward side. I had to find somewhere to make camp; the gusts were growing too strong to continue.

Ahead on the north shore, the one I'd been tracing out in my canoe, there seemed to be a small bit of grass between the ancient boulders. It was perhaps not what most people would consider an attractive campsite, but to me, just now, it looked inviting. I headed for it. Shoals jutted into the water, forcing me to paddle into the wind to get around them. It was fall now; the winds were fierce and steady and frost was in the air. Winter would soon be on its way. When at last I came to the grass amid the rocks, the first such place I'd seen for many inhospitable kilometres, I made camp and staked down my tent, securing it with extra guy lines.

Then I carried up my canoe—worn, battered, almost paper thin from months of grinding against the rocks and ice floes—and overturned it beside the tent. Just a little longer, I thought, looking at my old friend, if you can last just a little longer without puncturing, we can finish our journey. The wind's howling grew louder, whipping up whitecaps that smashed into the barren shore. I was thankful to have found this lonely spot among the rocks when I did.

Across the lake's turbulent water rose a range of gracefully sloped mountains, their lower flanks a brilliant red and orange, the fall colours having transformed the slender leaves of the arctic willow and of dwarf birch, bearberries, cloudberries, and other tundra plants. A flock of snow geese passed high overhead. They seemed to only accentuate the emptiness of the landscape. In the past month I'd seen one other human being: a bush pilot who'd briefly resupplied me on a deep, cold lake, one of tens of thousands of such lakes that lay scattered across the central Arctic—so many that no one has ever counted them all.

I'd heard of canoeing parties being windbound on these vast stormy lakes for weeks at a stretch. It was not an encouraging thought. Ahead of me, to the east, lay powerful rapids; unlucky travellers had been known to drown in them. And if I were to complete my journey I'd have to navigate them late in the season, when the weather was bad.

That night the wind blew ceaselessly, shaking my little tent as I lay huddled inside. I pinned my hopes of escape on the morning calm. But the dawn brought no respite; the skies were grey and dismal, the gales as unrelenting as ever. All day I waited anxiously for a break in the wind that would enable me to launch my canoe and leave the point I'd camped on. None came. The frigid gusts seemed only to grow stronger, howling eerily across the lifeless tundra.

A second night passed with me still stranded in the same spot. Growing more anxious, I watched as yet another day slipped away without any break in the wind and waves, which made paddling impossible and me trapped on that rock-strewn point. And each day lost, I knew, was a day closer to winter's onset.

× 1 ×

PLANS

My passion was paddling wild rivers and lakes, and wandering silently through quiet forests, indulging my curiosity about plants, trees, and the mystery and enchantment of the natural world. Adventures I'd had and would continue to do so, because it came with the terrain of wandering alone through wild places. But I didn't anticipate making any particularly long journeys in the Arctic.

Then, in the spring of 2010, I happened to visit a local nature club in the Short Hills—a region of wooded, rolling hills, tumbling streams, and waterfalls south of Lake Ontario—which put in motion a chain of events that led to my becoming windbound alone on an arctic lake. No doubt that's a common occurrence stemming from nature club meetings, and a prudent reason to avoid them. As far as nature clubs went, this one had a youngish membership, the average age being barely more than mid-seventies.

It was there at the nature club's meeting hall, after my presentation on canoe tripping had wrapped up, that I first heard the word "sesqui-centennial" used in a sentence. I'd been chatting with a white-haired man, a retired professor of chemistry.

"Well, you know," he said, "2017 is going to be Canada's sesquicen-tennial."

"Oh," I said, nodding. In fact I hadn't known this.

He kept looking at me, apparently awaiting a further response.

I wasn't sure what "sesquicentennial" even meant.

"The 150th anniversary of Canada's Confederation," he elaborated.

"That's right," I replied.

"It's sure to be a big deal. Huge celebrations," he said with emphasis. "I remember the Centennial celebrations back in 1967. We went to Expo 67 in Montreal for that. 'Course, that would've been well before your time."

The connection between my canoe trips and a 150th anniversary, which was still seven years away, wasn't immediately obvious to me.

"It'll be a very big occasion," the old man resumed. "Have you given any thought to doing something special for it?"

"Er, no, I haven't."

He shook his head, evidently dismayed at the lamentable failure of my education. "Back in '67 I remember there were people who canoed across Canada. Maybe you should think of doing something similar in 2017? There's bound to be lots of funding opportunities and groups interested in that kind of thing."

"Well, anything's possible," I said.

Still, 2017 seemed a long way off, and I thought it unlikely that something as obscure as a sesquicentennial would attract much notice beyond the ordinary July 1 fireworks. I soon put it out of my mind and returned to paddling wild rivers, observing plants and animals, wandering the woods, and, for a while, pursuing a passion I'd developed for the study of rare mosses found on certain rocks, especially the species *ptychomitrium incurvum*.

But a few years later, the old professor's supposition proved correct. As 2017 neared, "Canada 150" seemed to crop up more and more in conversations and news stories.

A great many plans were underway. There would be public infrastructure projects. Free access to national parks. A ship travelling around Canada with a hundred and fifty passengers chosen from across the country. Trees planted in every province and territory. Tulips bedded in Ottawa's public gardens (300,000 of them, a unique species) that resembled the country's flag. An actual flag (a massive one) raised to the top of a pole (fourteen storeys high). Eventually, the federal government would fund nearly six thousand of these Canada 150 initiatives.

Meanwhile, over three years had passed since my encounter with the old professor at the nature club. I recalled what he'd said about the Centennial canoe trip. Maybe, I thought to myself, another cross-Canada canoe journey might, in some small way, inspire people to care more about the fate of the country's ever-diminishing wild places. I decided to look up what exactly had been done in 1967. It was fortuitous perhaps, that I did so at a time when I was under one of those spells of wanderlust and adventure that had a habit of stealing over me whenever I was shut up inside for too long.

It turned out that ten teams of canoeists had paddled from central Alberta to Montreal. Dubbed "The Centennial Voyageur Canoe Pageant," the journey involved ten people per team; six at a time would paddle on alternating days while the other four rested. The route included stops in cities and towns along the way, where parties and fanfare greeted the paddlers' arrival. By starting east of the Rockies and ending in Montreal, the hardest portages and upstream travel were avoided. When it was all over it took 104 days to complete and covered 5,283 kilometres, ending in celebration at Expo 67.

Now that's a remarkable journey, I thought to myself as I sat in my cluttered study on the ground floor of a rundown Victorian house I rented. And to recreate it fifty years later would be quite a thing. But nowadays, given that Canada's a lot less wild than it was in 1967, I figured somebody could probably retrace that canoe route and stop in at a Tim Hortons every third day. What could I do in 2017 that hadn't already been done?

I stared at the map of Canada on the wall above my desk (a dangerous thing—staring at maps, that is). What if, I wondered, I shifted the canoe route north? Roughly, say, two thousand kilometres north, beyond the trees to the tundra?

Unlike the 1967 route, a canoe journey that far north wouldn't have a line of cities or towns to break up the journey and allow for resupply, not to mention hot showers and human encouragement. Instead of travelling through farmland and cottage country, it'd mean travelling across arctic terrain. The elements would be much harsher, with sub-zero temperatures, snow, bitterly cold winds, shifting ice floes, and probably no Tim Hortons. If something went wrong, help would be far away and a long time coming. To further complicate matters, there was no easy or obvious water route across the mainland Canadian Arctic. Four major watersheds would have to be crossed, meaning a lot of overland and arduous upstream travel would be required.

I suppose it was a mad idea. On the other hand, it was exactly the kind of undertaking that appealed to me, or at least appealed to me in my more adventurous moods. After all, as I often remarked to myself, you only live once.

But such a project could never come to fruition without consider-able funding. And it was one thing to daydream of an expedition from the comfort of my desk chair, with maps spread out before me and a steaming cup of tea at hand, and quite another to translate it into reality. It seemed unlikely that I'd ever be able to afford such an undertaking. Reluctantly, I set it aside as one of the many hypo-thetical projects I'd like to one day attempt if I had the funds. In the meantime, I went back to my rare moss. That, at least, didn't require any money.

Some months later, in November 2013, I found myself in Ottawa having a conversation with some of the staff at the Royal Canadian Geographical Society, a non-profit organization devoted to modern exploration and geographic education. I'd led a few expeditions for the Society focused on mapping northern rivers, and was now hear-ing the first inklings of possibly doing something special for the "150th" in 2017, perhaps involving the Arctic, or maybe a great jour-ney. Naturally I was enthused, but in my excitement I think I con-flated their two ideas into a single project.

"You're thinking of a journey across Canada's mainland Arctic by canoe?" I blurted out.

There was a moment of hesitation and confusion in the room, as that wasn't exactly what anyone had in mind.

"Is that possible?" asked one of *Canadian Geographic*'s editors.

"Well," I said, slouching back in my chair, "possibly it is. Hard to say. It'd be difficult. Most of the rivers drain north to the coast rather than east–west or west–east. Anyway, it'd be enormously expensive. Air charter, resupplies, et cetera."

"Hmm, actually that might not be a problem," said Gilles, the publisher. "There'll likely be funding opportunities for 2017."

That was a change. I was used to doing expeditions on shoestring budgets, with gear I fashioned myself or picked up second-hand.

"Well, I'll have to think about it. Do some research. I'll get back to you," I replied.

We adjourned our little meeting, with the notion that we'd follow up at some unspecified date. After all, it was still only 2013. 2017 seemed rather far off and hypothetical.

Over the following weeks I mulled over the idea. Now that I was actually compelled to come up with a plan and a budget, I had to look at things in more detail. I studied maps and atlases and satellite images, consulted with pilots in the Arctic about costs, and sketched out various plans. And I came to a disheartening conclusion—I was unlikely to succeed. No matter how I calculated things, I couldn't see any realistic plan that would allow for a long enough ice-free canoeing season to get even halfway across Canada's mainland Arctic territories on a west–east axis, let alone the whole thing. Everything I researched was discouraging. There were the August snowstorms, the ice that persisted on lakes well into July, and the polar bears that ate canoeists. Not to mention a lack of navigable water routes that actually lead east–west or west–east across the Arctic. Much of the rivers would have to be navigated upstream, against the current. A five-month journey seemed optimistic, and that would entail travelling in the shoulder season with plunging temperatures. Of course, I was no stranger to any of these things. But the odds were not good. I suppose if I'd been an ancient Roman I'd have looked at the bird signs, said it boded ill, and concluded that the gods did not approve of the idea.

Fortunately, I wasn't an ancient Roman.

So I decided to go forward with the plan. After all, at least it seemed I wouldn't have to worry about the funding. And that certainly counted for a lot.

Then, as fate would have it, a few months later I found out that the Royal Canadian Geographical Society couldn't promise any money. The funding they'd hoped to obtain through a strategic partnership never materialized. Such are the vagaries of non-profits.

That threw a wrench in my plans. To gamble with your life is one thing; to gamble with your money quite another. As a rule, I didn't do that—one needs standards, after all. The cost of such an Arctic journey spanning five months would run around $35,000, much of it toward air charter. An impossible sum for me to come up with on my own. Maybe, I wondered, I should focus my energies on something more manageable for 2017. I might, for instance, do a study on rare moss. Somehow, though, that didn't quite capture the imagination in the same way.

I needed to do some serious thinking. Whenever I was confronted with some momentous decision, I preferred to go where my mind was clearest—to the place I knew best, where I'd grown up, the woods of my childhood. It was a large forest south of the little rural village of Fenwick, Ontario, made up of ancient oaks, maples, ash, beech, and cherry, and intersected with swamps of black water, brambles, and sarsaparilla. It was there in those woods surrounding my family home where I'd first learned to recognize trees—to know them, along with the plants and the birds and the other wild things. It was where as a child I'd slept in shelters cheerfully built during bright days, and huddled in during fearful nights as I listened to the wind in the swaying branches of the great oaks and sassafras. In these familiar woods I'd known and loved, where I'd fished in creeks, slept under the stars, and wandered by night and day, I felt sure I'd know what to do.

And out there, among the oaks and sycamores, the ferns and sarsaparillas, the nuthatches and woodpeckers, my heart felt the pull of wild places. Something seemed to whisper to me that I ought to attempt the Arctic journey in 2017, regardless of the odds. I also felt something else with terrible clarity—that if I wanted to wander across a vast wild, the time to do it was now. It might be a last chance to make a journey like this across a portion of the earth's surface that had largely remained in its natural wild state, undeveloped by humans, one of the few places where large animals still roam free and it's possible to wander for months without seeing another human being.

So that settled it. I resolved that in three years' time I'd attempt my journey across the Arctic, come what may. I put this in writing as soon as I returned home, which was a custom of mine when vowing to tackle some daunting prospect (it's less painful than making blood oaths). I didn't know if I'd succeed on such a journey; I didn't even know the details: what route I'd follow, when exactly I'd start, or whether I'd be doing it alone or with companions. But I'd made up my mind to try.

Slowly, as the months unfolded, I began to prepare. I tested out various gear and clothing and researched different routes, average ice melts, weather patterns, and past trip reports. The challenge was to design a route and a stratagem that would allow me the greatest ice-free canoeing season at minimal financial cost.

My best chance seemed to be to start in the mountains of the west, in the northern Yukon. The ice breakup is earlier there than in the east, near Hudson Bay, so starting in the west would let me get my canoe in the water sooner. In the west is also Canada's most northern highway, a narrow gravel road known as the Dempster that winds through the Yukon's wilderness. It would provide a convenient jumping-off point for an expedition. (It would also be the only road I'd encounter on my entire journey.)

After hiking through the Richardson Mountains along the Dempster I'd reach the Mackenzie River, the world's thirteenth longest river. Much would depend on when its ice broke up. Its annual spring breakup varied, ranging from early May to mid-June, and a difference of a few weeks could make or break my expedition. When the Mackenzie broke free of its winter ice, I'd start canoeing. The problem was, following the Mackenzie's winding course downriver wouldn't help me. That'd merely take me out to the icebergs of the Beaufort Sea. Instead I'd have to somehow go the opposite direction, *upriver* on the Mackenzie, against its powerful current.

Whenever I shared this idea of travelling upriver on the Mackenzie, the response I heard from fellow canoeists acquainted with the North was, "Are you insane?"

It was a question I'd become accustomed to hearing.

And that would be the easier part of my journey. Once I'd ascended the Mackenzie for a distance of some three hundred and forty kilometres, the real work would begin. I'd have to strike east, laboriously working my way against the current up the mysterious Hare Indian River, of which little was known. From its headwaters I'd have to undertake a series of long portages, spanning several kilometres each, over difficult terrain with no trail to follow. I hoped these would bring me within sight of the vast, icy waters of Great Bear Lake—the world's eighth largest lake, making it larger than two of the Great Lakes. I planned to paddle across it in my fifteen-foot canoe.

If I could cross Great Bear, more hauling, wading, and dragging would await me on its eastern shores, up more rivers against the current. This would take me northward in the direction of the windswept Dismal Lakes. A series of long portages would be needed to reach these wild lakes set amid mountains. From there I could continue working my way east until reaching the fabled Coppermine River—a river with a current far more powerful than the Mackenzie's. Once again I'd have to fight my way up it, battling whitewater, canyons, and rocks that might puncture my canoe. If I could canoe the

Coppermine in reverse—a prospect that in comparison made paddling up the Mackenzie sound perfectly sensible—the next task would entail lengthy portages and paddles across the big icy lakes of the central Arctic.

From there I'd cross into the Hudson Bay watershed. Now the rivers would be flowing east. My plan was to paddle down the Hanbury River, with its deep canyons and thunderous waterfalls, to the Thelon River, which would bring me to another series of large, stormy arctic lakes, each of which I'd have to paddle across. By that time it'd be late in the season—well into September—with frost and fierce winds sweeping off Hudson Bay.

Finally, with any luck, I'd descend the last section of the Thelon and arrive in the little community of Baker Lake, Nunavut—the first human settlement anywhere in this vast route since the banks of the Mackenzie River thousands of kilometres to the west.

In total, including the doubling back I'd have to do on all the portages, it worked out to a distance of almost four thousand kilometres. That is, nearly four thousand kilometres across the largest expanse of wilderness, free of roads and cities, yet remaining in the terrestrial world outside of Antarctica.

Next I had to decide whether it was better to attempt the journey alone or with a partner. It's true that travelling alone is considered more dangerous, even reckless. But I had a natural affinity for solitary wandering, and I liked the freedom and simplicity that came with it. On the other hand, there was no question having a partner would make things easier and minimize risks. Two paddlers could travel twice as fast, or nearly so. Labour could be divided—one person could make the fires while the other set up the tent, a useful thing when a storm threatens. When needing to track a canoe with ropes up treacherous stretches of rapids, or around boulders when the current is strong and dangerous, two people are nearly essential. And there'd be two sets of eyes to watch for any hazards, like hidden rocks or hungry bears. In the case of some unforeseen medical emergency, two people would also make things much safer. But experience had taught me that it was better to go alone than to undertake a venture with someone who was only half committed to it.

And who'd wish to commit to such a journey anyway? Most of my past expedition partners I knew wouldn't be able to take the time required. They'd gradually settled down with lives, careers, and families, and could now seldom get away for more than a week or two. In the three years since making my vow in the forest, I'd undertaken many expeditions independent of what I had in mind for 2017, and these ventures had brought me into contact with some excellent expedition partners.

There was my old friend Travis, an elite athlete and two-time silver medallist in the world lacrosse championships with the Iroquois Nationals, who could laugh at adversity while trudging up an arctic stream in the icy domain of polar bears or while in the teeth of an arctic gale. That first summer after I'd made my resolution, the two of us canoed a nameless High Arctic river some five hundred kilometres north of the Northwest Passage. After that adventure, Travis and I spent time climbing snowy mountains together in the Adirondacks.

Whereas Travis and I were old friends of more than ten years, my other expedition partner during these summers was a person I'd never previously met before plunging off with. Nearly thirty years my senior, Chuck was an American, an avid angler and outdoorsman who'd once raced canoes back in the 1980s. He was sensible, congenial, and undaunted whenever confronted with some horrid journey. He joined me to trace an obscure river to its headwaters deep in trackless muskeg in the subarctic. There, in polar bear territory—over a hundred miles from the nearest human settlement, in a swamp home to the highest concentration of blood-sucking insects on earth—our friendship blossomed. The next summer, 2016, Chuck and I reunited for another journey, this time in the Northwest Territories, where we headed beyond the Arctic Circle to the windswept tundra in order to trace another winding river to its source.

Either Travis or Chuck would make an ideal partner for a journey across Canada's Arctic. But Chuck, I knew, wouldn't be able to take anything like five months off from his career and his family. He also said that, all things considered, it might not be wise to walk long distances over rough terrain with a heavy pack in polar bear territory. He was sensible like that. (Chuck did, however, offer his help when it came time to shuttle myself and my canoe up to the Arctic Circle.) As for Travis, when I told him of my idea for an Arctic journey in 2017, he was tempted. Very tempted. But Travis also had a steady job, a mortgage, a dog, and a girlfriend. These things all made a potentially five-month expedition difficult. Ultimately, he concluded he couldn't commit to it.

In contrast, I had little to hold me back. My own beloved dog, Riley, who'd been my companion and shadow, had died three years earlier; I'd never had another. My income, such as it was, came from grants for my doctoral research plus whatever I made from writing—things that allowed me to wander. My rent was seven hundred a month for the ground floor of an old decrepit house in St. Catharines. It was enough for my landlords that I paid the rent and was quiet; they didn't ask questions about my prolonged absences or the muskox skulls in the backroom. And with Travis and Chuck unavailable and my other past expedition partners tied down, there wasn't anyone else I could see myself spending five months with in the Arctic.

So that settled it. I'd be going alone. The prospect didn't much trouble me, at least not the idea of solitude. But from a practical point of view, one person instead of two would amplify the physical dimension of the journey. To make up for this, I'd need to do some careful strategizing and devise a few novel techniques, especially since I'd be racing against the seasons.

But first I had to confront a more immediate and alarming challenge: coming up with the funds. Though I'd heard about grants being handed out for Canada 150 projects, I'd also heard they were reserved for groups, not individuals. In any case, it seemed doubtful that a project like mine would win government funding. So, in the spirit of the times, I opted for crowdfunding. This was not something I'd had any experience with. My penchant for the woods left me estranged from social media. I didn't have a smartphone, a Twitter account, or an Instagram page. Regardless, eight months before I planned to set off, I launched a GoFundMe page for the expedition. My goal was to raise at least $12,000 of the $35,000 I needed that way, with the remainder (I hoped) coming from sponsorships.

The same month I launched my fundraising page I moved to Sudbury, Ontario. There I spent my days training and prepping for the expedition—rock climbing, skating laps on the city's outdoor oval or on hockey rinks I had all to myself, and ransacking the archives of Laurentian University for old canoe exploration reports and other useful information. Besides this, I took long daily hikes through spruce and pine forests, culminating with scrambles up barren summits of the high rocky hills that envelop the city. From those gloomy peaks, scarred by acid rain, I brooded over my plans for the journey, pondering the challenges to come.

Meanwhile, my fundraising proceeded slowly. Three days after I'd launched my funding page the sum total of donations came in at only $0.00. I didn't find it a particularly encouraging sum.

Then one Theresa, whom I didn't know, broke the ice by donating $25. Soon after a certain Mallory gave $45, then Meg gave $25, and one Cody tossed in another $20. Amazingly, I was up to $115. On the other hand, I'd spent $300 on hiring a graphic design artist to make a poster promoting the expedition. But small donations continued to trickle in: from a couple of Canadian expatriates who wished me well, from an old school classmate, from past archaeological dig colleagues, from readers of my first book (one of whom appended a note to his $10 donation requesting that I write another book, if I should happen to live). Mostly, though, support came from total strangers. By the date of my departure in May, I'd received through my GoFundMe page $5,310 in donations. Minus GoFundMe's handling fees, that left with me with almost $4,800.

In other words, well short of the thirty-five grand I needed. Just as I was beginning to despair, I received an unusual and unexpected phone call. It was from someone I didn't know, someone who promised to fund my entire expedition on one condition—*that I take him with me.* This prospect, camping with a stranger you meet over the internet in exchange for money, was not as appealing as it might sound, given that the individual admitted to having little to no previous canoeing experience. I could foresee all too well where that might lead, so I felt I had no choice but to decline his offer.

That put me back at square one.

Fortunately, much to my surprise, McMaster University's alumni association offered to partly sponsor my journey. I'd done my master's degree at McMaster and was still finishing (from afar) my doctorate there, so I was only too happy to have their support. Then Brock University, where I'd gone as an undergraduate, also offered to sponsor me. Apparently universities considered the image of a penniless adventurer to be an excellent recruiting tool for prospective students. Meanwhile, the outdoor chain MEC (that is Mountain Equipment Co-op) offered to outfit me with gear, clothing, and much of my dried rations. Nova Craft Canoe, a made-in-Canada canoe company based in London, Ontario, built me a custom canoe for the journey and shipped it to Whitehorse. A number of other companies and individuals also made donations of gear or cash toward the expedition.

By April, as the snow started to melt around Sudbury, I was pacing my small rented rooms in an old Depression-era apartment building, anxiously piling up my accumulated gear for the journey: seven watertight plastic barrels crammed with dehydrated energy bars, hundreds of photocopied topographic maps covering my route, more electronics than I used on a daily basis to cover my satellite communications and filming, clothing of various sorts, and my tent, sleeping bag, and assorted waterproof bags. But I was still short of the funds I needed, and I'd run out of outdoor companies I could approach about sponsorship. What was I to do? Time was running out: in less than four weeks I needed to be in the Arctic if I were to get underway when the ice melted. None of the remaining options I could think of were at all encouraging.

Then, out of the blue it seemed, came a generous donation from another stranger—a remarkable woman in British Columbia, who'd read my first book and wanted to assist me in this project. She provided the funds I needed through a donation to the Royal Canadian Geographical Society, and like that, my expedition was a go. The Geographical Society bestowed symbolic support by honouring me with a flag bearing its coat-of-arms. The flag was presented to me at a ceremony in Ottawa by the Society's honorary president, Alex Trebek, who a few readers might also know from his television show *Jeopardy!* He wished me well.

With that, I rolled up the flag and stashed it in my backpack, bid farewell to my friends and family, packed up my gear, and headed to the airport to catch a flight to the Yukon.

× 2 ×

LAND OF THE MIDNIGHT SUN

I arrived in the Yukon on May 13, 2017, but it'd be Mother Nature that would dictate exactly when and where I'd begin my journey. If it was going to be an early spring, I'd launch my journey from the tiny northern community of Old Crow (population about three hundred) on the banks of the Porcupine River, which drains out to the Bering Sea. If it proved to be a late spring and the rivers were still swollen with shifting ice floes, I'd have to begin southeast of there to avoid the ice, in an even smaller community, Eagle Plains (population about nine). In either case, I'd still need the Peel and Mackenzie Rivers to be ice-free by the time I reached them on foot through the Richardson Mountains. Otherwise I'd be stuck waiting for ice to melt.

You might be thinking that if the rivers were still frozen, why not just walk across them? The trouble is, they were in the ice breakup phase, when they're no longer frozen solid enough to safely cross and not yet open enough to traverse by boat. During this period, which can last weeks, large chunks of ice drift swiftly downstream like gigantic jigsaw puzzle pieces—posing hazards to any watercraft. The result is a kind of purgatory in which travel of all kinds is difficult and the crossing of rivers well-nigh impossible. Even today, with modern transportation, this fact remains largely unaltered in the western Arctic. No bridges have ever succeeded in spanning the northern reaches of the great rivers of Canada's far northwest, the Mackenzie,

Peel, and Porcupine. In the long dark winter months snowmobiles ply these frozen arteries of the North; in the summer months, motorboats and canoes. But during the spring breakup these rivers become impassable barriers.

In recent years, with warmer average temperatures, the Yukon's ice breakup seems to be getting earlier and earlier. Partly it was this realization, that the ice-free season in the North was becoming longer and longer, that had led me to think a trans-Arctic canoe journey might be theoretically possible—something that in the past would have been dubious at best. But as luck would have it, by the standards of recent decades, the spring of 2017 did not prove to be an early one. It looked like it'd be an unusually late breakup, which would necessitate starting my journey from Eagle Plains. But with the rivers still clogged with ice, I had time on my hands, so rather than hang around in Whitehorse watching weather reports, I decided to take in the sights of Old Crow.

Old Crow sits tucked away in the northwest corner of the map of Canada, a remote fly-in community of some three hundred people, mostly members of the Gwich'in First Nation. Despite its geographic remoteness, it's connected to Whitehorse by daily commercial flights. I waited there, biding my time while the ice broke up, in an isolated cabin in the woods east of town. The cabin was the home of Betty, a Giwch'in elder in her mid-seventies, who largely shunned town-life in favour of the isolation of her cabin and the company of her two sled dogs, Winston and Vicki. I hadn't known her beforehand, nor had she known me—chance brought us together.

When I'd arrived at the airport, northern hospitality soon made me feel welcome. I was given a ride into town, invited to a barbecue, and offered a place to store my things. Later that day I accompanied a local fellow up the slopes of barren Crow Mountain, a low hill that overlooks the town. He brought his rifle in case we encountered any caribou, but despite some fresh tracks in the melting snows, we saw none. After a few days in town watching the ice drift by, I became restless and decided to see if I could scout conditions farther out. I ended up wandering along the riverbanks for a ways. I'd been hiking through dense thickets of black spruce, fording streams, and scrambling down high bluffs when I unexpectedly came upon a little cabin set deep in the woods, near the banks of the still ice-choked Porcupine River. Two sled dogs were tethered outside and wreaths of smoke were rising upward from a chimney.

I heard the cabin door slowly unlock from the inside, then an elderly woman cautiously peeked out. She had a rifle clenched in her hands.

"Hello," I said. "Sorry to bother you. I was just passing by."

"Oh," the old woman said in a surprised tone. She opened the door wider. "I thought you were a bear."

"No," I replied, "I'm not."

"What are you doing here?"

"Waiting for ice to melt."

Betty invited me in for tea, and before I knew it I'd spent the whole week as her guest, sleeping in her woodshed. At seventy-three years old she still hunted caribou and red squirrels, though age had reduced her mobility. She didn't tend to venture far from home, and during the ice melt was cut off from human contact altogether. I'd only reached her cabin by traversing the ice-clogged Crow River on an inflatable pack raft beneath a bend where the ice had jammed enough to allow for a spot of open water. In fact, Betty informed me, I was the only visitor she'd ever had who'd arrived in that manner. Most people came by motorboat or snowmobile, but none during ice breakup.

For the most part, Betty now chose to live alone. Though to my surprise, she did have an old flip-style cell phone that, amazingly, had reception at her isolated cabin. Her battery had died, and she hadn't any means to recharge it, except on her visits to town. Luckily I had a battery charger, which I offered to her.

We discovered that we had a fair number of overlapping interests, from a love of wilderness and solitude to an enjoyment of old *Reader's Digest* issues (of which she had a collection). While I chopped wood and gathered blocks of ice for her water supply, Betty offered me soup and lemonade and told me stories. Among other things, she recounted her family history, some of the great fishing successes she'd had with her net, her experiences hunting bears and caribou, and feeding whisky-jacks from her hand. Betty also shared some of her wisdom for my upcoming journey. She suggested that for nourishment I try eating the inner bark of willow shoots—in springtime, she said, it was full of nutritious sap— as well as spruce gum, which she collected from the trees around her cabin. Betty also advised that crossing rivers on small pack rafts between ice jams was liable to shorten my life expectancy.

For hours each day outside her cabin I listened to the stream of ice floes, bumping and crashing into each other, making sounds like glass shattering. It was mesmerizing to see them drift swiftly downriver, the sun glinting off thousands of pieces, some large enough to hold stranded, doomed caribou. This went on for days, night and day, so that it seemed extraordinary that so much ice could exist at all—but it was ice coming from hundreds of kilometres of river, all of it breaking up and now drifting in seemingly endless procession downstream like a kind of ice parade. Betty said it was the latest ice breakup she could remember since the 1980s.

Some days I took Betty's dogs, Vicki and Winston, for walks in the encircling subarctic forests, where we met with arctic hares and grouse. Winston seemed to take a particular liking to me. This may have been a result of feeding him half my lunches.

I was surprised by how gravely Betty took the threat of bears. She never went anywhere without a whistle around her neck, and usually her rifle. Her dogs, she said, were to help keep bears away and sound the alarm if any approached. I had the vague idea, sleeping as I did in a small tent for months out of the year in bear territory, that such worries were perhaps overstated. But several times in the night bears did come into the camp. I could hear them outside the woodshed, sniffing around for caribou meat. When the dogs caught wind of them, they'd bark furiously.

One day, when we were sitting by the river watching ice floes drift by, I asked Betty if she'd ever had a problem with grizzlies breaking into her storage shed to steal food.

"Oh, they broke into my house," she replied.

"Into your *house*?" I said.

"They broke the door right in half," she explained.

Betty motioned me to follow her behind the shed, where the discarded door now lay. I was expecting to see some flimsy, rickety old thing. Instead Betty pointed to the mangled remains of a heavy, steel-plated wooden door.

"He just took one paw"—Betty gestured with her arm to imitate a bear swipe—"He folded it right in half." The door was bent over double, the metal plating twisted and curled up like car wreckage. The wood inside the steel plates had been partially ripped out, the grizzly's claw marks plainly etched into it.

Fortunately, Betty hadn't been home at the time. The grizzly ended up gutting the cabin's interior. After that Betty had an electric fence, powered by a car battery, installed around her door and windows, which she turned on each night. Staring down at the ruined door, I reflected that I'd been sleeping in a small shed whose only door was a sheet of tarp. Nevertheless, on my journey I wouldn't be carrying a gun. Travelling as light as possible was an absolute necessity, and anyway, I figured, it must have been the smell of caribou meat that had attracted the bears to the cabin. Betty did give me some dried caribou meat as a gift, but this I ate (with Winston's help) before setting off.

After a week together watching ice floes drift by from atop the high banks of the Porcupine River, it was clear that I'd have to begin my journey from Eagle Plains. Betty wished me well, and asked me to stay in touch once I'd finished my journey.

＊

I returned to Dawson on the next outbound flight. From that ghost-haunted place, rich in lore, I could await Chuck's arrival. He was driving north from Whitehorse with my canoe and the watertight plastic barrels I'd tightly packed with rations. Accompanying Chuck was his friend Mark and some filmmakers who intended to record the start of my journey with a drone along the Dempster Highway.

The Dempster Highway winds like a great ribbon across the northern Yukon, snaking between the awe-inspiring mountains of the Tombstone and Ogilvie ranges as it heads northward beyond the Arctic Circle. It is the only road, as far as roads go, to penetrate the immensity of the Yukon's north, and Canada's only road access to the Arctic Circle. On either side of it, for hundreds of miles, you'll find no other roads, cities, towns, or even mines—only a vast mountainous terrain extending to the horizons. The highway, really only a narrow gravel road, stretches some 740 kilometres from Dawson to Inuvik in the Northwest Territories, partly following a historic dogsled route once used to carry mail between these isolated settlements. Construction began on it in the 1950s, but was soon abandoned. In the 1970s work resumed when it was thought the road might serve as a supply route for oil exploration in the Beaufort Sea. The oil never materialized, but the highway was officially opened in 1978 and named for Sergeant Jack Dempster of the Royal North-West Mounted Police, who'd led dogsled patrols from Dawson to Fort McPherson in the early 1900s.

Our drive along the Dempster took us first through subarctic forest north of Dawson, where the dark spruce woods crowded close to the gravel roadway, hiding their secrets from prying eyes who only drive the road and don't venture beyond it. In places where the road gained elevation, vistas opened up, revealing spruces extending in seemingly endless expanse, covering millions of acres. As we continued north the spruces thinned, aspens appeared in great clusters along the shoulders, and the forests gradually disappeared into meadowlands and wind-swept, jagged mountains, their upper slopes covered in snow.

Our progress north was slowed by a sudden thick snowfall as we passed through the Tombstone Mountains. But by early evening, the sun still high in the sky at these latitudes, our little two-vehicle convoy arrived at the outpost of Eagle Plains. It's the only inhabited place between Dawson and Fort McPherson, if a fluctuating population of six to nine people may be said to qualify as an inhabited place. Opened in 1978, Eagle Plains was established as a private venture to service and maintain the Dempster Highway, providing fuel, lodging, supplies, a restaurant, a bar, and a garage, as well as living quarters for its residents. The entire settlement is contained within a single sprawling compound set on a plateau overlooking vast spruce forests stretching away to distant mountains.

A lone transport truck sat parked beside the gas station. Perched nearby were three ravens, looking slightly ominous as they stared at us. Our intention was to refuel, have a last meal, and then head north to the Arctic Circle a short distance away. We parked outside the hotel, and then the seven of us headed into the lobby: Chuck, his friend Mark, the four filmmakers—Francis, Marty, Patrick, and Barclay—and me. Over the front entrance was a faded, painted sign with the words *Eagle Plains Hotel: An Oasis in the Wilderness.*

Eagle Plains seemed like a place lost in time—the decor, carpets, paint, signs, furniture, towel dispensers, bathrooms, and even bedding apparently hadn't been updated since it was first opened in 1978. Beside a vintage Pepsi-Cola vending machine were a wall-mounted payphone (there's no cell reception anywhere nearby) and a large painted map showing the Dempster's route. According to the map, we were now 409 kilometres from Dawson and 181 kilometres southwest of Fort McPherson, the two nearest inhabited places along the road.

Well, I thought, taking it all in, this would be a great setting for a horror movie.

The lobby was a grand-looking space, complete with dirty old carpets, a worn leather couch and easy chair, and a side room adorned like a fur-trading post that functioned as a kind of canteen and office. I didn't often stay in motels, but when I did, this was the sort of place I preferred.

The crew headed into the cafeteria, where a third of Eagle Plains' population worked. After looking over the menu, they decided on the chili. Meanwhile I'd wandered off down an empty, dimly lit corridor, attracted by the faded black-and-white photographs thickly plastered along the walls. The first one I came to showed a corpse with a half-frozen grimace on its gruesome face. It was the death photo of the infamous Mad Trapper, alias Albert Johnson, who'd trapped along the Rat River in the 1930s. Johnson, alone in the wilderness, had gone insane, murdering at least several people. A manhunt by the Mounties tracked him to the mountains north of here, culminating in a gun battle that ended with Johnson's death.

"This is a cheerful place," said Chuck from behind me. "Who's that?" He pointed to a faded, grainy image of a well-dressed man seated in a chair.

"Hubert Darrell," I replied. "A solo explorer who disappeared in the wilderness east of here in 1910, never to be heard from again."

"Hmm . . ." Chuck took a closer look. "Maybe one day they'll have a picture of you in here, with the caption 'Adam Shoalts, disappeared in the wilderness east of here, in 2017, never to be heard from again.'" Chuck laughed. I laughed too. It was obviously absurd to think they'd ever update the decor.

The crew had finished the chili, which they pronounced excellent and encouraged me to try. I instead sampled an oatmeal raisin cookie, for sale alongside a few other baked goods, and wandered from the cafeteria into the empty bar and lounge. It was a wondrous place: decked to the rafters with all manner of mounted Yukon animals and other curiosities.

Although Eagle Plains had a certain bewitching charm, we didn't intend to spend the night there. I'd been in the Yukon for two weeks already and was eager to begin my journey.

On the drive north I'd become better acquainted with my companions. It turned out that Chuck and Mark had met each other years earlier, when their sons were in Boy Scouts together and they'd organized the group camping trips. In his youth Mark had spent some time as a fisherman off the U.S. east coast. He'd told some fascinating stories of the sea, like when his fishing trawler had been hit by a rogue wave, or the time they'd pulled up a dead body in one of their nets, or the strange, unknown creatures of the depths they'd occasionally haul in.

After refuelling the vehicles and checking that the ratchet straps still held my canoe securely, we left Eagle Plains and continued north for another thirty-seven kilometres to the Arctic Circle—the true start of my journey. The Arctic Circle is an imaginary line that corresponds to latitude 66°33'47"N and runs around the top of the world. North of this line, the sun never sets for at least one day in summer and never rises for at least one day in winter. The farther north you go, the more days there are of either continuous daylight or darkness.

Ecologically, though, the Arctic doesn't fit into such a precise category. Permafrost, for example—the frost beneath the ground that never melts—doesn't correspond very closely to the Arctic Circle. As one nears Hudson Bay, it extends far to the south, all the way down to fifty-five degrees north latitude, where there's still tundra, along with polar bears and other species characteristic of the arctic environment. In other places, the treeline extends considerably beyond the Arctic Circle. In western North America, a lack of permafrost means black spruce, tamarack, and aspen can grow hundreds of kilometres north of the Circle. In short, among geographers, "Arctic" doesn't denote any single agreed-upon definition beyond a vaguely cold, northern region—but then geographers are fond of arguing.

Beside the gravel road was a conspicuously large wooden sign proclaiming the traveller's arrival at the Arctic Circle. But the sign seemed insignificant, even absurd, compared with the awe-inspiring, almost magical landscape visible beyond it. Across a wide meadow rose the Richardson Mountains, an otherworldly range of high, dune-like peaks. Their unique, dreamlike appearance is partially owing to their escape from glaciation during the last ice age. While the rest of Canada was buried under a mile of ice that gouged out the continent's modern landscapes, here, at the northwest end of the world, the glaciers never reached—leaving the Richardson Mountains unscarred.

We camped just beyond the Arctic Circle sign. Amid the rocks and the clumps of willow, lingonberries, and a few stunted spruces, each of us set up a tent wherever we could find a reasonably level bit of soil. I found a particularly inviting patch of caribou lichens and settled down for a comfortable night's sleep. Come morning, I'd begin my journey.

× 3 ×

THROUGH THE MOUNTAINS

Frost had settled over the tents in the night. The morning dawned cold and clear, the thermometer hovering around freezing. Still, with daytime temperatures over the past two weeks climbing up to double digits, most of the winter's snows had melted away, exposing the meadow-like tundra. It was now May 28. Three and a half years of planning, preparing, and visualizing had led to this moment. Or maybe it had been thirty-one years. All my life I'd chased after adventures, and now I was about to embark on the biggest one I was ever likely to attempt.

I soon had my tent down, rolled up, and put away alongside my sleeping bag, all stuffed into my expedition backpack. My plan was to follow the Dempster through the Richardson Mountains until I reached the banks of the Mackenzie River just over two hundred kilometres away. Chuck and Mark would see to the delivery of my canoe and barrels there, where I could pick them up to begin the water phase of my journey. Meanwhile the film crew intended to record with the drone what they could of my initial progress along the gravel Dempster. They were operating under tight schedules, as they had to make the nearly thousand-kilometre trip over rough roads back to Whitehorse in time to catch their flights to more remunerative jobs.

With the six of them assembled beside the parked SUVs to see me off bright and early, and the drone hovering overhead like something out of a science fiction movie, I strapped on my backpack, grasped my ultra-light trekking poles, and started walking. Clasped to my belt was a can of bear spray in case I should meet with any bruins that were less than accommodating. Of course, owing to the fierce winds, most of the time bear spray would be of no use. A blast of it would be just as likely to catch the wind and hit me in the face as anything else. So as a secondary measure I'd pocketed three bear bangers—essentially fire-crackers that can be screwed onto a pen-sized launcher that when unleashed will scare off any bear getting too close. In theory, anyway.

I set a quick pace, eager to put behind me as many kilometres as I could. The distance between me and my final goal, Baker Lake, Nunavut, felt daunting to the point of impossibility. What if the weather went against me? The ice, the winds, the snows? I'd never make it. Maybe I should have done that study on moss after all. I struggled to banish these thoughts from my mind. But it was difficult, knowing as I did that this hike would be the easiest part of my journey—the only place on my entire route with any kind of trail to follow. Here, all I needed to do was put one foot in front of another. Nearly everywhere else I'd have to be ever vigilant. Without any trails to follow, navigating thousands of kilometres of often fogbound, serpentine lakes, or endless thickets of chest-high willow, or black spruce bogs, or boulder-strewn tundra would require careful calculation.

As it was, the breathtaking scenery held me entranced as I hiked silently along. I fixed my gaze on a dreamlike range of bluish moun-tains, their smooth, pyramidal sides barren of vegetation and culminat-ing in snowy peaks half-hidden in thin, wispy clouds. They seemed enchanted, like a scene from some ancient fairy tale or sword-and-sorcery story—a place where wizards might happily reside. I couldn't help thinking of the almost inconceivable ancientness of such hills, formed eons ago, older by far than the Rockies. They came from a time when unknown dinosaurs stalked the earth—126 million years ago. In contrast, the environment I most often explored, the vast swamps and pathless bogs of the Hudson Bay Lowlands, were formed a mere eight thousand years ago during the retreat of the Laurentide Ice Sheet.

These ancient mountains no longer hid dinosaurs, but there were still nearly thousand-pound grizzlies to be reckoned with. When it comes to arctic bears, polar bears normally come to mind. But they're seldom encountered much more than a hundred kilometres inland from the seacoast, where seals, their main prey, are to be found. Grizzlies, meanwhile, are widespread across Canada's western and central Arctic. In fact, polar bears are thought to have evolved from these grizzlies some 200,000 years ago, as they spread farther onto the arctic ice. The two species are still closely enough related that in places where their ranges overlap interbreeding can occur, producing adorable little grolars.

The arctic grizzlies around here hibernate in the mountains during the winter, but now they'd be coming down from the hills, hungry after a long winter fast. It wasn't long into my lonely trek before I came across tracks of an unsettling size, sunk deep into the gravel roadway. Their sheer size was heart-stopping. As I bent down to inspect them I fidgeted with the bear spray clasped onto my belt. Just now the wind was blowing hard from the northeast, making the spray of uncertain application. The tracks were fresh. That much was obvious, for nearby were unmistakably fresh bear droppings—also enormous. The bear, evidently, had been feeding on grasses and last year's mountain cranberries, which remain on the plants over winter. I could also see in the scat some half-digested crowberries and bearberries. The tracks continued along the narrow road for about a hundred metres before veering off and disappearing into a thicket of willows.

I decided, just in case, to screw a bear banger onto the pen launcher and keep it in my pocket, ready to go. Then I walked on, scanning the open meadows on either side of the roadway for any hint of grizzlies. The road felt very quiet, and very empty. Hardy motorists will drive the unserviced Dempster in the summer, but in May there's little traffic at all, particularly if the river ferries aren't yet operating, as was the case this spring, given the late thaw.

The road eventually took me into flatter territory, the mountains declining into merely large hills set back several hundred metres from either side of the road, with open meadowlands in between. Arctic ground squirrels, looking rather plump and playful, appeared and disappeared, scurrying from burrow to burrow—they're one of the arctic grizzly's favourite foods. An occasional bald eagle soared high overhead. Later I glimpsed a snowy owl as it glided elegantly over the grassy tundra, perhaps hunting a snowshoe hare that appeared briefly on a slight hill. But most of all there were more and more grizzly tracks and fresh droppings. Evidently the bears were numerous here.

At one point, scanning to the right of the road, my eyes were greeted by the sight of what had left some of the tracks: a large, magnificent-looking grizzly bear about three hundred metres away, with a big hump crowning its broad shoulders and a wide, almost heart-shaped, face. Its back was to me as it crossed the meadows toward the encircling hills. Instinctively I unclipped the bear spray from my belt. But with the bear upwind from me, and with the wind as strong as it was, the spray would be of little use—other than to add flavour to myself. So I also took the bear banger out of my pocket. Meanwhile, the grizzly must have either heard me or caught my scent. It suddenly turned, rose on its hind legs—towering some nine feet tall—and seemed to be sniffing the wind, scanning the horizon. It was certainly a big, fully grown grizzly; it didn't look at all famished, as one might expect in the spring, when bears have typically shed weight from their winter slumbers. The grizzly remained standing on its hind legs for what seemed an amazingly long time—until, that is, it spotted me, a lone figure on a long, empty stretch of gravel.

Then it dropped to all fours and charged.

It came barrelling across the meadow straight at me. Three hundred metres separated us, a matter of perhaps thirty seconds. I begin shouting hoarsely at it, waving my trekking poles about, and even jumping in the air—all in an effort to appear as large and menacing as possible, hoping to deter the bear's charge. I wasn't sure it was going to work. I'd had polar bears and black bears come at me before and had always driven them off, but this was my first grizzly charge, and I wasn't entirely sure what to expect. But I knew this: I had only three bear bangers, and I couldn't afford to use them all up on the morning of the first day of my journey. So I held off on firing a banger and instead kept waving my trekking poles, shouting at the grizzly as it approached. I also knew this: when a bear charges, never run. At least, that's my philosophy. You can't outrun a grizzly anyway, and north of the treeline as I was, there are no trees to climb. Some people advise playing dead, but that's not a tactic I'd recommend unless the grizzly in question is a mother with cubs, and it's clearly a case of having startled her.

At about two hundred metres, with me still waving my poles and shouting, the oncoming grizzly suddenly halted its charge, wheeled around, and began running back in the direction it had come. As it ran back toward the hills, it glanced over its broad shoulder in my direction several times. For a long while it remained in sight as I cautiously resumed hiking along the road. The grizzly, it seemed, had lost interest in me. It skirted along the edge of the hills, apparently searching for berries. Eventually it disappeared from view.

This was only the first day of my journey, and I knew I'd have to face more bears before it was over—likely many more. I took heart in the fact that most bears when left alone are generally harmless. The majority seek to avoid human contact whenever possible. And the behaviour I'd just witnessed, a so-called "bluff charge," was a well-known characteristic of these arctic grizzlies. They are, it seems, wonderful practical jokers who delight in seeing whether they can scare hikers or paddlers with one of their bluffs.

As part of my academic research I'd spent years studying bear attacks, compiling a database involving hundreds of fatal attacks on humans stretching back over several centuries. What emerged were some clear patterns. It was obvious that bears were intelligent creatures that seldom attacked a human blindly; rather, they seemed to calculate carefully before attacking, weighing their chances of success. When attacks on groups happened, bears would consistently single out the smallest member of the party for attack. In almost all cases, it seemed clear that grizzlies would avoid a fight if they could—since for any wild animal the mere possibility of an injury is often enough to deter an attack, as any injury is likely to bring fatal consequences if it impedes hunting or food gathering. That's why playing dead with a grizzly makes sense only when the bear is clearly acting defensively (such as a mother bear with cubs or a bear defending a fresh kill), and not when the bear is acting aggressively. In those cases, playing dead, running away, or attempting to hide might simply trigger the bear's predator instinct to see you as easy prey. In one of these scenarios, the best thing to do is to look big, make noise, and not flinch.

On my first day, I hiked forty-one kilometres along the Dempster. The second day the winds were bad, knocking me around on the road, and I covered only thirty-nine. The third day I increased the time I spent hiking and upped my distance to fifty-nine. The fourth day, my best, I managed sixty-two kilometres over thirteen hours of hiking.

The film crew had departed on the second day in order to make their long drive back to Whitehorse. The filming, they reported, had gone well. Other than when the drone had crashed into a mountain and was destroyed. Meanwhile Chuck and Mark had been investigating with a fishing rod some of the streams the Dempster passed over. Chuck reported that they were completely devoid of fish. This I could well believe, for if there were fish in those streams, Chuck would surely find them.

As my lonely trek continued, the landscape varied. Mostly it was tree-less tundra framed by majestic mountains, with quilt-like patches of snow on their slopes interspersed with exposed rocks and meadows. However, in places where the road crossed rivers and creeks, black spruces and aspens reappeared, as the trees were able to take root in these sheltered valleys. It was in one of these valleys, in 1932, that the Mad Trapper had met his violent end after a prolonged firefight with a posse of RCMP officers and hired guns. It'd taken no less than seven bullets—one of which struck spare ammo stuffed in the Trapper's pocket, causing an explosion that blew off part of his thigh—to finally bring him down (may that be a good lesson for us all not to store spare ammo in our pant pockets). The mystery of his true identity, and his motives, was never satisfactorily solved. A drifter who'd come north some years earlier, he'd given the name Albert Johnson, but that seemed to have been a made-up alias, as others knew him by different names. On his corpse was found a considerable quantity of cash and gold, including gold teeth that weren't his own. That's never a good sign, in my experience. Perhaps he'd been a dentist before taking up fur trapping, a common enough career transition. But there were alarming rumours that in places he'd drifted through—the Nahanni Valley, for instance—unsolved murders and headless corpses had a tendency to show up.

That first night I camped in one of those sheltered patches of black spruce, where there was ample wood for a fire—and perhaps, I liked to think as I lay in my tent and watched through the screen door the flames flicker and the shadows dance, the ghost of Albert Johnson. I soon drifted off to sleep to these cheering thoughts.

✳

My trek along the Dempster continued early the next morning. The weather was colder, and rain fell intermittently. I'd switched into my warmer blue waterproof jacket. Fierce winds knocked me around as I marched. The gusts were so strong that I had to lean into them to maintain my footing, making full use of my trekking poles to keep me upright. Even so, my progress was significantly slower. I spotted another grizzly on a mountain slope, but it seemed to pay me no attention. Then, as the route began to steeply ascend, I felt the burn in my legs. Crossing now from the Yukon into the Northwest Territories, the Dempster climbed through the windswept McDougall Pass, one of only two passes across the Richardson Mountains.

This lonely pass, over bleak and icy mountains, was a scene of desolation. Scant vegetation grew amid the tumbled heaps of grey boulders and barren slopes, while large patches of snow remained in the shadows cast by the peaks. The wind howled violently as I trekked along. Somewhere to the north, I knew, the Richardson Mountains reached their apex, with the highest peaks exceeding 1,700 metres.

The Yukon's mountain passes have seen their share of mysteries, murders, and adventures, none more famous than the Mounties' doomed "Lost Patrol." On December 21, 1910, a dogsled patrol consisting of four Mounties set off from the outpost of Fort McPherson to make the long, perilous journey south to Dawson. The weather was a balmy minus twenty-nine Celsius, so the Mounties, under the lead of Inspector Francis Joseph Fitzgerald, were optimistic, carrying food for only thirty days. With Inspector Fitzgerald were Constables Richard Taylor and George Kinney and Special Constable Sam Carter, as well as fifteen sled dogs divided between three sleds. To break a trail through the deep snows, the men took turns snowshoeing ahead on foot.

The elements soon turned against the Mounties. Blizzards blinded them and temperatures plunged to a mind-numbing fifty below, the wind chill sometimes making it seventy below. The human body cannot long survive such extreme temperatures. The only thing to be done in such conditions is hunker down, take shelter, and stay warm. The Mounties, however, pushed on, battling frostbite and deep snows that slowed their progress. Given such conditions, they failed to find the frozen creek that pointed the way to Dawson. Unknown to them, they'd overshot the mark. When they realized their error, they still couldn't locate the correct creek, losing valuable time and food as they searched.

On January 18, with their food supply dwindling, they made the desperate decision to turn back to Fort McPherson, giving up any hope of reaching Dawson. That night they butchered one of their own dogs for meat, but the other sled dogs refused to eat it. Without food, there was little hope. But desperation drove them on. The dogs, starving, now began to eat their own when offered it. One by one they killed and ate their dogs, until by February they had only five left. This kept them grimly going for a time. But frostbite and starvation closed in on them—and there was to be no escape from winter's icy grip. Taylor, Carter, and Fitzgerald perished from starvation and hypothermia, while Kinney, surrendering to despair, shot himself with a carbine. Fitzgerald was the last to die—having used a piece of charcoal to scribble out his will on a scrap of paper, leaving all he owned to his mother in Halifax. His body was later found just forty kilometres outside Fort McPherson by Sergeant Dempster, for whom the highway was subsequently named.

I kept hiking. Below the windswept McDougall Pass were narrow canyons the road cut through, mountainous walls rising high on either side. There was barely any vegetation, altogether the impression was of a moonscape. Yet there was life in these desolate mountains. Dall's sheep, a type of hardy mountain sheep native to the northern Yukon, range among these precipitous peaks. The rams weigh several hundred pounds, with big, fantastically curved horns up to three feet long. They favour lonely crags and cliffs, bounding up seemingly impossible slopes with ease. When the opportunity presents itself, grizzlies and wolves are known to make meals of them—and even the great golden eagles that live in these mountains, with their huge wingspans, carry off the little lambs occasionally. I was hoping to spot a Dall's sheep bounding among the stony slopes, since in my mental checklist of animals I most wanted to see, they were in the top three (along with a giant squid, and a sasquatch).

As I came out of the barren, treeless Richardson Mountains, I found myself hiking past forests of dwarf tamarack and black spruce. Then, from a small prominence where the road rose up, I took in a vast panorama. To the north were imposing walls of snowy mountain ranges; to the south endless wild land cloaked in stunted forest stretching to a far distant horizon, broken only here and there by placid blue lakes. To the east I could see glimpses of the twisting course of the Peel River, and could just barely spot a scattered collection of white rooftops that made up the tiny hamlet of Fort McPherson (population 785). It had been founded as a fur trading post back in 1840. The town, however, wasn't on my route, as it lay just a little north of the main road I was following.

Willow and alder bushes grew thickly along the roadside, reaching heights of eight or nine feet. Concealed in these thickets, I knew, were grizzlies—their fresh tracks, sunk alarmingly deep into the gravel, littered the roadway. They might spring out at any time, but hopefully only to spook me for the fun of it.

I kept marching. One foot in front of another. Slow and steady wins the race, I told myself. Another ten kilometres or so and the road dropped into the lowlands of the Peel River. Here, conditions were less harsh than higher up; the trees were bigger, and now included white birch—though the birch were still far too small for canoe-making. Foxtail barley, horsetails, yarrow, and fireweed all grew in abundance along the roadside. Along this stretch, my third day hiking, the weather became misty, with intermittent rain. A big grizzly appeared, sauntering along the road in the most casual manner possible. It was a striking animal, with blond tips on its thick, rich coat and impressive curved claws. For a moment it looked as if it might charge me, but then the bear dipped back down into the willows, disappearing from view.

Late on the third day I could see up ahead the waters of the Peel, about two hundred metres wide. Nearby was a miscellaneous collection of shacks, trucks, and rubbish scattered about. Chuck and Mark were parked by the muddy bank, and Chuck had set up his tent there.

Chuck and Mark had already made friends with the ferry operator and told him something of me and my plans. The ferry operator, Morris, a native of Fort McPherson and veteran boat captain familiar with the strong currents of the Mackenzie, expressed the opinion that upriver travel alone in a canoe was impossible. Only a motorboat with a strong engine could make it upriver, and even that was difficult and time-consuming.

When Morris saw me arrive, somewhat wearied from my hike, he looked me up and down and asked, "What kind of drugs are you smoking?"

"None," I assured him.

"So you're just crazy, then?"

I thought I'd demonstrate my sanity by invoking a different subject. Morris, I'd noticed, sported an Edmonton Oilers hat. I alluded to the team's having made the playoffs for the first time in eleven seasons. Morris livened up. Yes, he assured me, the Oilers were back—they'd shown real promise. Morris, it turned out, had lived in Edmonton and was something of a fanatical Oilers fan. But now that Edmonton was eliminated, Morris explained, he wanted the playoffs' only remaining Canadian team, Ottawa, to win—he couldn't stand the thought of an American team claiming the Cup again. The Senators were playing that night, so he had to be off soon so as not to miss the puck drop.

Having noticed Chuck and Mark's lack of interest in our discussion, Morris asked me what the deal was with them.

"Americans," I explained.

The original plan was to have Chuck and Mark deposit my canoe and two barrels on the banks of the Mackenzie River, where I could pick them up. To do so they'd have to take the car ferry across the Peel River, which the Dempster crosses. The ferry, though, was out of service for repairs. I'd planned for such a contingency by including among my expedition gear a small wheeled cart. That way, in the worst-case scenario with the river-ferry closed on the Peel (thereby preventing Chuck and Mark from crossing in the vehicle), I could still transport my canoe and barrels to the Mackenzie River by wheeling them along the Dempster behind me. But this prospect was not at all appealing, as it'd be slow-going and time-consuming.

Fortunately, Morris eliminated the need for the cart by offering to transport the canoe and barrels to the Mackenzie River. While the ferry was out of commission, he still had a motorboat at hand and a pickup truck on the opposite side of the Peel. I gratefully accepted this offer, and wondered if my favourable words about the Oilers had facilitated it.

Chuck and Mark, meanwhile, had to take their leave. I owed them both a debt of gratitude. Besides helping transport my canoe and supplies to the river, Mark had given me his hiking boots. (They were a size larger than my own, and my feet had swelled slightly from all the hiking, causing me considerable discomfort. He'd told me I could keep the boots, so I did.) Chuck, too, had been overly generous—he'd given me his waterproof neoprene waders, lighter than the ones I'd packed. As they prepared to make the long drive back to Whitehorse, the two of them wished me well. Before they left I rifled through my pack and discarded anything I didn't need, so as to travel even lighter and repay them in some way for their kindness—I had a pair of wool socks (worn), a pack of matches (half-used), and two granola bars (unopened) that I could spare. I handed them over.

The Mackenzie River had cleared of its winter ice just as I'd hoped it would, by the last of May. On June 1, five days after setting off from the Arctic Circle, I arrived on its muddy banks where the Dempster crosses it. As promised, Morris dropped off my canoe and two barrels, then wished me well on my fool's errand upriver. Nearby was the little community of Tsiigehtchic (population 195), where Morris had gone to visit his sister before returning to his post at the Peel River crossing. His was the last face I'd see for a while.

Now the real challenges would begin.

UP THE MACKENZIE

U p close, the swirling, rippling waters of the vast Mackenzie River did look alarmingly swift. At 1,738 kilometres long on its main branch, the Mackenzie is Canada's longest river and North America's second longest. It was understandable why pretty much everyone judged trying to canoe upriver on it an indication of insanity. It wasn't just that I was attempting to do it alone; it was also that I had over a hundred and seventy pounds of dead weight to transport in the canoe—two barrels crammed with food rations and a backpack holding my tent, camping gear, camera equipment, and miscellaneous other things—all of which would have to be propelled upriver against a powerful current still swollen with the recent ice melt.

Even if I could maintain a paddling pace of five kilometres an hour—no mean feat with a hundred and seventy pounds of dead-weight against a four-kilometre-an-hour current—that'd translate into only one kilometre an hour progress. At that rate it would take me well over a month to get upriver to the point I'd needed to reach. Not at all feasible, if I were to have any hope of success. So instead I'd thought up a different plan.

I hoped to rely on an ancient, though now largely forgotten technique for upstream navigation: poling. Sticking close to the river's steep banks, I planned to delicately balance myself in a standing position while pushing a long pole off the river's bottom—advancing the canoe steadily upstream. It's an eloquent illustration of Newton's third law of motion: "When one body exerts a force on a second body, the second body simultaneously exerts a force equal in magnitude and opposite in direction on the first body." My pushing down with the pole would meet with a second body, the river bottom, simultaneously exerting a force equal in magnitude and opposite in direction to my initial thrust with the pole—thus propelling the canoe upriver. A pole used in such a manner is far more effective than any paddle.

But first I had to find myself a suitable pole. The Mackenzie here was about one kilometre wide, and across its icy, swirling waters I could see a stand of trembling aspens. One of these hardy trees, I figured would serve my purpose admirably. I shoved my canoe into the water, hopped in, and pushed off with my paddle in what was the first stroke of my journey across Canada's Arctic. To traverse it to reach the aspens my canoe would have to be broadside to the current, meaning I'd have to paddle twice as hard. To compensate for the current pushing me back I first headed some ways upstream, pointed my canoe farther yet upstream of where the aspens were, and then began paddling across, the current swirling around me, forming little whirlpools as I went. Fifteen minutes of hard paddling later, I'd landed on the opposite bank beneath the stand of aspens.

A plump muskrat sat on the bank cheerfully chewing some willow shoots as I scrutinized the trees. About ten feet long, I figured, would be enough to reach bottom if I stayed close to shore, where the current was slacker. With my hatchet I chopped down my chosen tree and then shaved off its branches, smoothing it down into a pole that could be easily wielded. The muskrat, meanwhile, finished his meal and plopped into the water with a splash, heading upstream in a steady dog paddle, or rather muskrat paddle, as if to show me the way.

Steadying myself upright in the canoe, I began pushing against the river bottom with the pole, propelling myself along after the muskrat. Slow and steady wins the race, I told myself again. Another thrust, then another, each one flinging the canoe against the oncoming current, with me repeating the manoeuvre before the current could overcome the boat's forward momentum. The muskrat, for his part, now seemed to think better of the exercise. He took a gulp of air, sank beneath the swirling waves, and passed under the canoe, emerging a short way downriver, letting the current carry him back to the willows. Glancing over my shoulder, I saw him scramble up the muddy bank, give his coat a good shake, and then resume feasting on willows.

I cast my eyes back upriver, in the direction I had to head. I couldn't see very far. Towering grey banks a hundred feet high, like some kind of huge canal carved out by a giant long ago, curved around to the west, blocking the view. On top of these heights I could make out lines of little trees: spruces, tamaracks, and in a few places aspens. The skies were blue, with the sun beating down and glaring off the rippling waters.

I kept on poling. I had to—otherwise I'd drift right back downriver—but it seemed to be working. At times I'd bend my knees and pivot my body, giving the canoe an extra strong thrust. In a few places, though, large rocks beneath the water blocked my path. Here, I'd have to cautiously thrust out farther from shore, into the deeper water where the current was much stronger, then rapidly pole myself back in, skirting the rocks.

I poled my way into the enormous canyon known as the Lower Ramparts, which I'd seen from downriver. Pushing along, I soon fell into a rhythm. After the river rounded a sharp bend, the view opened up down a straighter stretch that extended for over twelve kilometres. It was a magnificent sight—no other great river in the world, not even the Amazon, is so free of human development and traffic as the Mackenzie still is. No buildings, radio towers, transmission lines, cottages, pipelines, or any other human-made objects appeared to litter the view. Just high grey cliffs crowned with rich, dark green forest, beyond which were rolling hills extending for hundreds of miles in either direction.

Poling wasn't my only strategy for overcoming the river's powerful current. Some six hours into my upriver battle, I found the chance I'd been waiting for to implement another tactic. The wind had shifted;

it was blowing from the northwest now, just what I needed to try out my second trick—a specially designed sail shaped like an umbrella that could be sprung open to catch the wind and just as quickly collapsed when the wind shifted or died.

If I could successfully harness the power of the wind, it'd be a nice help. But sailing a heavily laden canoe upriver on a wilderness expedition is easier said than done. Canoes aren't designed to be sailed. Not only are they light, shallow vessels without much means of rigging up a decent mast, but any such mast becomes a liability on portages, in rapids, or if you have to suddenly change direction, as happens a lot when going up a winding river. On an expedition, when time is critical and shifting quickly from one mode of travel to another is essential, a mast becomes a potentially dangerous thing to fiddle with. Which brings me to the secret of my sail's design: it didn't require a mast. It could simply be flown like a kind of kite, with one end secured firmly to the canoe's centre thwart and the other end tied with a string toward the back of the canoe.

Just now the wind seemed favourable. So with a tinge of excitement and trepidation I set aside my pole and gave a pull on the slipknots holding the little sail I'd reefed to the canoe's thwart. In an instant the tightly coiled sail sprang out and caught the wind. I felt a sudden tug—it was pulling me upriver! I could hardly believe it: the canoe and I were shooting straight up the current. Hurriedly I tied a shoelace from the sail to my canoe seat, securing it so that my hands might remain free. Then I snatched up my paddle and used it as a rudder to steer. In that moment I felt what all sailors must feel when they first learn to harness the wind—an exhilaration that's half revelation, half jubilation at the wind carrying you along.

With the sail up, I steered with my paddle and added strokes of my own to further improve my pace. It felt marvellous to sail a canoe upriver. Alas, this triumph lasted only thirty minutes before the wind shifted again. The sail abruptly fluttered and then fell flat over the canoe. It was back to poling.

On the bright side, the sun was shining, the temperature was hovering around nine degrees Celsius, and this early in the year there were still no blackflies and mosquitoes to torment all living mammals. Better yet, lots of birds were around to keep me company.

Along the river's banks hopped little shorebirds, mainly sandpipers, which glide gracefully over the water. Also on the banks, chirping away, were robins, which during the summer are indeed found north of the Arctic Circle. They're one of the most widely travelled birds in North America, ranging from urban parks to northern tundra. As I was poling along I also spotted a stately looking bald eagle. Perched tall and proud on its spruce throne, high atop the banks, it seemed to survey the vast river lands that formed its domain with a touch of aristocratic disdain. Any fish, muskrat, baby beaver, arctic ground squirrel, duckling, or other small bird that attracted its fancy might furnish it a meal.

But most intriguing of all were the great sandhill cranes stalking along the mud flats. These giant birds, standing three and a half feet tall and with a nearly seven-foot wingspan, are one of the eeriest birds in the North. Their sheer size, along with their thick grey plumage that almost looks like fur and the bright red bands around their eyes, as if they're attending a costume ball, make them unmistakable. Their most peculiar characteristic, however, is their call. It's a kind of nervous, rattling sound—something like a French horn mingled with a rusty gate opening and closing.

The first time I ever saw one of these cranes was as a teenager. I'd been wandering in the wilderness with my best friend Wes for three weeks. One evening, while gathering firewood, I spotted a couple of these giant, spooky cranes near a clearing on the edge of a spruce bog. I had no idea what they were; to me they looked like a ghostly mirage. Back at our campsite I hesitated to even tell Wes I'd seen them, so bizarre did they appear, like a kind of Canadian emu. Maybe I'd been dreaming? In fact, sandhill cranes are not uncommon, and can be found across much of North America's wild places, from the Gulf of Mexico, where they overwinter, all the way up to the Arctic coastline in summer. But in dark and gloomy subarctic forests, or on deserted tundra, there's something peculiarly striking about these distinctive birds with their red masks and eerie calls. Poling up the Mackenzie that afternoon, I saw more sandhill cranes than I ever had before: a trio on a mud flat, a half-dozen more wading along the shores, and another nine or ten soaring over the river.

That night I made camp along the river's eastern bank on a patch of sand that promised to make for a comfortable night's sleep. The Mackenzie was nearly three kilometres wide at this point, although its current seemed just as strong, with eddies, ripples, and driftwood swirling by. I'd put in only eight and half hours my first day, not having slept much the night before. Examining my maps, it seemed I'd made it about twenty kilometres upriver. This was fairly encouraging, and I was optimistic that in the days ahead, as I refined my methods and increased my hours, my daily distances would increase. Of course, much would depend on the wind.

I gathered up some driftwood and fixed myself a nice cheering fire. With the driftwood crackling loudly, it wasn't long before my kettle boiled, giving me enough water to make tea and cook a freeze-dried meal. From my packed rations I selected "Forever Young Mac and Cheese" from the brand Alpineaire. I found it particularly savoury as I sat on a driftwood log and watched the great river rolling by, shorebirds soaring gracefully along it.

Nearby on the mud flats were wolf tracks as well as some grizzly tracks. It was quite interesting to see how clearly their giant claws registered in the mud, unlike their much less vivid imprints on the Dempster. Some people think you should never camp in an area with signs of bears. Such people, I presume, wouldn't find camping along the Mackenzie River very agreeable. Signs of grizzlies are nearly everywhere in springtime.

Survival books tend to advise all kinds of precautions when camping in bear territory, such as never bringing food anywhere near your camp, or even toothpaste. A few even go so far as to advise not sleeping in the same clothes you cook in. And some, if you can believe it, will tell you never to camp alone. I've always taken this kind of advice with a grain of salt. My packed food was the kind that doesn't give off much odour: a mix of dehydrated meals (rationed to one a day), and things that didn't need preparation, like high-calorie energy bars, granola bars, and protein bars supplemented by some jerky and dried fruits. Since these dried foods were all in sealed packages inside watertight plastic barrels, there didn't seem much likelihood of attracting bears. At night I'd move the food barrels just a short distance away from my tent. Unlike in heavily visited parks farther south or near towns, the bears in remote wilderness areas are much wilder, and much less accustomed to stealing camp food. On the other hand, wild bears are said to be more likely to attack humans. You can't have everything, after all.

Seeing how there was ample driftwood at hand, before turning in I did make a nice cheering fire on the beach. Most wild animals instinctively fear fire, and the scent of it is sometimes enough to keep bears away. Of course out on the tundra there wouldn't be wood for a fire, and I'd likely sleep months without one. But that needn't concern me now. So I slept peacefully under the midnight sun, listening to the river murmur and the robins sing.

＊

The next day, June 2, I put in nine and half hours of upriver travel: a combination of poling, some paddling for variety, and yet another technique meant to overcome the difficulties of upstream navigation. I experimented briefly with walking along the shoreline and dragging the canoe with a rope behind me. This method worked indifferently, and wasn't as fast as poling proved. I also managed to do a bit more sailing when the wind was favourable. All in all, my progress that second day was better than my first: I made it twenty-five kilometres upriver.

Partly what gave me the idea of experimenting with these different methods was reading a 228-year-old diary by Alexander Mackenzie, a hardscrabble adventurer and fur trader. In 1789, at the age of twenty-five, he ventured down the river now bearing his name along with some dozen companions—mostly Canadian voyageurs, Dene hunters from lands to the south, and a stray German tossed in for good measure. After reaching the Arctic Ocean, Mackenzie and his companions retraced their route all the way back upriver, returning to their fur trade post on Lake Athabasca. Mackenzie's diary describes them as fighting their way upriver using various means, with some men hauling their large canoe with ropes along the shore while others remained in the canoe, working to paddle and pole it together. Obviously I couldn't replicate this combined approach on my own. But I did try out each method individually, and found poling to be the most effective.

I was hoping to keep improving my pace, but June 3 saw a stiff headwind blow against me. Battling the current and the wind together was doubly difficult, yet I forced myself to keep poling regardless. Ten hours of hard effort saw me advance another twenty-four kilometres. This left my arms and back feeling pretty sore. There could be no thought of resting, though. The next day saw me again equal this distance, with more of the same headwinds that prevented me from raising sail.

In the course of this fourth day struggling up the mighty Mackenzie, I felt my aspen pole crack after one hard push off the river bottom. This was a bit disconcerting, as scanning the banks I saw no sign of aspens from which to fashion a replacement pole. There were spruces and tamaracks aplenty, but to use a conifer would mean getting my hands coated in sticky resin. The conifers also have a lot of branches along their trunks, not ideal for a fashioning a pole. Still, putting into shore and searching for a suitable aspen would mean a costly delay. Then suddenly help arrived from an unexpected source.

I could hardly believe my luck when I saw a perfectly sized stick already cut and lying a short distance away on the bank. The teeth marks on either end of it showed plainly that it had been cut by a beaver. It seemed to be of balsam poplar, and likely had come from somewhere far upriver, drifting down with the current until it lodged where I found it. It was just the right length and thickness I needed; the water had already worn it smooth. After mentally thanking the beaver gods I grasped the pole, leapt back into my canoe, and resumed poling with renewed vigour. That beaver-fashioned pole worked even better than my old one, and I was able to establish my best pace yet, making it twenty-eight kilometres upriver that day.

Over the following week I continued my solitary journey upriver. Most of the time the wind was against me, including a three-day stretch in which I battled ceaseless headwinds that left me unable to use the sail at all. In places I found great mounds of ice still piled up on shore. In one spot where the river curved, the ice formed a continuous wall some twenty to thirty feet high, which was slowly melting in the June sun. I was somewhat apprehensive that, poling along these massive blocks of haphazardly stacked ice that formed caverns and caves, they might crumble and collapse onto me as I poled by. The odd block of ice in the river showed clearly where some of the mounds had already collapsed, and the steady drip coming off the ice mounds in the noonday sun suggested that more might collapse at any time. If a block should topple over just as I passed it, I'd be crushed, or at least knocked clean into the river. Neither seemed appealing.

This massive ice wall, forming towers and turrets, extended along the river's shore for about half a kilometre, looking in my imagination like some enchanted ice palace. Ideally it'd be safer to stay outside the range of the ice mounds if they were to collapse, but this I couldn't do. It was too deep for my pole farther offshore. So in the spots where the ice seemed particularly precariously stacked and in danger of toppling over, I just poled past as quickly as I could, passing by before the ice could fall. There's nothing like falling blocks of ice for maintaining a good travelling pace.

Other places presented hazards of a different sort along the banks. One morning I came across a young blond grizzly. The bear had its head down as it sauntered along the bank, apparently searching for food, and didn't notice me. When I saw the bear, I switched from my pole to my paddle, in order to stay a safe distance offshore. Here, the current wasn't too bad, so I paddled along for a bit. Eventually, the young grizzly noticed me, and after curiously looking at me for a few seconds, abruptly ran off into the woods. It seemed I'd terrified him.

Three days later, still poling along, I saw near a small stream a mother grizzly with two cubs. To my surprise, contrary to what you might expect a mother grizzly to do, she simply took one look at me and immediately turned around and ran off. Her two bewildered cubs, seemingly caught a bit off guard by their mother's sudden flight, looked wide-eyed at me a moment longer, then turned around and hurried after their mother. I got the strong impression that the cubs received a stern talking to that evening about how they'd been raised to know better than to linger staring at humans. In fact, as the days went by, it seemed to me that the grizzly's reputation for aggressiveness was somewhat exaggerated, as I found the grizzlies generally more timid than my experiences with both polar bears and black bears.

In contrast to the grizzlies, landslides were a more serious concern along the Mackenzie's high banks. There were many dozens of areas where the banks had collapsed into enormous landslides that buried everything in their path. Some slides were over a hundred metres wide and the height of a three-storey building, with full-grown spruces and aspens knocked over and now sticking out of the mud every which way like pins in a pin cushion. As far as I could ascertain, the slides were triggered by some combination of stream-caused erosion, melting ice, rainfall, and the thawing out of the ground. At night, when selecting my campsites, I had to be extra cautious for any signs of impending landslides. To have an avalanche of mud and rocks slam into my tent and bury me while I was sleeping would really put a damper on things. (Later I learned that CBC News reported that the same summer I was poling along, a landslide on the Mackenzie River obliterated an entire log cabin, which was, fortunately, empty at the time.)

The landslides, because of the huge quantities of mud they wash into the river, caused other obstacles to upstream travel. When I tried to pole alongside one giant slide, I found that I could no longer push off the river bottom. The pole, rather than striking a hard bottom, simply kept sinking deeper and deeper into the soft, quicksand-like mud, failing to give any purchase for the thrusts required to drive the canoe against the current. Nor could I get out and walk along the shoreline: I'd just sink into the mud if I tried. There seemed no other option but to try paddling. The current, however, was very strong, and the landslide of mud and tumbled spruces extended out into the river, forming a sort of weir that amplified the current's strength.

Nevertheless I began paddling, battling the current with each stroke. The mudslide stretched for about a hundred and fifty metres, so if I could just manage to overcome the current for that long, I'd be able to resume poling. But as I edged away from shore to skirt around the slide, it felt like paddling on a treadmill. Then, as I began to tire, the current overwhelmed my efforts and I drifted back to where I started.

Until now I'd been using a traditional paddle with a straight shaft—the familiar kind of paddle you see most everywhere. Mine had been crafted from ash for a strong shaft and spruce for an extralight blade. I loved my paddle, as only a canoeist can. But now it was time to try something different. Stored in my canoe, as yet unused, was a second paddle. It was shorter than my other one, with a wider, rectangular blade. But the real difference was the shaft: its blade was set at an eight-degree angle. This odd-looking design, developed in the 1960s, is based on the principle that an angled blade will remain vertical in the water longer through each stroke than a traditional paddle. The result is increased power and efficiency. Bent-shaft paddles are now the standard among competitive racing canoeists, although they're still uncommon among wilderness canoeists. I suspect that's partly because most canoeists are at heart romantics. Still, I'd thought it prudent to acquire one, and now I'd see if it could make the difference I needed.

With the bent-shaft paddle I kneeled down in the canoe and threw all my effort into fighting the current. My strokes were quicker and shorter than before—each one pulling through the water with maximum efficiency. I edged around the fallen spruce, paddling furiously as I went. The bent-shaft design was more awkward than my traditional paddle, and not as good for steering. But for sheer power, it had the advantage. My furious strokes propelled me upriver until I was safely past the landslide and able to resume poling.

✳

Five days into my journey upriver on the Mackenzie and I still hadn't seen another soul—an experience that would be hard to replicate on any other great river of comparable size, whether it's the Mississippi, Amazon, Nile, Congo, or Yangtze. But then, late in the evening of June 8, I heard the distant sound of an engine coming from somewhere downriver. A small motorboat materialized with two men on board. They were gunning the engine hard, battling their way right up the middle of the river, about half a kilometre offshore. When they spotted my tent they steered in closer and hovered in the current. Over the roar of the engine and the distance between us, one of the men shouted, "Do you have any marijuana?"

"No!" I shouted back.

This important inquiry out of the way, we discussed other matters, bellowing back and forth to be heard. They'd come from Inuvik, they told me, a small town about three hundred kilometres downriver, and were on their way to Fort Good Hope, which lay another couple hundred kilometres upriver. It occurred to them the oddness of seeing me camped where I was on the bank so early in the season after the ice breakup. Normally, canoeists wouldn't arrive this far down the Mackenzie River until much later in the summer. They wanted to know, shouting to be heard over their boat's engine, how I'd managed to make it so far downriver this early in the year. I explained, shouting back, that I hadn't come downriver at all.

"I came upriver," I shouted.

This revelation caused some bewilderment, and it was as much as I could do, shouting back and forth, to explain things. When they realized that I'd indeed been travelling against the current, they now seemed to think I must be in some kind of trouble. They offered to help, explaining they had a satellite phone and could call for rescue if I was injured. I explained I was fine, but this only prompted an offer to take me in their motorboat to wherever it was I was going, though they said, my canoe would have to be left behind, as there wasn't space for it. When I insisted I was perfectly happy, they at last relented.

"Well," shouted the man at the engine, "enjoy the Mackenzie! And if you ever make it to Fort Good Hope, come see us and we'll give you a place to stay and a good meal!"

With that, they waved goodbye and roared off upriver.

The only other people I encountered along the Mackenzie during my eleven-day journey up it were in two other motorboats. The first was another small boat, also battling the current upriver, this time carrying three men and a snowmobile. They were too far away to communicate with, as where I spotted them the Mackenzie was over three kilometres wide. The other boat I saw was a much larger one, also in the distance. Scanning through the zoom on my camera, I made out that it was the coast guard ship *Eckaloo*. On its three-tiered deck were two smaller boats covered in tarps and a crew swarming about. To me in my little red canoe, the giant, noisy coast guard ship, powering up the river with its mighty diesel engines, was an odd sight. As far as I could tell, the *Eckaloo* was steaming along the river in order to lay out navigational buoys, to open it up for boat traffic, now that the ice had cleared. Without buoys, the Mackenzie's shifting sandbars and mud flats pose a hazard for boats.

Meanwhile, my pace continued to improve. On June 6 I'd made it another thirty-two kilometres upriver, mostly by poling aided with a little sailing, and I managed to replicate this success over each of the next few days. As I became more adept at sailing, I experimented with trying to sail and pole together. This unorthodox method turned out to be quite effective when the wind wasn't too strong. I tottered a few times when gusts hit the sail, but with my beaver-made pole I was always able to stay upright and keep pushing along. The result was better progress upriver than even I'd dared to hope possible—a full thirty-seven kilometres in a single day, which I managed twice. That was accomplished in just ten hours, with three hours of combined sailing and poling and seven hours of only poling.

My progress might have been better yet had it not been for a costly delay. I'd come upon a long, flat, muddy island, and rather than pole the long way around by sticking with the river's main channel, I decided, not without some hesitation, to remain close to the eastern bank I'd been following. There was a chance the mud "island" might be only a dead-end bay. My maps indicated that it was an island, but maps aren't always to be trusted. Shifting channels and fluctuating water levels can make islands disappear and reappear. However, I reasoned that since it was still only the first week of June, given the recent ice melt, high water levels ought to indicate a clear passage. Moreover, the current on the near side of the island wasn't as strong, and this enticed me to chance following it to avoid the main current on the far side.

But the farther I went, the thicker the weeds and the shallower the water became until, after twenty minutes of poling, the channel abruptly terminated in a mud flat. It wasn't a channel after all, but merely a long narrow bay. I'd have to take off my hiking boots and wool socks, roll up my pants, and haul my canoe and gear across the mud flats that separated me from open water. But there was no way to haul over two hundred pounds across the quicksand-like mud flats, which I sank into as soon as I stepped out of the canoe. Instead, I had to carry each load across individually, sinking past my ankles into the cold mud with each step. A trio of curious sandhill cranes silently watched as I struggled across with the different loads.

The effort of hauling my gear across mud flats caused me to work up a thirst. Attached to my backpack was a small handheld water-filter. It was brand new for this journey, and I'd upgraded to a better model than the type I normally relied on. After all, you don't want to skimp on water safety. And it was certainly a comfort to have a top-of-the-line model at hand now, especially since the waters of the Mackenzie are exceptionally muddy and silty. I dipped the intake hose into the river and the output hose into my water bottle. Then I began pumping, marvelling at the efficiency of the contraption. Abruptly, the filter clogged. Then water burst out of the seams. I could hardly believe it: inspecting the device, it had ruptured and broken irreparably—apparently a result of how dirty the river was. The irony of this I found amusing, the thought of drinking untreated water for months to come as rather less so.

Still, there was nothing for it. I could boil my water at night but not during the day, when by necessity I'd be unable to stop (even my breakfasts and lunches were just energy bars that could be eaten on the fly). I took heart in the fact that I'd recently read the results of a new science study that had concluded, somewhat unexpectedly, that most water in backcountry rivers, lakes, and streams was generally safe to drink. On the other hand, I'd also read reports that contradicted this—though I preferred not to think too much of those ones at the time. At any rate, I was now offering myself up as a guinea pig to see what would happen from months of drinking untreated water across the Canadian North. If I were to get sick with giardia (a type of microscopic parasite found, among other places, in wild animal feces), my journey would end rather badly from a personal perspective, though perhaps well for medical science.

At the moment, though, my concern was in finding somewhere to make camp. Considerable stretches of the river were lacking in camping places, due to canyon walls, steep banks, mudslides, heaps of driftwood, and piles of melting ice. When travelling downriver, it can be easy to take for granted finding a suitable site to camp, as if nothing looks promising, one can always drift along with the current until something better shows up. Not so though when dealing with upriver travel, when at the end of a long, wearisome day of battling the current, one has to take whatever one can get. June 10 was such a day for me. For a long while I'd been passing high muddy banks that came right down near the water's edge, not leaving space enough to pitch my tent amid the driftwood. So when I finally happened upon a clear spot that looked level enough to camp, set back some way from the river edge on a partially sloping bank, I took it.

However, upon closer inspection, the spot wasn't as level as it'd appeared from the water, and there were wild rose bushes with thorns that weren't very comfortable for sleeping on. But scanning ahead upriver I couldn't see any more promising site, and there were huge quantities of spruce logs currently drifting downriver, which, presenting the obstacles that they did, made me indifferent to the idea of pushing on. So far the Mackenzie had kindly given me charming campsites on soft sand beaches, spoiling me with their ease of access. Now it looked like I'd have to haul my gear and climb the high bluffs to find a site in the woods above. If it'd been only a matter of sleeping on a slope and some thorns, I might have tolerated it for one night, but I'd also noted that the banks here looked partially susceptible to a landslide. Such slides were very common, as I'd passed many during the day. I carefully inspected the soil—it seemed fairly hard-packed and dry, and there hadn't been any rain lately—but still, for peace of mind, I decided not to chance it. So, after securing my canoe and barrels on shore, I took my backpack and climbed up the high, steep banks to the forest above. It was thickly grown with dead black spruces, their ghostly, claw-like branches reaching out every which way, as well as aspen, poplar, and even a few dwarf birches. Amid them I spotted a patch of sphagnum moss that was just big enough for my tent.

After dining on freeze-dried shepherd's pie, I crawled into the tent, rolled up my second pair of clothes for a pillow, and stretched out in my sleeping bag. It was a cooler night, three or four degrees above freezing. Strangely, as I'd been setting up my tent beneath the dead spruces—something I'd done hundreds of times before—a vague sense of unease had come over me. There hadn't been any sign of grizzlies about, as far as I could tell, and so I tried to dispel the feeling by talking out loud. Yet as I drifted off to sleep, at some suppressed, almost unconscious level, that odd premonition remained.

× 5 ×

EASTWARD BOUND

round two-thirty a.m. I awoke to the sound of snapping branches. Something was out there, moving through the spruces. Rather than remain silent and still, as instinct might suggest, I yelled, "Hey, hey, hey!" in a deep voice. As I did I sprang from my sleeping bag, grabbed my knife and bear spray, and unzipped the tent's door on the side nearest the noise. In the eerie twilight gloom of the arctic summer night, I saw through the dead spruces something moving—a huge grizzly thirty feet off.

Then as my eyes focused I realized it wasn't a grizzly but something else entirely: a massive, prehistoric-looking creature—an arctic muskox, with huge curved horns. The great muskox, weighing half a ton, glared at me. My goodness, I thought, I'd almost rather it *was* a grizzly.

I dropped my bear spray and instead grabbed my bear banger. Hurriedly, with the muskox staring at me, I fired a banger into the air. It launched up like a firework, exploding with a bang above the trees. The muskox, startled by the bang, paused for a moment, still looking at me, then galloped off, smashing and crashing through the fallen spruces as if they were mere matchsticks.

I waited until I could no longer hear the muskox anymore. Then I waited some more, casting glances every which way, trying to see through the ghostly grey spruces. Finally, when I'd convinced myself it was safe to do so, I climbed back into the tent and my sleeping bag.

I'd met with muskox before—strange and eerie-looking beasts, a sort of arctic bison—but only in the far north of the High Arctic. Up there on the windswept, desolate snows of the arctic islands, owing to the harsh conditions the muskox were smaller. I'd found them to be mostly gentle giants that left me alone as I camped and paddled along. But here along the Mackenzie, the more hospitable climate allowed the muskox to grow much larger. The big bull that had stirred me from my sleep was the largest I'd ever seen.

After a few more hours of uneasy sleep I was on my way. Leaving that spot among the bluffs, it was one campsite I'd be happy not to see again. Later that morning as I poled along I spotted another muskox half-hidden in some poplars; then, a few kilometres on, deposited on the mudbank was a muskox skull. My curiosity was such that I couldn't help but stop to look at it. The enormous thing, horns and all, I estimated weighed fifty pounds! At the front of their skulls is a mass of hard bone, forming a kind of protective shield. The shield helps protect the males when they gallop and charge into each other, smashing their heads together with thunderous force. Such fierce contests are used to determine mating, sometimes inflicting severe and even fatal injuries on the losing muskox.

✳

By midday on June 12 I'd reached the end point of my journey along the Mackenzie: a smaller tributary flowing in from the east known as the Hare Indian River. This little-known waterway would, I hoped, lead me eastward for several hundred kilometres—almost to the vast, icy waters of Great Bear Lake itself. It wasn't, however, the obvious route into Great Bear from the Mackenzie. Looking at a map or satellite image, you'd almost immediately see that the obvious choice for getting from the Mackenzie River to Great Bear Lake is a larger river farther south— that's the Bear River. It connects directly to the lake, and has in fact been used for centuries as a traditional travel route. In contrast, the river I planned to follow, the Hare Indian, doesn't reach all the way to the lake, but instead terminates in a dead-end, which bars the way forward with miles of mosquito-infested swamps, tangled willows, and boulder fields. Why then—assuming I wasn't crazy—would I go that way? Simple: in keeping with the spirit and intention of my journey, I wanted to stay as far north as I could, whereas the Bear River lies a further two hundred kilometres south. Besides, my curiosity naturally inclined me to the lesser known route, despite the difficulties.

I was happy to bid goodbye to the Mackenzie not only because I was eager to push on with my journey, but also because I didn't relish drinking silty, untreated water along it (I'd filled my water bottle from clear feeder streams whenever I chanced to camp near one). Given all the sediment that washes in along its great banks, the Mackenzie is a naturally muddy, silty river. But where it meets the clear waters of the Hare Indian River, an odd effect is produced. It looks something like water and vegetable oil being poured into a bowl together. An abrupt division between the two rivers' waters is plainly visible, similar but on a smaller scale to the famous "meeting of the waters" in Brazil, where the coffee-coloured Amazon joins the dark waters of the Rio Negro.

My progress up the Mackenzie had been better than expected, but I knew that could easily change if wind, ice, or any number of other factors turned against me. Still, before setting off up the Hare Indian, I planned to make a detour south on foot to Fort Good Hope, population about 500, where the two men I'd met in the motorboat had gone. It was the last inhabited place I'd see until reaching Baker Lake, Nunavut, still thousands of kilometres away across the immense wilderness forming the heart of northern North America. So the extra ten-kilometre hike seemed worth it, as I could pick up a few essentials, fresh batteries, boxers, and perhaps some yogurt . . . maybe even blueberry yogurt, should they have such a delicacy.

I paddled across the mouth of the Hare Indian River (it was too deep for poling) to its southern bank, where it joined the Mackenzie. A couple of small motorboats lay pulled up on shore; behind them, a gravel path led into the woods. I secured my canoe and then set off on foot for town.

Founded as a fur trade post back in 1805, Fort Good Hope was the scene of a famous clash in the 1970s over the proposed Mackenzie Valley pipeline. A consortium of oil companies sought to build what would have been the world's largest natural gas pipeline running right through the valley. The local Dene communities, like Fort Good Hope, argued passionately against it on the grounds that it would destroy their traditional way of life by disrupting wildlife habitats, especially caribou. Facing tremendous local opposition, the federal government shelved the project.

But times change, and a generation later, with the influence of the old traditionalists fading, the local Dene and Inuit groups now joined a consortium led by Imperial Oil, with a promise to receive one third of the profits from the mammoth pipeline. The approval process dragged on until, in 2010, the government finally gave the go-ahead. Construction was set to begin in the near future. Thus, as I'd poled my way up the mighty Mackenzie, I assumed, with an undeniably sad air, that I was bearing witness to the final days of the North's greatest river in its natural state. But, in December 2017, Imperial Oil opted out, bowing to changing economic realities that had opened up more promising reserves elsewhere. Still, most observers were optimistic (if that's the word) that the world's insatiable demand for fossil fuels will eventually revive the pipeline.

Despite its geographic remoteness, I found Fort Good Hope to be a thoroughly modern town: shiny new pickup trucks (brought in by ice roads) rumbled through the streets, while in a sign of the times people seemed to move about with eyes glued to their phones. (A giant transmission tower had been erected overlooking town to provide reception.) As I made my way down the main street, half a dozen planes suddenly roared across the skies performing aerobatic manoeuvres. They were there, I learned, as part of a touring Arctic air show that had been conceived as a Canada 150 project. Inside the store, I quickly picked up what I needed. Everyone I met was friendly, asking if I'd come for the air show. I explained about the yogurt and the boxers.

As I was leaving town, I happened to spot one of the men from the motorboat I'd met days earlier along the Mackenzie.

"You made it?!" he said, apparently shocked.

"Yes," I said. Now that there were no revving boat engines, conversation came easier. "You know," he said, "it's a lot easier to travel the Mackenzie the other direction?"

"I've heard that."

"You're the first guy I've ever heard of to canoe upriver. Are you nuts?"

I just laughed and shrugged. I wasn't actually the first, but the fact that he thought so reinforced the oddness of it. He again offered me a place to stay, but I had to be on my way. It was all I could do, pressed for time as I was and a little shy after weeks alone, to decline offers of a hot shower or a lift to the airport to see the assortment of planes up close. So we parted, he for the airport and me for the river.

My detour to Fort Good Hope had taken less than three hours. There was still plenty of light, but rather than face the uncertain prospect of paddling up a new river where decent camping places might be difficult to find, I decided to make camp where I'd left my canoe. I'd get an early start in the morning.

It had been a cold, windy day with some light snow that later gave way to rain, followed overnight by more snow. Inside my little tent on the riverbank I was warm and snug, despite my sleeping bag having lost much of its warmth through regular use. But I wasn't troubled, as whenever it was cold I always slept fully dressed. Normally, I didn't even bother taking my jacket off. The great thing about this method, I find, is not only does it keep you warm, but you also lose no time getting dressed in the morning. You can just spring up and go.

Occupying my thoughts that snowy night was what might await me on the Hare Indian River. The people I'd spoken to in town weren't able to say much about the river beyond its first shallow rapids, as it wasn't possible for motorboats to get beyond that, and their focus was naturally on the vast Mackenzie. However, in winter there was a seasonal ice-road that at one junction crossed the river, so trucks and snowmobiles could pass near that point when it was buried under ice, though that didn't really apply much, given it was June. I hadn't been able to locate any canoe reports on the river from the usual sources.

The only canoe description I'd found of it, back in Sudbury while digging around in Laurentian University's library, was in a canoe book issued by the federal government in the 1970s. This report, however, was of a rather nebulous character, especially when compared with the other northern rivers in the book. There are a few reasons why this river attracts little notice from canoeists. The giant Mackenzie River, stretching for thousands of kilometres, naturally monopolizes canoeing attention in its vicinity. And if someone is after the splendour of a more wild and majestic river with gorgeous scenery and exciting whitewater, the dozens of rivers draining down from the nearby Mackenzie Mountains are the obvious choice. For most of these waterways, as well as the Mackenzie itself, hundreds of trip reports are readily available. But not so for the river I was now to embark upon.

*

From the air, the river known as the Hare Indian seems to wind like a giant anaconda through the sparse subarctic forests west of Great Bear Lake, stretching over two hundred kilometres before emptying into the Mackenzie River just south of the Arctic Circle. It's a much smaller river than the Mackenzie, measuring only about two hundred and fifty metres near its mouth, and this decreases the farther up it one ventures. Its waters I found swift and clear, but with a current even more powerful than the Mackenzie's. Again, my plan entailed travelling upriver, paddling, poling, and wading through rapids against the current. I hoped it'd take me no more than two weeks—three if conditions were really bad—to struggle upriver and then hike overland to the coastline of Great Bear Lake, hopefully just in time for that mighty inland ocean's ice melt.

Despite the stronger current, in the river's lower reaches I found my paddle could be used effectively by using a technique I'd experimented with previously when needing to paddle up rivers from Hudson Bay. This method consisted of capitalizing on the river's undercut banks, which could be used as a springboard to push off from with my paddle while I remained seated in the canoe. A hard push off the undercut bank was then followed by several more strokes, and then another thrust off the bank, and so on repeating the manoeuvre, alternating between thrusts and paddle strokes while hugging the shoreline. This strategy allowed me to travel quite rapidly against even strong currents when conditions were right for it.

A potential drawback did occur to me, though, as I was springing cheerfully along the banks with my paddle. Those same undercut banks are often thickly grown with willows—exactly the kind of willows that conceal anything lurking within them. A grizzly or a muskox could be three feet away and I'd never know it (which I found was occasionally the case). Battling upriver hugging the banks, should a muskox take a sudden fancy to charge out from its concealment, it would land right on my passing canoe. Or should a hidden grizzly reach out from a willow thicket to swipe its powerful paw at my head—well, I'd seen what that did to Betty's steel-plated door. But I reasoned the odds of such a thing happening were quite minimal, so I tried not to let such thoughts trouble me too much as I paddled along, enjoying the plump little yellow warblers singing their songs along the banks.

Beyond the willow thickets enclosing the river were black and white spruce, tamarack, poplars, and trembling aspens, hardy trees that can tolerate the extreme cold of these northern latitudes. In places where the banks didn't lend themselves to my paddling method, I switched to poling. It was hard work; my muscles were feeling the ache and burn of continuous hours of non-stop poling, especially when forced to pole up rapids.

Difficult as paddling and poling could be, a more serious challenge lay in navigating the river's bigger rapids. This was a problem I'd largely avoided on the Mackenzie, which has few real rapids, and even those I could avoid by hugging the shorelines. But here, in sections of fast-moving water, that wasn't an option. With hard effort I managed to pole up some of the shallower rapids, although driving a canoe through rapids while standing upright in it is always a precarious proposition. Deeper, more powerful rapids required getting out of the boat and hauling the canoe as I waded through the rushing water. For these I wore the neoprene hip waders Chuck had given me.

Some sections weren't too bad. I'd slosh along, dragging the canoe behind me with a rope. The river was clear, so I could at least see the rocky bottom and be sure of my footing. The exception was in the largest rapids, where the torrent of churning whitewater made it impossible to see where I was stepping. Here, I had to be extra cautious to avoid twisting an ankle or losing my footing and smashing my head on a rock. My careful plans, worked out in advance, had been very clear on the need to avoid smashing my head off rocks.

The key was to read the water correctly—to make the right decision as to where to haul the canoe. I needed the weakest point in the racing waters, where it wasn't too deep. Otherwise I'd lose my footing and be swept away. One stretch gave me particular trouble. The river cascaded around different gravel bars, causing swift rapids. I had to struggle to maintain my balance in the rushing water, holding on to the canoe's bow to steady myself. I edged forward cautiously, barely lifting my feet off the river bottom; it was more like shuffling forward, trying to avoid being knocked over by the force of the water. Just a bit farther, I told myself, if I can just overcome this surging current, I'll get there . . . But it was too deep: another step and the water would be over my hip waders. Reluctantly I retreated to shore.

Fortunately, I'd packed in addition to the hip waders a separate pair of chest waders in the event of meeting with deeper stretches. The extra weight of having to pack two pairs of waders wasn't ideal, but chest waders are very impractical to wear all the time. From past experience I'd found that smaller hip waders allowed for much greater agility, such as when needing to leap from rock to rock or across fallen logs. So it was only with reluctance that I packed the ungainly chest waders as a kind of worst-case-scenario measure. Both sets were the kind worn with detached boots, so at least I didn't need two pairs of those.

On the bank I switched into the chest waders, then plunged back into the river, taking the canoe and retracing my steps into the deeper waters. I didn't dwell too much on the particulars of the situation: standing nearly chest-deep in a swollen river with frigid water rushing past that just a few weeks earlier had been ice-covered, far from any help, hauling a heavily laden canoe behind me. I just put one foot in front of the other and kept going. That's often the best approach, I find, when dragging canoes upriver.

Lurking in the deep, weedy pools along the banks were northern pike. These stealthy hunters hover in calmer sections, waiting for smaller fish, or even unsuspecting ducklings, to happen along. Pike weren't the only wildlife about. In one winding stretch of river, after I'd left the rapids behind and switched out of my chest waders, I caught sight of something small, dark, and furry moving on the opposite bank—a black bear cub.

Most of my route was outside the range of black bears, but here, where the treeline surged northward, black bears reach the northern limit of their natural range, which extends right up to the Arctic Circle. As such, these black bears are the hardiest of their kind in the world, putting up with long, dark, brutally cold winters. However, unlike grizzlies, black bears avoid the open tundra, preferring to remain south of the treeline. My route here partly overlapped with their range, but as I continued east, the black bears would disappear as tundra came to predominate. This little cub was apparently alone. I watched it wander along the bank for several minutes until it disappeared from view. I hoped it wasn't lost and that its mother was merely hidden somewhere nearby.

That night I made camp on the riverbank. It wasn't my most pleasant campsite, as the shoreline was filled with pebbles and rocks, which

I hadn't much choice but to sleep on. That old report had warned that the Hare Indian River was mostly covered with willow thickets along its banks, which made camping difficult. Thus, I felt I couldn't afford to be too choosy when it came to finding any spots free of willows. At any rate, sleeping on rocks isn't the worst thing in the world, especially when you've got a wild, majestic place all to yourself.

With my tent set up on the rocks, I dipped my head into the cold, rippling waters of the river. It felt wonderfully refreshing—on the Mackenzie, I hadn't done anything of the sort. Its waters were so silty and muddy that when I dipped my hands in them, they quite literally came out dirtier than when they went in. But here the water was clear, allowing me to see right down to the pebbly bottom and the vivid green reeds dancing in the current.

Refreshed, I crawled into my tent and stretched out on the rocks, I felt around with my hands through the tent floor for any particularly troublesome ones and, grasping them through the tent floor, tossed them aside as best as I could. Then I pulled out my maps to study my progress. In total, my route encompassed hundreds of topographic maps. When I reached the end of one map and the start of a new one, I'd set aside the old map to be burned in my fire—thus literally burning through my maps as a measure of my progress. Just then I heard something pass over the tent. It made a kind of swooshing sound, as of wings flapping, and a strange call, like someone knocking. If you've ever had a raven fly over your head you'll know the odd, unnatural noise they make, and how unnerving it can be if you have a superstitious turn of mind.

Judging from the sound, the raven outside continued to swoop back and forth around my tent, as ravens are wont to do, making other surreal noises, but mostly that odd knocking sound. Although ravens are most famous for their deep croaking calls of the sort featured in horror movies, they have an amazing vocal range that includes not only knocking noises but also shrill cries, raspy chatters, and even mimicry of other birds' calls.

In my rambles around the hills of Sudbury ravens would often pass over me, making the same eerie knocking noise I now heard coming from outside my tent. I poked my head out and caught a glimpse of a large, glossy black bird flapping across the river before it vanished over the spruces. I thought to myself, when camped alone in the wilderness one can certainly appreciate why ravens feature prominently in horror stories. I took it as a good sign, then laid back down on my rock bed and fell asleep—dreaming of ravens.

INTO THE SWAMP

The farther up the river I went, the wilder it became. Each bend I rounded, each rapid I waded through took me farther from the haunts of humans and deeper into a land of wolverines and muskox. The shallow, rocky rapids along the river's winding course ensured that no motorboats could reach up it, leaving it as an oasis for wildlife. There were bald eagles perched in spruce thrones and in the waters swam green winged teals, mergansers, and goldeneyes. Sandpipers hopped along the pebbly banks while robins and yellow warblers provided music, the robins singing *cheerily, cheer up, cheerily, cheer up* and the warblers chiming in with their whistling *sweet-see-see-swee*. Beavers loudly slapped their tails in the water as I passed by, and muskrats were also about. In one spot I heard a moaning cry—a little baby beaver, lost among some reeds, searching for its parents. I hoped it found them; if not it might provide lunch for a fox or passing eagle. There were signs of moose along the banks, as well as caribou. Meanwhile wolves stalked along, hunting the numerous muskox.

On my third day poling upriver I saw a total of four muskox, each of whom stared curiously at me. One was barely ten feet away, concealed on the riverbank as I poled by; neither of us noticed the other until we were directly opposite each other. The muskox snorted, apparently shocked to see me, and then glared with its enormous eyes, seemingly mystified by my presence. I apologized for the intrusion and poled hurriedly away.

More interesting perhaps was what I couldn't see from the river—inland, I knew, stalking like phantoms amid the shadowy gloom of the black spruces, were lynx. These living ghosts are the North's most elusive creature: beautiful big cats with sphinx-like faces, thick grey coats to endure the harsh winters, and giant, oversized paws that act as snowshoes so that they can move soundlessly, spectre-like, across deep snows.

The farther up that twisting, windy river I ventured, the more I began to wonder about that old 1970s government canoe report. It had described the river as lined with willows along its entire course and flowing through a "subdued and gentle rolling landscape." But I kept seeing things that didn't match that description. In the first place, the willows weren't as numerous as the report suggested. Perhaps that kind of change might have happened through natural processes like regeneration after a forest fire, though the evidence on hand didn't seem to support such a theory. But when I started to encounter towering tabletop mountains with sheer cliffs hundreds of feet high, it became hard to reconcile such cliffs and rocky uplands with the report's description of "subdued and gentle" terrain. I wondered whether the authors had actually explored the river, or if perhaps they'd lost their field notes and couldn't remember what they'd seen. I found it a landscape to give free reign to the imagination—a place where one could daydream for hours while poling to the point of numbness against the current.

It was in the midst of one such daydream, of dinosaurs stalking amid the towering limestone crags overlooking the winding river, while poling near the bank that I noticed an odious stench wafting on the wind. Something was dead—very dead, judging by the smell—somewhere nearby. Another pole thrust and I saw what was giving off the stench: a dead muskox lying on shore, half-concealed by willow shrubs. A rapid analysis of the fly-covered carcass suggested that it had most likely been ambushed by a grizzly that had ripped open its neck. Large as they are, muskox are occasionally killed by grizzlies when they're caught unawares. In this case, the grizzly had apparently eaten its fill, leaving the remains to be picked over by ravens and other scavengers. I doubled my pace, poling hard to get back to pure northern air.

That night I made camp within sight of a big sandstone outcrop crowned with little spruces. What wood there was I gathered for a fire to make spruce tea. In the last four days I'd made it some hundred kilometres up this mysterious river, the waterway becoming narrower and the trees thinning steadily. Though diminutive in size many of these spruces, I knew, were quite ancient. The harsh conditions and short growing season meant that, despite their size, some were centuries old. Soon they'd disappear entirely and I'd be back on the wind-swept tundra. In the meantime I enjoyed their shelter, reminding me as they did of a childhood spent wandering woods.

I slept peacefully that night, until branches snapping around twelve-thirty jolted me awake. I grabbed my bear spray and unzipped the tent's screen door. Under the midnight sun I could see all too clearly a bear's face staring right at me. The bear's body was hidden in willows, with just its head visible, about twenty feet away.

Camped alone in the wilderness, many miles from any other human, with a bear outside my tent—I thought to myself that's the very stuff of childhood dreams (if your dreams at all resembled mine). It wasn't a grizzly or polar bear at least—merely a black bear. It's not that I dismissed black bears as of no particular concern, but they're familiar animals, and though still big (say about 300 pounds), they don't have quite the intimidating dimensions of grizzlies and polar bears.

Still, there was something in this black bear's face—staring as it was at me—that I found unsettling. It looked uncomfortably like it was sizing me up. I tried talking to it, telling it gruffly to not even think about it. In the meantime I fished out my bear banger and stepped outside the tent. Fortunately, my canoe was lying overturned between the bear and me, forming a psychological barrier separating us, if not an actual one.

"All right," I said. "I've asked you to leave and you haven't, so now I'm going to fire a banger and give you the scare of your life." I pointed the banger toward the sky, then pulled on its end, unleashing a flare that shot up high and exploded with a bang. It was so abrupt and loud, echoing across untold miles of wild, silent country, that it startled even me.

The bear barely flinched. He remained exactly where he was, staring straight at me with an icy look in his dark eyes. Apparently, bears don't find bear bangers as frightening as muskox do. So I grabbed my paddle—it was lying beside the tent—and started shouting to scare off the bear. After all, such tactics had worked with the charging grizzly. As I did so I spun the paddle round in my hands, then swung it violently against the overturned canoe, banging against it like a giant drum to add to my intimidating display. Surely, this would work.

The bear, however, responded by growling in a low, guttural way, his gaze still fixed on me. Apparently, he wasn't easily frightened. I thought of my bear spray nearby, but I didn't want to use it if I could help it. So I mustered up an even louder barrage of shouts, deeper and more menacing, and really swung the paddle now, threatening the bear should he try anything. This finally seemed to work: the bear, huffing and puffing, now edged back, and slowly, very slowly, started walking away. He shuffled off along the river, remaining partly concealed in the willows. I kept my eyes on him, gripping my paddle as I did so, until he moved out of sight.

Then I kindled up a blazing fire nearby on the rock-strewn bank. The fire, I hoped, would keep the bear from returning. I waited a while for any sign of it, but it seemed to have gone. So I crawled back inside my tent and forced myself to fall back to sleep. Difficult as sleeping alone in bear territory might be, particularly after you've just had a bear growl at you, I knew that without sleep I wouldn't have the energy needed to continue. Sleep was a necessity, plain and simple. And thus I slept—with my bear spray handy.

✳

As the days went by, each one taking me farther from the world of emails, phones, screens, laptops, and incessant news cycles, I felt as if I were poling back in time. It felt relaxing to turn my back on those things, even in spite of bears interrupting my sleep. Personally, I think the more we can step away from our society's deepening addiction to digital screens, to 24/7 connectivity, to unnecessary clutter, the healthier we'll be. Immersed in nature, one feels alive. Shut up indoors all day, staring transfixed at a screen, one loses something.

But to return to the peace and tranquillity of nature: as the temperatures warmed, immense, suffocating hordes of blood-sucking insects filled the air. My throat was soon pockmarked with blackfly bites, my beard smeared with bloodstains, and my wrists, waistline, and anywhere else the flies could get at covered in itchy sores. Prior to mid-June, the weather had been cold enough to keep away the bugs, but now they were out with a vengeance. I didn't suffer alone: thick clouds of insects hovered around the muskox, caribou, and moose, feasting on them mercilessly. One moose I spotted must have had a million mosquitoes and blackflies on it—the poor animal took to the water to escape them, but above the waterline the bugs still swarmed its head and ears. Having grown up on the edge of a swamp I had a particularly high tolerance for mosquitoes, though blackflies are a torment for everyone. I told myself now, as I fetched my mesh bug net out of my backpack to get some relief, to take heart that these storms of bugs were merely temporary—if I could just put up with them for the next two and a half months, the return of cold weather would take care of the matter.

Three weeks since setting off on my journey, and now fully eight days of travelling up the Hare Indian River, my body was feeling the ache and wear of continual travel. My legs were bruised from stumbling into unseen rocks beneath the water's surface. The tendons in my fingers were sore from poling for long hours each day. (At night I'd stretch them out gingerly, but I knew there wasn't much I could do—I was at the mercy of the elements, and so to take any time off was out of the question.) My feet were blistered from the waders, and my big toenail on my left foot had fallen off. But otherwise, I felt fine.

The river was getting smaller, little more than a creek now. The water continued to alternate between calmer sections I could paddle up and faster, swifter sections that could only be navigated by pain-staking wading and dragging the canoe behind me, often for hours on end. This wading, given the rocky bottom, took a toll on my toes, but I made light of it—toenails, after all, grow back.

The shallow sections were full of arctic graylings, a beautiful fish with a vibrant rainbow hue to their big dorsal fins. I'd happily eaten graylings in the past, but alas on this journey, if I were to reach my goal, there was no time for fishing—food was mere fuel, to be con-sumed as I marched and trudged along. Even my customary morning oatmeal I'd forsaken in order not to lose time setting off early. To stay healthy though, I did occasionally make spruce tea—since spruce is high in vitamin C, something my dried rations lacked.

Caribou, wolves, eagles, muskox, and bears were all plentiful in the wild upper reaches of the twisting river. One beautiful arctic wolf, his white coat streaked with black and grey, was particularly curious about me. He was a big, lanky animal, and followed me along the riverbank for over a kilometre as I paddled along, so drawn by curios-ity that he almost seemed to wish to speak with me. He'd cock his head to the side, eyeing me up and down. There wasn't any hint of malice in his look. Indeed, the wolf—a true symbol of wildness in a world with ever less of it—was shy and skittish. The slightest noise by me, such as a simple "hi there," or my paddle bumping against the canoe, caused him to jump back, startled. But then, as I quietly contin-ued on, he would follow. Finally he vanished into the spruces. Never in my life had I ever seen anything so perfect, so magical, as that great arctic wolf—it filled me with awe and wonder.

✳

It was a rainy morning when I crawled out of my tent at five a.m. on June 22 to get a start on the day. The sound of a caribou swimming across the river had stirred me from a pleasant dream. I'd camped on a sandbank within sight of some cliffs. In the rain I soon had my tent down and rolled up, my barrels carefully loaded into the canoe, and my day's rations set out so I could grab them as need be from the bottom of the canoe. I was eager to be underway, as I sensed I'd was at last nearing the end of the Hare Indian River. Soon I'd be facing the prospect of travelling on foot across trackless and unknown terrain, transporting in stages my canoe and barrels, in order to reach the coastline of Great Bear Lake.

Before it came to that though, I knew from my maps that the Hare Indian River flowed through two long lakes, connected by what was left of the river. These lakes I referred to as the Headwater Lakes, since they were the river's source. Beyond them was one more long narrow lake, after which lay terrain of uncertain character blocking the way to Great Bear's coastline. Whether it'd be possible to make it all the way to each of the lakes by water, or whether the interconnecting river would dry up before then into a tiny trickle or become clogged with natural debris, I didn't know. The satellite imagery I'd examined beforehand was insufficient to determine such details, and I'd lost all faith in the reliability of that old 1970s canoe report. At any rate, those authors were canoeing downriver, not up, and they'd only started at the first of the Headwater Lakes (supposedly), whereas I'd have to go well beyond that to reach Great Bear Lake.

Poling, wading, and paddling saw me advance another twenty-four kilometres that day. Things were getting much harder, though. The river's upper section wasn't much more than a beaver creek now, and increasingly unnavigable. The first hints of change came the next day, when I hit a long, marshy lowland. The grassy marshes were quite unexpected, and reminded me of the tidal marshes along coastal rivers in New Brunswick. The water here was too shallow for poling as the heavily-loaded canoe hit bottom. So I had to get out and wade, listening to shorebirds calling in the marsh as I hauled the canoe with rope behind me.

In the distance a blue ridge rose high against the clear sky; somewhere beyond that I figured were the Headwater Lakes. I pressed on, sloshing through shallow stretches, forcing the canoe over them. Then I saw something glinting along the marshy stream banks—something that made a shiver go down my spine. It was the remains of river ice, clustered on the shore and melting in the June sun, a reminder of how recently these waterways were still frozen. The remnant ice boded ill for what I might find on Great Bear Lake: if it was still ice-covered, I'd be faced with a delay that might spell the end of my journey's hope of success. I pushed on to find out.

The first of the Headwater Lakes, fortunately, I found free of ice. I paddled straight across its five-kilometre expanse in forty minutes—seeing how in nearly eight hundred kilometres of travelling it was the first water I'd paddled on without an opposing current. I'd almost forgotten what it felt like to paddle a canoe normally, without battling wind and current—and that such things could be peaceful and pleasant. Alas, it was but a brief respite from the increasingly punishing nature of my journey, now that I'd quite run out of anything resembling a navigable water route. On the far side of the lake the river continued. It widened into a swamp filled with dead spruces and tamaracks protruding from the water at odd angles, after which the remains of the river rapidly diverted into several channels, each thickly grown over with spruces and willows. The day was warm, sunny, and windless, making the clouds of mosquitoes and blackflies extreme.

The tangled jungle of alders, willows, spruces, and tamaracks gave the creek a claustrophobic feel as I followed its snaking course. The thick clouds of biting insects didn't improve things much. Dead trees across the waterway forced me to climb carefully onto them and then haul my canoe up and over so that I could resume paddling on the opposite side. It was hard work, given that the heavily loaded canoe weighed more than I did.

Soon I arrived at a place where the swampy creek forked in two: it wasn't immediately clear which fork I should take. My maps and GPS were no help—neither had the kind of detail needed to accurately discern swampy channels. It was clear they weren't terribly precise, as my plotted position on the GPS showed me on dry land somewhere, which wasn't the case. I was smack in the middle of the remaining waterway.

So I set aside the maps and GPS and instead read the landscape. Neither fork looked promising—both led straight into logjams. The bushes and fallen trees had become so thick that I couldn't see much beyond twenty feet in any direction. But examining the current I detected a stronger flow from the left fork, so I resolved to follow it. I was still heading upriver, and sooner or later it seemed, this waterway was going to dry up and disappear. There was barely room to swing a paddle inside the thickets, but I jabbed and pushed along as well as I could.

I'd gone only a short distance before a logjam formed of dead spruces barred the way forward. There was nothing for it but to get out of the canoe and into the water. Carefully, knowing how easily I could slip and cut open my leg on one of the logs' sharp, snapped-off branches, I began the backbreaking labour of clearing a passage—first shoving, heaving, and pushing with the weight of my body to get the logs out of the way, then lifting, hauling, and ramming my canoe to get it through.

The jam continued as far as I could see. The sight of such a nightmarish string of obstacles before me, combined with the relentless hordes of blackflies, made me briefly wonder if on balance it might not be wiser to quit now, point my canoe downstream, and paddle with the current back to the Mackenzie. Fortunately, this was but a passing delusion, and saner heads prevailed: I banished such thoughts and instead plunged into the river up to my waist, heaving with renewed force to batter the canoe over the logjam. I smashed branches aside, and forced the canoe through like a medieval battering ram against a fortress gate. Then, to squeeze under the next jam, I had to get down into dark water that rose above my waist, flooding my hip waders and drenching me. There wasn't anything to be done but to keep going.

I was in the zone now—you know that zone you get into when you've been canoeing up rivers alone in the wilderness for a month? That was the exact zone I was now in. With renewed vigour I shoved, heaved, and twisted my way up and under successive logjams. One fallen spruce formed a kind of bridge across the narrow creek; to get around it I scampered up its trunk, balanced on my chest on top of it, and threaded the canoe underneath with my legs dangling in the air. But this triumph was short-lived. Around the next bend lay a logjam that made a mockery of all others. It was massive, impenetrable, and utterly demoralizing—a colossal pile of dead trees that looked as though a beaver the size of Godzilla had heaped them up. To hack through it with my hatchet would take months. I had no other option but to portage around it through the swamps of alders and black spruces.

Since it wasn't possible to carry everything at once, it'd have to be done in stages. My easiest load was my backpack, which held my tent, spare clothing, tripod, hatchet, and other survival essentials. I strapped it on and plunged off into the green alders. They were almost as tall as me, making seeing ahead difficult, but they didn't last long, as the vegetation abruptly gave way to a foul bog.

I picked my way elf-like across it, trying not to step in the wrong place, seeking out the mossy patches of firmer ground wherever they existed. Next the ground sloped up, revealing more fallen spruces to climb over and alders to push through. Once through these obstacles, having managed to bypass the giant logjam, I could see where the creek resumed. It wasn't exactly clear sailing—there were more jams ahead, but they weren't so bad as to rule out relaunching the canoe.

But first I had to retrace my steps back to where I'd left the rest of my gear. So far I'd only completed the easiest load, my backpack. Next I'd have to transport my two barrels across the swamp. These would have to be taken across one at a time, as any more weight would just cause me to sink into the muck. The bugs in the midst of the swamp were dreadful, swarming me as I laboured back and forth across it, transporting each load successively. The bug net I was wearing overtop my broad-brimmed hat didn't make much difference—blackflies always seem to find a way to squeeze through eventually. Finally I went back for my canoe, dragging it behind me through the alders and across the morass. When I came to the ground that sloped upward, I lifted the canoe over my head and carried it in order to get around the toppled dead spruces. At last, panting and sweating, I reached the spot where my backpack and barrels were waiting.

No sooner had I repacked the canoe and launched it back into the swampy creek than I arrived at another logjam. Wearily I climbed back out of the vessel, summoning up whatever strength I had left. Grabbing hold of the canoe's bow I hoisted it up onto the first of the fallen spruces. Then I began heaving it across the barricade of dead trees. The jam continued for some ways. Luckily, though, I was able to slip back down into the water where a spot opened a bit, crouch down, and then wade under the fallen trees as I dragged the floating canoe behind me. The water once more rose above my waist and flooded my hip waders. Soaking wet, I kept edging under the dead spruces by kneeling in the water, forcing the canoe to scrape beneath their claw-like branches.

At last I emerged from the swampy logjams to a welcome sight before me—the blue waters of the second of the two Headwaters Lakes. Like the first, it was long and narrow and enclosed by towering, spruce-clad ridges that in places had vertical rock outcrops amid heaps of tumbled boulders. There were caves visible on the rocky slopes, making me wonder whether grizzlies or windigos might inhabit them.

A Pacific loon cried hauntingly from somewhere across the water. Despite their name, Pacific loons are found in the Arctic, and are cousins of the common loons farther south. I made camp on the lake's north shore, knowing I was now getting close to the mighty, frightening expanse of Great Bear Lake.

In the meantime, I enjoyed the soul-filling splendour of a wild, lonely lake I had all to myself. My soaked clothes I left drying in the branches of a dead spruce. Then I found a pleasant place on some soft moss and lichens, and I stretched out and slept.

✳

Hard as the previous day had been, harder challenges yet awaited me. After paddling across the lake in the early morning I headed down a short swampy stream that promptly dried up, meaning yet another portage. Back and forth I went through the willow swamps, transporting each of my four loads—the two barrels, backpack, and canoe, mosquitoes and blackflies swarming horrendously. The incessant biting of the flies and mosquitoes was almost maddening, since my hands were full and unable to swat them away. A high rocky ridge remained in sight to the east; I used it as a guide so that I wouldn't lose my way amid the willows and suffocating clouds of swarming insects.

Eventually I came to a small, nameless pond amid the willows. This little pond, I realized, was the true headwaters of the Hare Indian River, that's to say, its farthest source, lying beyond even the two lakes. The little pond was barely more than two hundred metres across, but I decided to spare myself what little portaging I could by transporting my loads to its muddy edge, then paddling across, before resuming my struggles on its far side. It seemed probable that I was the first person ever to drag a canoe all the way from the river's mouth to its swampy, inaccessible headwaters—if only because under any normal circumstances to do so would be utterly impractical, if not completely mad. When it came time to transport the canoe, I simply dragged it behind me through the willows, mosses, and grasses. The dragging was made more difficult than it ought to have been owing to the fact that inside the canoe, adding to its weight, were my hiking boots (I'd kept my waders on for the portage), as well as the beaver pole (which I knew I'd still need), fishing rod (my emergency food plan), and the wheeled cart (a dubious idea). Why did I have a wheeled cart? It was the cart I'd bought in advance in case I needed to wheel my canoe along the gravel of the Dempster Highway. That hadn't been necessary, but I kept the cart in spite of its bulk and extra weight, because of a report I'd read of an Arctic canoe trip done a few decades ago by two paddlers. They'd reported using a wheeled cart to great effect to lessen their loads on portages, and I'd hoped to do the same. So far the willows and uneven ground had precluded any hope of using it—and thus it became more dead weight for me to haul in the canoe. I consoled myself with the thought that I might yet meet with some favourable terrain where it could be of use.

Once across the small pond I portaged on, not entirely sure which way to head. Again my maps and GPS weren't of much use here. I hoped to find a stream flowing in the other direction, out to the last of the three long lakes, since this would mean I'd reached the Great Bear Lake watershed. The willows gave way to sparse woods of tamaracks and black spruce, the uneven ground cloaked with caribou lichens and aromatic shrubs of Labrador tea. As the name suggests, the leaves of that plant have long been used to make tea, and in springtime their pretty white flowers add a touch of beauty to sombre subarctic forests.

I navigated intuitively, rounding some swamps and trudging through alternating terrain, until I happened upon a welcome sight—a tiny creek not more than a ditch, where the water flowed the opposite direction, *east*. That could mean only one thing—I'd crossed a watershed divide (or else become hopelessly lost). A few steps behind me, all the water was draining west, down into the Hare Indian River and onto the Mackenzie, and from there out to the Beaufort Sea. A couple of steps the other way the water flowed east, through tiny creeks and lakes to the vast waters of Great Bear Lake itself.

The little stream, less than a foot wide and ankle-deep, was too small to paddle. But the sight of it cheered me all the same, as I at least now had something to follow. Several hundred metres farther on it widened into a shallow creek that twisted around through an open sort of meadow before disappearing behind a willow thicket. The water here looked as though it might be deep enough to at least pole my canoe, so I dropped my backpack by the bank and returned for the other three loads, swatting hordes of mosquitoes as I went.

Transporting each of my four loads individually meant that to advance just one kilometre I had to travel *seven times* that distance on foot, as not only did I have to carry the four loads separately, I had to retrace my steps back to the start each time to get the next load. This depressing arithmetic made me especially eager to find any water-course that would allow me to resume travel by canoe. The little creek flowing east offered that hope, so I pushed myself hard in order to get everything to its muddy banks.

But I'd met with too many creeks in my life to pin my hopes on one. They often come across as charming at first, but then, once you've gotten to know them a bit, they dash your hopes. Such was the case with this little stream. After I'd poled along for just a few hundred metres it led right into a willow thicket that blocked any passage for-ward. The bugs here were among the most intense I'd ever seen. Unable to press forward in the canoe, I reluctantly stepped out into the mud, sinking to my knees as I staggered toward firmer ground.

The willows were impossibly thick; portaging through them wasn't an option. I had no choice but to unload my gear from the canoe and struggle across the deep mud with it to more solid ground, outside the willow swamp. Here the ground sloped upward, with black spruces and a few tamaracks. Scanning ahead, I couldn't make out any clear water, just a tangled mass of willows that seemed to suffocate the little creek I'd hoped to follow. I sighed, realizing that my longest and likely most difficult portage yet now lay before me.

With my backpack and a paddle as a walking stick, I set off to seek the end of the willows and the return of navigable water. The ground was uneven, rising and declining into small gullies. In some places I had to claw through thick clusters of black spruce; in others I plunged through willow thickets taller than me, making me apprehensive grizzlies or muskox might be lurking about. I tried to do the polite thing and announce my presence by talking out loud so as not to star-tle them. Hopefully they'd do the same for me.

After about a kilometre I finally reached a point where the stream looked navigable. I set down my backpack on the bank, then returned to fetch my next load. It was a warm, sunny day, the temperature climbing to the mid-teens. All the portaging, perhaps combined with the bugs that were incessantly draining my blood, gave me a terrible thirst. I'd filled my water bottle before leaving the lake that morning, but it was empty now. Nearly three weeks had passed since my water purifier had broken, and so far, drinking untreated water had no apparent ill effects on me. But I drew the line at drinking from a beaver swamp. Thus, I pushed on without water, continuing the long, gruelling portaging.

Yet the painstaking effort required to carry each of the loads over rough, uneven terrain became increasingly difficult to maintain without water. By this time I was sweating and nearly exhausted. I slouched down to rest and thought the matter over: it seemed on balance that the odds were greater that I'd pass out from dehydration than get sick from drinking untreated water. So upon such logic, I filled my bottle from the little creek. Before drinking I held the bottle up to the sunlight, making out tiny organisms in it. "That's just extra protein," I told myself, before taking a gulp.

It may have been that I was badly dehydrated, but the water seemed to taste especially delightful. At first, I thought, I'd only drink a small amount, enough to keep me going. But then I drank a little more, again reassuring myself that the odds of anything bad coming of it (based on that science paper I'd read) were minimal.

By late afternoon I'd finished the portage and was able to relaunch my canoe in the creek. The narrow creek was still tightly hemmed in by willow bushes, but it was deep enough to float a canoe in. But despite the depth, the narrow banks made it impossible to paddle in the water. So to make progress I had to stand upright in the canoe and jab with my paddle at the banks, propelling myself onward. Still, I kept hitting bottlenecks, where I couldn't squeeze through. Here, I'd have to climb out and struggle among the willows and clouds of biting insects to haul the canoe and my gear around, until the stream widened again. In a few places I found that I could stand on the bank, wedge the canoe sideways, and with hard effort heave it through the bottleneck. This spared me from unloading and reloading, the trick being not to turn the canoe too far on its side and spill everything out.

Gradually the twisting little stream led me onward through the willow jungles and sedges until it widened out and tamaracks and spruces reappeared. I didn't want to get my hopes up, but then I saw some goldeneye ducks, a cheering sign, as it surely meant there must be larger water nearby. Sure enough, a few more strokes and the creek emptied into a beautiful lake set amid low hills. After the swamps it almost seemed like a mirage. I paddled out onto the narrow lake after the goldeneyes, filling my water bottle over the side of the canoe. Then I made camp happily on the lakeshore amid clusters of Labrador tea, sphagnum moss, caribou lichen, and black spruce—familiar things that always made me feel at home.

That evening, recuperating with a freeze-dried meal, I listened to distant thunder. A storm was on its way, probably gathering strength over Great Bear Lake, which I hoped to finally reach the next day. I took shelter in my tent, drifting off to sleep while the storm passed away to the west.

※

The morning dawned with a fierce wind blowing from the northeast under grey skies. The wind brought relief from the bugs, but made me somewhat apprehensive about paddling to the end of the lake I'd camped on. It was about six kilometres long, and I needed to reach its far end before I could begin the final phase of my quest to reach Great Bear's coast. My maps indicated a small stream draining from this nameless lake, twisting and snaking southward eventually into Great Bear Lake. I doubted it'd be large enough to paddle, but with luck, I might at least be able to wade through it and drag the canoe behind me, thus sparing me a difficult portage over rough terrain that, with all my loads, would total over eleven kilometres to reach Great Bear.

But first I had to somehow overcome the headwinds that were sweeping across the lake. I lingered taking down my tent and packing things up in the hopes that the wind might slacken a bit, but it seemed only to grow stronger. "Well," I thought to myself, "there's nothing for it but to give it my all." That's my general approach to things.

I packed up the canoe, took up my bent-shaft paddle for the extra power, and shoved off into the wind. All my effort and energy I threw into paddling, fighting the wind with every stroke. Progress was painstakingly slow, but gradually, stroke by stroke, my canoe edged forward. What motivated me was the thought that if I couldn't succeed in overcoming these gusts, I'd have no chance at all on the vastness of Great Bear Lake—and thus by such logic I paddled on. An hour later I reached the lake's end.

The small stream that drained from the lake I located without difficulty. It was shallow, with rocks protruding from its rippling waters. There wasn't any chance of paddling it, but I was at least able to heave and drag the canoe over the rocks while sloshing through the water. This went on for some ways, but my hopes that the stream would deepen after a few kilometres were dashed. Instead, it became shallower, to the point where dragging the canoe any farther seemed unwise.

My canoe had been designed to be extra strong and tough for me by Nova Craft Canoe. They'd manufactured its hull from a cutting-edge composite material made of basalt fibres, melted down from basalt rock, and Innegra, a flexible polypropylene fibre. The two materials were then woven together and infused with a high-impact, waterproof resin. The result was an ultra-strong canoe sturdy enough to withstand all kinds of abuse from rocks and ice that would puncture and destroy a traditional canoe.

They'd demonstrated this to me when I visited their factory in London, Ontario, by showing me a video of the canoe prototype being pounded repeatedly with sledgehammers and emerging unharmed. Then, for good measure, they'd thrown the canoe off the roof of a six-storey building to the asphalt parking lot below. My own early experiences with canoe construction had been somewhat more traditional. My father and I had built canoes from cedar and birchbark sewn together with spruce roots, along with other materials found in the woods surrounding our home. I had a great fondness for those traditional canoes, but they weren't designed to withstand constant gouging by rocks and ice (or being tossed off buildings).

Yet, as remarkably strong as Nova Craft's canoe was, I noticed with some alarm that the rocks were beginning to tell on it. The frequent pounding and grinding it had undergone as I'd hauled it upriver had begun to wear away some of the fabric. There were no leaks yet, but if the canoe punctured, I'd be in serious trouble. I could improvise a field repair to keep me afloat, but any patch I devised wouldn't be remotely strong enough to withstand the thousands of kilometres of harsh terrain that still lay ahead of me. It'd require delicate handling and daily repair—things that were simply impossible given the difficulties of the route and the time constraints imposed by the arctic seasons.

Thus, after a kilometre of dragging the heavily-loaded canoe over the rocks, and listening with some consternation to the sound of it scraping against them like nails on a chalkboard, I decided I hadn't any choice but to go back to portaging. There wasn't any sign of the stream deepening, and I didn't want to risk puncturing my boat with further dragging.

I'd come to a vast, open rocky plain stretching off into the distance. It was a strange, barren sight, devoid of plant life aside from a little moss and some scattered clumps of sedges and dwarf willows. This rocky plain, it seemed, was an old riverbed that had drained into Great Bear Lake; all that was left of it now was the tiny stream. The stream, from what I could see, wound around it—meaning I could cut across the rocks on a diagonal, meeting up with the stream on the far side.

The better part of the day was taken up with this wearisome portage. The stream on the far side was just deep enough to paddle, and there I reloaded the canoe. Alas, it was but a short paddle before it narrowed too much to squeeze through amid willows and high banks. I once more had to empty the canoe, carry my gear ahead, then delicately turn the canoe on its side, squeezing it through the narrow creek that was in places only a foot wide, though surprisingly deep. Eventually, the creek widened out into a waterway I could paddle.

By evening I could see ahead of me something in sharp contrast to the demoralizing swamps I'd been passing through: high sand dunes, with arctic terns and gulls soaring above them. I paddled on with anticipation, realizing that Great Bear Lake must be near at hand. The temperature had dropped considerably in the face of an icy wind that was no doubt blowing across hundreds of miles of Great Bear's frigid, arctic waters.

With gloved hands I paddled on, passing by sand dunes until a surreal sight suddenly revealed itself to me—like an ocean, the vast, seemingly limitless expanse of Great Bear stretching beyond the horizon. I'd reached it at last.

× 7 ×

ACROSS AN INLAND SEA

beached my canoe on shore, then cut across the white sand, passing clumps of dune grasses until coming up a slight sand ridge. From the ridge I saw the immense, ocean-like extent of the world's eighth largest lake: Great Bear. My route now lay across it.

A huge, towering iceberg loomed up out of the water in the shape of a pyramid. Beyond it, farther out across the vast, cold waters, I could make out several more bergs. Their white sides were tinted blue, and from a distance they almost looked like the sails of ships. Grey skies stretched away to the horizon while a cold arctic wind swept across the lake, whipping up surf along the beach. The beach extended as far as I could see up the coast in either direction, miles upon miles of fine white sand that made it look like Nova Scotia—aside from the fresh grizzly tracks I'd stepped over to reach the ridge.

The icebergs were somewhat unexpected, since they're normally associated with saltwater, not inland lakes. In the ocean, they form when chunks of ice break off from glaciers or an ice shelf of the sort seen in Greenland and Antarctica. Examining the nearest berg from the sand ridge, I concluded it most likely formed as a result of the surf piling up drifting pieces of ice one on top of another. Once they'd piled up out of the water they'd partly melted to form the solid, twenty-foot-high pyramid I now saw.

The Arctic Circle cuts across Great Bear's deep, clear waters, making it by far the largest lake in the world's arctic regions. It covers an immense area, some 31,153 square kilometres: that's much bigger than Lake Erie or Lake Ontario. And at nearly half a kilometre down, it's deeper than all the Great Lakes, even Superior. Such profound depths combined with its northern latitude keep Great Bear's waters frigid even in midsummer, when the water temperature hovers just a few degrees above freezing.

But what really makes Great Bear unique isn't its size, depth, or northern latitude, but its wildness. Of all the world's giant lakes, Great Bear is the one least touched by humans. Africa's Lake Victoria's watershed is home to over thirty million people; North America's five Great Lakes have along their shores such sprawling cities as Chicago, Milwaukee, Cleveland, and Toronto. Siberia's Lake Baikal, remote and isolated as it seems, now has some two and a half million people residing in its basin. Great Bear Lake's vast watershed, meanwhile, boasts one tiny settlement that could fit into a single high school gymnasium.

These facts I knew beforehand, but standing alone on the lake's desolate shores, staring off at distant icebergs in a place that felt so wild and remote, stirred in me feelings of awe and wonder at Great Bear's grandeur that no facts could ever capture. Now more than ever, I could feel the solitude of my journey.

I was excited and eager to begin paddling, but I concluded that conditions ruled out setting off until the wind died down a bit. I made camp near where the nameless creek I'd followed emptied into the lake. Beyond the beaches was mostly windswept tundra dotted by clumps of low-lying willow bushes and occasional clusters of black spruce. The cold wind had thankfully dispersed the clouds of bugs. I set up my tent just beyond the beach on a level patch of sand, bearberries, and lichens, where there was plenty of driftwood for a fire.

The fresh grizzly tracks made me a little wary, so I kept an eye out as I boiled water for some tea and a freeze-dried meal. Since my waders were still wet from the swamps I hung them to dry on a small though ancient spruce. With the nearness of the lake the temperature had dipped considerably, and now I wore my heavier waterproof jacket, fleece sweater, thermal base layer, and gloves.

With a steaming cup of tea in my hands, I stared across the water at the horizon. In a straight line it was nearly three hundred kilometres across that vast expanse of open water to where I needed to get to: a small river on Great Bear's eastern shore. But there was no way to paddle straight across the lake in my canoe—not if I wanted to live, anyway.

Instead, my plan was to hug Great Bear's north shore, following it all the way across the lake. Given the heavily indented nature of the rugged coastline, with its array of bays, inlets, peninsulas, and islands, the actual distance would be much longer. If I played it safe and never risked any big open-water crossings, the total distance would increase to approximately 443 kilometres. How long that would take was impossible to say, depending as it did on wind and ice—maybe two weeks, maybe three. If the wind was bad, paddling would be impossible.

Lying inside my tent that cold night, listening to the waves lap against the shore, my mind ran through different scenarios, though mainly that pounding surf and fierce waves would make paddling fraught with danger, capsizing my canoe in the icy, storm-tossed waters. I envisioned shivering with hypothermia as the waves swept over my head and I struggled in vain to reach the shore before sinking into the depths. But, like with anything, at times you just have to set aside negative thoughts. Whether it's a case of a rough day at the office or the jobsite, getting stressed out about an exam, confronting a difficult boss or client, or crossing Great Bear Lake, sometimes you just have to tell yourself, "Everything will be fine. An icy wave isn't going to flood my canoe." That's the power of positive thinking—it really does make all the difference.

※

A storm gathered over the lake in the night. Thunder bursts and rain pattering off the tent kept me from sleeping too soundly—although actually, I didn't wish to sleep too soundly. Up until now my days had followed a set pattern: rise early, set off, travel all day, make camp, sleep. Then do it all over again. But now the lake would determine my schedule. If it was too rough to paddle, I'd sleep. Otherwise I had to be prepared to set off whenever conditions allowed: whether it was night or day made no difference. Thus I didn't want to risk missing a calm spell by falling into a deep sleep (which probably isn't wise anyway when grizzlies are nearby). What made this strategy possible was the fact that I was in the land of the midnight sun. I hadn't seen a star in a month. Continuous daylight meant I could paddle all night if need be, while sleeping during the day if the wind was bad.

The storm blew itself out shortly after three a.m. A dead calm, eerie in its near perfect stillness, settled over the lake. I'd slept only three hours, but by three-twenty I was up and by three-fifty-five I was paddling hard over Great Bear's icy waters in my little fifteen-foot canoe. I followed the shore, hoping to make the most of the calm conditions.

The water was clear as crystal; despite overcast skies, in places I could see thirty or more feet down. The lake's cold, oxygen-rich waters breed monstrous lake trout that can live for decades and grow to fantastic sizes. The biggest ones reach in excess of four feet and weigh over a hundred pounds. Lean as I was from a month of rations and hard travel, my mouth practically watered at the thought—but I wasn't here to fish. I had to keep paddling.

I passed landscapes of varying description: white sand beaches, rocky coastlines, stunted spruce forests, and open tundra that looked almost park-like given the natural short vegetation. In places the fierce winds had sculpted the dwarf spruces, bending them low and leaning them away from the lake. Along the northern shores of Newfoundland, one sees these kinds of gnarled, twisted spruces where they've been shaped by the Atlantic gales and where they're known as "tuckamores." Such tuckamore trees testify not only to the power of the wind but also to the resiliency and adaptability of tough northern conifers.

My route took me north up the lake's western coastline. Once I'd reached the north shore, I would turn east. The skies remained overcast and grey as I paddled, with rain falling intermittently. Twice rainbows formed across the water. The sight of them felt almost bewitching, given the sudden infusion of vivid colours over grey skies and dark waters combining with the isolation of the place, its utter vastness, and the all-encompassing solitude.

Five hours of paddling without a break brought me to the extreme northwest corner of Great Bear Lake's Smith Arm, one of the five great arms, or gigantic bays, that give Great Bear its distinctive shape. This is the loneliest of all lonely corners of the lake. It had an almost indescrib-able feel to it—well not physically, I can describe that no problem: it was wet and cold. But spiritually it had a kind of magic to it—a place seldom visited by humans, where the rocks seem as old as time, so old as to be almost beyond human conception. Drifting on the still, clear water, I breathed in the solitude, the beauty of dark spruces, and quiet hills—finding it all refreshingly peaceful, especially after the swamps.

Rounding this wild bay marking Great Bear's extreme northwest corner, I crossed over to the lake's north shore, leaving behind the west-ern end of Smith Arm. I paddled on for another fifteen kilometres before abruptly stopping. What brought me to a halt wasn't the return of the wind or waves, or even my own exhaustion. It was *ice*, and lots of it.

Ice floes of varying thickness, some thin and clear, others still thick and snowy, formed a pack extending from the shore far out into the lake, blocking the way forward. It looked like there was open water beyond the ice, deeper out in the lake, but I knew that at such dis-tances appearances can be deceiving, and that what I thought was open water might only be more ice.

Half a kilometre on, a headland jutted out into the lake, blocking the view farther along the shore I'd been following. Pack ice clustered all around it—but whether the far side of the headland was more ice or open water I didn't know. To risk paddling far offshore in the hopes of evading the ice, and then gambling that there wouldn't be more pack ice on the far side, was too dicey. If I ventured out there in my canoe only to discover the passage blocked, and the wind or the waves picked up while I was far offshore along the ice—I'd be trapped, and could be swept out by the shifting ice into the heart of the lake.

With my route blocked, I made camp on shore near the start of the ice floes. There was no way forward until either the ice melted or the wind shifted and blew it farther into the lake. Normally Great Bear's ice is nearly all gone by late June or early July. In planning my route I'd had to calculate on reaching Great Bear at just the right time—not too soon, when it was still iced up, and not too late either. It wasn't easy to forecast when the ice would melt and how long it would take me to arrive at Great Bear, given the number of variables involved, but it seemed I'd reached the lake at more or less the opportune time. I was optimistic that this would be only a short delay.

I made camp on a small beach with plentiful driftwood washed up on it. Beyond the beach were spruce and willow swamps. The willow swamps, given the sandy beach in front, looked almost like the kind of mangrove swamps found along tropical beaches, at least if you ignored the ice floes. I calculated that I'd covered about forty-one kilometres from where I'd reached Great Bear. Not too bad, I figured, on only three hours' sleep. After a dinner of freeze-dried lasagna I lay in my tent, falling asleep to the peaceful sounds of squawking shorebirds and grinding, shattering ice.

✳

By two-thirty a.m. I was awake and rolling up my sleeping bag, packing the spare clothes that formed my pillow, and my other gear. I ate a couple of energy bars, and took down my tent and packed it in a waterproof bag. Then I flipped the canoe over and carried it back down the beach to the water's edge, packing the two barrels, backpack, and other miscellaneous items carefully. By three-fifteen a.m. I was on my way.

The ice had dissipated somewhat, leaving more open water between the hundreds of floes. Under bluish-grey skies the lake felt unnaturally calm—and with thin vapours rising over the ice where the warmer air met the colder water, it looked almost like a painting. Without wind, the temperatures had edged up somewhat, allowing a cloud of mosquitoes to buzz around me while I paddled among the floes. I weaved through them without too much trouble.

The floes ranged in size from less than a metre across to as much as seven or eight. In certain places, it was necessary to break up some thin or slushy ice to force a passage through; in other places, where thicker floes were in the way, I'd push off from them with my paddle to add some momentum.

Once through this initial pack ice close to shore, I found that the ice ahead formed a continuous field spreading over hundreds of acres. Fortunately, though, it was mostly melted, and was rather slushy as it half-sank into the water. I could break a passage through it with my paddle; jabbing away at the ice, ramming into it with the bow, and then pushing on through. It was slow, but it was progress. Beyond this thin ice the lake opened again, with bigger, more solid ice floes drifting about. They looked thick enough to stand on, though it seemed unwise to do so.

To avoid more ice and round the headland that had prevented me from seeing up the coast, it was necessary to paddle farther offshore. Once I'd passed the headland, I saw more ice lay ahead. For some distance I managed to snake between it, and in some stretches avoid it entirely, but after only about five kilometres it became too thick to proceed. I'd arrived at a deep bay, off which a great peninsula extended diagonally out into the lake.

Massed along the approaches to this peninsula were icefields that stretched far offshore. From the stern of my canoe I scanned for any passage through, but couldn't make any out. The ice, however, from the distance I was at, seemed weak enough that I might be able to batter a passage through it. It was a delicate matter though, as I had to balance not wishing to puncture my canoe with the necessary brute force to clear a passage. I was also acutely aware that if I were to sink out here in frigid water, far from shore, there was a good chance hypothermia would claim me before I could reach dry land. Still, aided by my lifejacket, which I always wore (I'm cautious like that), I figured I could just about manage the swim in time before my limbs seized up.

Amid the pack ice I noticed a narrow, maze-like channel. I headed for it in the canoe, but a bit of thin ice barred the way to it. As I neared the thinner ice, I spun the canoe around so that the stern, where I was seated, faced it. That way I could jab at the weak ice with my paddle, breaking open the passage. Then I spun back to edge the bow into the opening.

It was slow going, as I had to constantly shift from left to right, pushing off from the ice on either side to move the canoe forward. Onward I zigzagged, deeper into the ice, sometimes breaking up the weaker sections and other times managing to squeeze into gaps of open water between larger floes that were still as much as six inches or more thick. By now the wind had picked up a bit.

After only a short distance my progress was halted by a thicker patch of ice that didn't want to budge. So, I reversed, paddling backward, in order to take a second run at it. Building up a little speed, I rammed the canoe at it. But rather than break it, the canoe's bow just skidded up onto the ice and stuck there. Evidently this floe was thicker than it appeared. I tried reversing again with paddle strokes, but I couldn't dislodge the canoe.

Cautiously, I sprawled forward in my canoe, over my backpack and barrels, to try to free the canoe by pushing off the ice with my paddle. Putting my weight into it, a hard push at last dislodged us. Exhaling from the effort, I cast a glance around the ice labyrinth. This one was much thicker than the ones I'd already navigated, and it seemed I wasn't going to be able to force my way through it after all.

Seagulls passed in the distance over the ice, their raspy cries ringing out across the cold waters. I decided to back out of the ice and search elsewhere along the pack edge for an opening. But since the individual floes were constantly shifting on the rising wind, while I'd been busy dealing with the ice, the wind had closed the passages behind me after I squeezed through them. I was trapped.

My canoe was wedged between floes, unable to move forward or back, or side to side. This was a bit disconcerting. Locked in the ice like this, if the wind were to shift offshore and really pick up, I'd be blown out into the heart of the lake, miles from land. As romantic as drifting for miles on ice floes may sound, it wasn't something I had any great wish to personally experience just now.

To free up some space to manoeuvre I tried forcing the floe on my port side away from the canoe, digging my paddle into it and pushing as hard as I could while the boat stayed braced against the ice on the other side. The floe shifted about an inch. Then I turned around in my canoe to jab at the thick ice behind me; eventually I managed to smash some of it off. Still, I was surrounded. So I had to work cautiously all around the boat, breaking enough ice with the paddle to be able to manoeuvre it again. I needed to be able to slightly adjust the canoe's position so that it would point toward a weaker bit of thin ice between some floes—that was the escape route.

With hard effort, I freed the canoe enough to be able to push back through the maze in the direction I'd entered it, this time taking a different channel back. Gradually, paddling and pushing off the ice slabs, with relief I reached the open water again.

Once out of the labyrinth I tried paddling along the outer edge of the pack ice, striking at it with my paddle to test any leads. Again and again I jabbed at the ice; it was thicker than it looked. Finally, I found a short opening between some of the floes. But it was no use. I'd never make it all the way across the ice to the open water, nearly a kilometre away. So I pushed off again and rethought my approach.

It was a cloudy morning, still only about five a.m., with rain threatening. The rain, I hoped, might help melt the ice, making it weak enough to get through. But how long that would take was uncertain, and I knew I had to keep going.

As it was, with the ice having thwarted my advance, I was in a predicament. I could think of two options rather than just giving up and waiting for the ice to melt: on the one hand, a safe option, which would be painstaking slow and wearisome, and on the other, a riskier, dangerous one. The first, safe option was to paddle deeper into the bay I'd been passing by, which was free of ice except near shore, and then try to break a passage through to the shoreline. If I could get close to shore, it was conceivable that I might be able to proceed along it—assuming there was a bit of open water in close, as is sometimes the case on icy lakes in springtime. Failing that, I could land on shore and continue on foot: portaging all of my gear to beyond the ice, bypassing it altogether to continue my journey. But how long that would take I had no idea, as the ice field might extend for miles.

The second, riskier option was to paddle in the opposite direction, far offshore deeper into the lake, seeking the end of the ice. In terms of width, the ice floes didn't seem much more than half a kilometre, but in length I was rather less sure. I could see open water on the horizon, so if I paddled deep enough out into the lake, it seemed I'd be able to reach it and skirt round the pack ice. My mind toyed with which of these options to take. Should I play it safe? Would the wind pick up? How far did the ice extend? Two, maybe three, maybe more kilometres? What if on the far side there wasn't any passage back to shore? If an offshore wind picked up while I was along the pack edge I could be swept far out into the lake. Or if the wind blew onshore, creating waves, my canoe might be swamped or else thrown onto a floe.

The cautious side of me won out: I decided to paddle into the bay toward the shore. But as I neared the floe edge inside the bay it became apparent that the ice was considerably thicker than it had appeared from a distance. Worse, there didn't seem to be any open water near the shoreline. Seated in the stern in my canoe, it was hard to get a good view. So, cautiously, I stood up, allowing me to see better over the distance.

Standing up, I could see it was as I feared: the ice extended right to the shore with no break. Any hope of finding open water along the shoreline that would allow me to continue was dashed. Worse still, even my hope of portaging beyond the ice was, I could see clearly, not possible—for in order to do that, I'd first have to get to the shore, and the ice that separated me from it was much too thick to break through with my canoe or paddle.

I paddled idly, hovering around the pack edge, calculating my next move. The wind had increased a bit, but it still wasn't too bad. From what I could see—admittedly not much—the ice didn't cover all of Great Bear, just this one little corner of it, which was now tripping up all my progress. If I could just find some way around these icefields I'd be able to continue my journey. It seemed an awful shame to squander the relative calm spell, just waiting for ice to melt.

And thus, by degrees, the more adventurous side of my brain asserted itself, as if leading me by the hand toward the riskier option: paddling far offshore, deeper into the lake. How far the ice extended out into the lake was unclear—but it certainly did appear that there was an open passage out there. Perhaps, after all, it might be less than a kilometre, which I could skirt round quickly and easily, safely resuming my travels once round it close to shore—the whole thing taking less than half an hour. Surely, the wind ought to hold off for that long.

I began paddling toward the middle of the lake, setting a quick pace, as I wanted to get around the ice pack as fast as I could before the wind had a chance to pick up. Hopefully, I wouldn't have to paddle the whole way around it, as there might be a thin enough patch in it where I could simply plow through it, thus reaching the open water on the far side faster, which across the pack ice looked tantalizingly close.

But as I paddled along, scrutinizing the edge, I couldn't see a break in the ice open enough to make the dash through it. Ten minutes of paddling and searching had brought me more than a kilometre offshore—farther than was strictly comfortable, out here as I was on the world's eighth largest lake, alone in a canoe. But the prospect of finding an opening in just a few more strokes kept drawing me on.

Only when I glanced back at the increasingly distant shoreline did my cautious side finally reassert itself. The pack ice looked to continue for another kilometre, maybe more—and I wasn't going to risk going any farther to find out, not with the wind rising. It was time to abandon any thought of skirting round the ice pack, and instead retreat to shore. I drew a long C stroke with my blade, spinning the canoe around. Then I paddled rapidly back along the ice, shuddering a little at the thought of having been lured so far out.

Luckily, at the mouth of the bay I'd only partly explored was a tiny island surrounded by rocks and grown over with spruces and willows. The near side of the island was only a stone's throw from shore, whereas the other side faced out toward the vastness of the lake. From the island I'd be able to keep an eye on ice conditions. Besides, if I had to be stranded I figured I'd rather it be on an island, like Robinson Crusoe.

THE ICE LABYRINTH

T he island's shore was made up of fist-sized rocks that made landing somewhat difficult, especially now that I was more conscious than ever of the need to minimize wear and tear on the canoe. Smashing through ice had been a necessity, but I knew what ice could do to a boat, as I'd seen *Titanic*—twice. So I couldn't take for granted just scraping straight up onto the rocks, then climbing to the front of the canoe over my barrels. That sort of thing is well enough in cottage country, but here, sooner or later, if it put a hole in the canoe's bow I'd be in trouble. Instead I carefully spun the canoe parallel to the rocky shore, as close to it as the shallow water would permit. Then I stood up, slowly stretched out one leg, and set my boot down on dry land. Then, with one foot on shore and the other still in the canoe, I gently pulled the boat in close, avoiding any more scrapes than necessary.

My total progress had been barely more than five kilometres from my last campsite. But since I had set off so early it was still only eight a.m., and with any luck I might manage to be underway again before the day was out. In the meantime there was nothing to do but to wait—either for the ice to melt or for the wind to shift it enough to open up leads.

I left my canoe resting there, and went to investigate the little island. It was a charming enough place. The ground was mostly rocky, and overgrown with willows and small spruces. Among the willows matted low to the ground I noticed four lichen-covered rocks. The archaeologist in me noted that they were placed in an arrangement that was unlikely to have been natural. They were larger than the small cobbles strewn elsewhere across the island, and formed roughly a spread-out square. In the middle of the overgrown rocks, lying beneath the matted arctic willow, sinking into sphagnum moss I found a few old animal bones. Evidently, someone had once landed on this island and cooked a meal here, arranging the four rocks to shelter the flames.

The bones were clearly old—lichens had already begun to form on them. I pulled up what seemed to be the tibiotarsus of a goose—probably a snow goose or Canada goose, both of which are common on Great Bear's sheltered bays. There was also what looked like part of a goose femur and a few other bits, but the rest of the bones had likely been chewed away by mice. Judging from the various clues—the age of the willows, the presence of lichens not only on the bones but also the stones (which would have otherwise been burned off in a fire), how the bones had become half-embedded in the moss, and the absence of any visible ashes or charcoal—my best guess was that at least forty or fifty years had elapsed since whoever had been here and had the campfire. Perhaps it had been a hunter, a fly-in sport fisher with their guide, or even a passing trapper. But in the absence of other artifacts it was hard to know.

I sprawled out comfortably beneath a spruce tree in the middle of the island and dozed off. The cool breeze kept the mosquitoes to a tolerable amount. An hour passed before I stirred to check on the conditions.

The sun, which had crept out from the morning's clouds, was rapidly melting the thinner chunks of ice around the island. Farther out, though, the pack ice that had blocked my route remained very much an impassable barricade. It was shifting on the wind, edging westward, the direction from where I'd come that morning.

Since it now seemed clear that I'd be waiting for some time, I decided to fetch my kettle and make myself some tea. After more than a month of continual travel, it felt like a vacation to suddenly be able to rest, enjoy a cup of tea, and relax on the island. Perhaps being stranded in ice wasn't so bad after all. I lit a match and held it to a bit of dry sedge placed inside a tepee of spruce twigs. For the first time in perhaps half a century, the silent rocks once more sheltered a blaze.

As the hours drifted by I drank tea, daydreamed, made notes in my journal, and watched waterfowl fly across the bay. There were mergansers, pintails, and goldeneyes, freshly arrived in these latitudes from their migration north. Just off the southern tip of the island was a large ice floe, still thick with several big blocks of ice heaved up onto it by the wind. A flock of pintails landed on it, making me think of penguins drifting on an ice floe. Gulls of various kinds, too, soared above the bay's open water, hunting for fish. It'd been about a week since I'd last washed my face, so making the most of my island stay, I dipped my face into the ice-cold water along the shore.

One thing I didn't do much, resting under the spruce and staring off at the drifting ice, was wonder about what was going on in the world at large. The "news," I figured, never much changed, and I found I didn't mind not knowing what was up with the world.

As the morning and afternoon passed the pack ice shifted rapidly, the wind blowing it farther west. But more ice came along with it, keeping the route blocked. I was still hoping to push on that day should any break in the ice materialize. With that in mind I cooked up a freeze-dried meal, consuming the calories in the hopes that it would give me the energy needed to make a hard push that night along the lake.

But as the hours slowly ticked away the offshore ice to all appearances remained impenetrable. If anything, the evening had seen more ice drift into view. I'd assumed from what little I'd seen that the lake had largely melted, but the steadily drifting ice suggested that farther east much of the lake must still be frozen. Trouble was, without a bird's eye view, how much or how little of Great Bear's immense 31,153 square kilometres was open water or ice I had no real idea. From what I'd seen in the Yukon it had been shaping up to be a later ice melt than the previous year.

By late evening I'd resigned myself to the fact that for the time being I wasn't making it any farther through the ice. I set up my tent on the island in the only place there was room for it, squeezed between some willow bushes and a spruce. Then I lay down to sleep, hoping that when I woke the wind would have shifted the ice enough to resume paddling.

※

Around midnight I stirred from my sleep. It was cold enough that I could see my breath inside the tent. I crawled out of the warmth of my sleeping bag and unzipped the tent's door. It was still light out but the skies were clouded over, giving a twilit kind of gloom to things. I pushed through the willows to get a look at the lake, to find out what the ice had done since I'd been asleep. I was hoping that the wind would have blown it clear away, leaving me with open waters.

Instead, I could barely believe what I saw: the ice had multiplied, now the whole bay was iced over! The floes had drifted in all around the island, stretching off in all directions, entombing me on this little speck in the vast lake. I shook my head in surprise, but took heart in the speed with which the pack ice was plainly shifting on the winds. A few hours more and it might yet open up a passage for me. I thus climbed back inside my tent to sleep some more, hoping for better prospects the next time I woke.

Not quite three hours later, around three a.m., my eyes opened as I rolled over on a spruce root, which ran under the tent. I crawled out of my sleeping bag and back outside to find out what fate had in store for me now. Pushing through the willows, I was surprised to see . . . nothing at all. Thick fog had swallowed up the island, making it difficult to see much of anything.

Nevertheless, my hopes rose a little, as I knew fog must mean warmer air temperatures were melting the ice. I scampered down to the south end of the island, pushing past willows out onto the rocks for a better view. There was some open water here, extending out a considerable way, at least before the mist obscured things. I couldn't be sure, but it looked fairly encouraging. At any rate, a full day idle on the island had made me restless to push on, as what had initially seemed charming had now begun to feel more like an icy prison.

Anxious that the fast-shifting ice floes would close up the passage before I could escape, I raced to take down my tent, pack things up, and reload my canoe. By three-thirty a.m. I'd launched the canoe and was paddling away from the island back out into the lake. The fog limited visibility, but straight off from the island was a wide passage that was easy enough to make out. It brought me back in the general vicinity of where I'd tried previously to break across the ice. Pack ice still cloaked the lake as far as I could see eastward. An eerie, dead calm reigned, which at least would make things easier than they'd been the day before when the wind shifted the floes on me after I entered into them.

The ice had definitely thinned from what it'd been twenty-four hours earlier. I found a lead between two floes and began to weave into the pack. The core of the ice slabs, normally about the size of a big kitchen table, was still solid and opaque with white ice, but the edges had dissipated into clear ice that could be smashed and broken up. My canoe's bow broke through this thin ice as I proceeded along, while I smashed with my paddle any other ice. In certain places, I'd have to put a little more muscle into it to split in two some of the larger floes that stood in the way. This took repeated jabs, aided by putting weight on the ice to force it down into the water. The water then flooding onto the ice helped break it up.

But in spite of my best efforts, it was soon apparent that the ice was still too thick to get through. I sighed, alarmed at the thought that for the second day in the row I might be stranded in the ice—my daily distance amounting to almost nothing. The odds of me finishing my journey before the onset of winter were dwindling. Up until now I'd been ahead of schedule, but Great Bear's late ice breakup was a bad hand to be dealt. Even if I could get through the ice, wind and waves might still pin me down on the lake's north shore. With a sinking feeling in my heart I pictured the sands of time in an hourglass remorselessly running out, winter on the horizon.

The thought of turning back to exile on the little island, failing to advance any farther, was a disheartening prospect. Instead I resolved to at least force my way through the ice to the mainland across the bay, which I'd tried yesterday without success. That way I'd at least be able to console myself with having inched a tiny bit closer to my end goal, rather than accomplishing nothing at all. On the mainland I could also hike ahead on foot to scout out the ice conditions. Thus I pushed through the ice, shoving with my paddle the bigger floes away from the canoe and struggling slowly to get through the pack.

An hour later and I'd come to the bay's shore. It didn't appear at all inviting, with dense alder bushes six feet high cloaking the coastline. Rocks extending off the shore into the shallows, combined with the ice, made landing difficult. I couldn't parallel park next to the shore as I normally did, so instead I had to crawl carefully over my gear up to the bow and climb out that way.

Once on dry land, I crouched down to squeeze through the alders toward more open terrain inland. Here, away from shore, the ground rose up a small hill, thinly treed with spruces and some tamaracks, and carpeted with thick green sphagnum moss, blueberries, lingonberries, and lichens, although it'd be another five or six weeks before any berries ripened. On the bright side, there was ample wood for making fires, but on the downside it was much buggier, with swarms of mosquitoes that materialized as if summoned by black magic at my appearance.

I slogged my stuff through the alders, including my canoe, which was too dear a friend to leave all alone down by the shore. I always brought it with me to my camps, flipping it over near my tent if there was room for it. We'd sometimes have conversations about such things as which route to take, how the weather looked, the ice, and where to camp. I tended to do most of the talking, but the canoe was a great listener, very seldom interrupting.

Since it was still early morning I set up my tent and went back to sleep for a few hours. Thwarted as I was by the ice, I intended to make the most of it by sleeping and resting as much as I could. That way, when the ice finally did shift or melt, I'd be prepared to put in extra-long days of hard paddling to make up for lost time.

Light rain fell off and on during the day, while I occasionally crawled through the alders to stare pensively at the unmoving ice. Thick mist made seeing much of anything difficult, but again I consoled myself with the thought that the mist was vapour rising from the ice. Little by little, it must be melting.

Later I scouted north along the peninsula to get a better idea of how much water ahead was still frozen. The thick sphagnum moss, which I sank into as I walked, coupled with the uneven ground and mosquitoes, made hiking difficult. But I was hopeful that I might discover that open water lay just ahead.

Alas, I saw only more ice, miles upon miles of it, stretching off to a misty horizon.

After this disheartening exploration, I returned to my campsite, wondering how many more days I'd lose before being able to escape the ice. I decided to count my rations—I figured it might be a good idea to get a handle on how long they'd last. It turned out that there was enough for another four weeks, which might be made to last longer with some fresh fish. After that I'd need to arrange for a resupply with my satellite phone.

That evening, when I crept back down to the lakeshore through the alders to fetch some water for tea, I marvelled with surprise at a beautiful rainbow that had formed across the ice-covered lake, its bright colours standing out against dark grey skies. The rainbow disappeared into the mists rising above the ice in the distance. The floes, meanwhile, were a mix of snowy ice interspersed with pools of water, creating a dreamlike landscape. The rainbow I took as a good sign.

Hours later, as I lay in my sleeping bag with my head resting on my spare-clothes pillow, my ears detected a change. There was still the familiar drone of hundreds of mosquitoes trapped under my tent fly. But something else sounded different—I thought I could hear the faint sound of lapping water. Immediately I sat up in my sleeping bag with excitement; if I could hear lapping water, it must mean that the ice had shifted or melted! Quickly, I dashed out of my bag, tossed on my jacket and bug net, and went to investigate. Pressing through the green alders, I could barely believe my eyes—open water, and lots of it. The ice had mostly all melted; just the odd piece floated about. I glanced at my watch: two thirty-five a.m.—time I was on my way.

It took forty minutes to pack up camp and portage the loads one at a time through the thick alders to the rocky shore, where I carefully loaded the canoe. I needed to pack it just right, as I wanted to be optimistic that I wouldn't be coming back to shore for a good while. By three-thirty a.m. I was at last on my way, paddling once more out onto the vast clear waters of Great Bear Lake.

It felt wonderful to be back on the water, paddling hard. The skies remained cloudy but my spirits soared. With open water on all sides, the closed-in, claustrophobic feel of the pack ice was gone, and I now had the thrill of wide-open vistas once more. I paddled on, passing mile upon mile of wild, beautiful tundra where the permafrost prevents trees from taking root. Elsewhere the landscape varied with stupendous cliffs, green hills, and rocky shores. It was the kind of scene that always refreshed my spirits.

The lake itself was remarkably clear and free of aquatic vegetation; looking down into those cold, clear waters was like looking into another world. The frigid, oxygen-rich water prevents underwater weeds from growing. The result is a lake that looks deceptively empty, with sand bottoms that in places have great, silent jumbles of boulders and rocks resembling a kind of sunken moonscape.

After hours of paddling without any a sign of life below the placid waters, suddenly I was startled by a glimpse of an enormous creature—it jerked violently then dove off into the depths as I passed by in my canoe. So abrupt had it appeared and so unbelievably massive it looked in the vast clear waters that it felt as if I'd just seen a shark. In fact it was only a lake trout, though one weighing perhaps seventy pounds or more.

Above water, especially when I came across sheltered bays, birds were plentiful. I saw pintails, loons, mergansers, Canada geese, bald eagles, arctic terns, and sandpipers; I suspected that as temperatures warmed I'd see even more kinds. At the close of each day, stretched out in my snug little tent, I'd tally up the birds and other wildlife I'd seen during the day, and it was always a thrill to add a new species that I hadn't seen before.

Birds and fish weren't the only things about. Paddling silently along, my eyes spotted a herd of five shaggy, horned muskox wandering the coast, looking like creatures from another time. A couple of them swam in the icy water, something I'd never seen before. Their thick fur, however, is reputed to be the warmest in the world, which I could appreciate from personal experience. Some years earlier, while canoe-ing in the High Arctic, I found my jackets and clothing totally inade-quate for the biting cold of the fierce arctic winds. It seemed to cut right through my three layers to the bone. Scattered all over the arctic tundra in easily collected quantities where I was camping was muskox fur, which they shed in summertime. So I gathered up handfuls of it and stuffed it down my jacket and pants like a scarecrow, and never again on that journey did I suffer from the cold.

Paddling on, hour after hour, in places I encountered more pack ice, but I weaved through it without much trouble, as the leads between the floes had become larger. There were also more large icebergs, looking magical as they drifted in the clear water. I paddled by them, marvelling at the beauty; one was nearly forty feet long. Out on the lake, there weren't any bugs once I was paddling, as the wind blew them away.

I finally stopped after fourteen and a half hours' travel, during which time I never once touched shore. When I needed to stretch, I'd simply stand up in the canoe, while my lunch, as usual, was energy bars. The extra rest had paid off. I'd managed to cover approximately

sixty-seven and a half kilometres, or an average of just under five kilometres an hour.

To cap off such a physically exhausting but rewarding day, I camped
on a beautiful tundra site amid pink and white wildflowers. Looking
out across the lake, I could see far out in the centre that large amounts
of ice still remained. I hoped it would stay where it was, either melting
away out there, or if it was to shift, that the wind would carry it to the
far shore, and not the one I was paddling.

※

Living outdoors, you get to appreciate nature in all its moods. The
morning after my long paddle, the day dawned cold, wet, grey, and
dismal. I got out my balaclava and my warmer pair of waterproof
gloves. I was back to three layers: the wool-blend base layer, then
khaki pants and wool sweater, and finally my outer rain pants with the
warmer of my two jackets.

Fog and stiff headwinds slowed my progress, and I soon came
across more ice. Fortunately, I was able to navigate the ice without
too much delay, though there was still some icebreaking required to
get through it. By midday the skies had mostly cleared, but the wind
remained unfavourable. I put my back into it, paddling as steadily as
I could.

To save the time it would take to snake down into a deep bay, I did
chance one largish open-water crossing. It wasn't by normal standards
much of a big crossing, merely 1.3 kilometres in a straight line from
shore to shore. In more temperate places or with a canoeing partner
I'd often ventured far greater distances from shore. But things were
different alone in the Arctic, when I could still see sheets of ice drifting. Remote as the prospect seemed, I had to consider what might
happen if, in the middle of a big water crossing, I suddenly suffered
some freak muscle spasm or cramp, leaving me at the mercy of the
wind. Sometimes, though, you just have to play the odds.

By July I figured the last of the ice had almost all melted, and I'd have open water from here on out across Great Bear. The first of the month, Canada Day, I crawled out of my tent before seven a.m. and was pleased to see clear skies and calm waters. That morning I passed a long, sandy white beach where a lone grizzly was quietly wandering among the dunes. The beautiful beach extended for over six kilometres, and I thought it would be a wonderful place to rest, but I knew I couldn't afford to stop when the wind was still down. So I kept paddling, snacking on some high-calorie energy bars to keep me going.

Rounding the beach and continuing along the shore, I was surprised to see the sun glinting off vast fields of ice! It hadn't all melted, after all. This ice pack extended from the north shore out into the lake at least several kilometres, and it stretched as far as I could see along the coast ahead of me. In the midst of this giant ice field was one iceberg that rose up high out of the water, towering over the rest like a snow fort.

But surely, given it was July, I figured I could push through this ice. Paddling, however, soon proved ineffective: the ice pack was too thick. Trying to force my way through it was exhausting work—to advance just a few hundred metres involved continuously smashing and breaking up the thinner ice with my paddle combined with pushing the bigger floes far enough away from the canoe to squeeze between them. An hour's effort had seen me advance only a kilometre into the ice.

Clearly I needed a different approach. So I tried poling through the ice, as I still had my trusty beaver pole that I'd found along the Mackenzie. Standing up in the canoe, I grasped the pole and used it to push off the floes, propelling my canoe along over thinner ice. The ice crunched and shattered as I moved along, breaking a channel as I went. Canoes are perhaps not intended to be used as icebreakers, but mine I found quite effective at it.

However, it soon became too thick to push through, and at the rate I was going, I was exhausting myself with little to show for it. I began to wonder, given that the shoreline here was not choked with willows and alders like earlier on, whether it might actually be faster to just portage along the shore. The shoreline was a mix of tundra plants, sand, and pebble beaches. Maybe, just maybe, I thought, that wheeled cart sitting in the front of my canoe might at last come in use.

I forced the boat through the ice to shore, alternatively zigzagging through the icy labyrinth or else breaking a passage when there was none. I pushed and prodded my way across the ice, occasionally causing floes to sink beneath the canoe, until I reached the shore. The underside of my canoe was looking rather scratched up, with some deeper gouges that somewhat unsettled me, but no fatal punctures, so far. Leaving the rest of my gear on the beach to pick up later, I strapped the canoe onto the cart, which consisted of two hard plastic wheels specifically designed for rough usage. Then I began dragging the cart, weaving between juniper bushes, willows, and rocks. It sort of worked. For a little ways. But overall, the cart wasn't much of an improvement over simply dragging the canoe over the ground or carrying it over my head. The terrain was too cluttered with obstacles for it to work effectively.

So after half a kilometre of this I stopped on a stony beach surrounded by treeless tundra. I hadn't even come close to bypassing the icefields, and I'd concluded that it was simply not worth the energy and calories expended to push on with portaging. My time was better spent resting, waiting for the ice to melt or shift.

Over a driftwood fire, I boiled water for a freeze-dried dinner while gazing out on the icefields that had foiled my progress, wondering when they'd dissipate. Things seemed encouraging when that night, lying in my tent, I watched through the screen-door as the ice began to smash up and shift, partly breaking off waves that were rolling in. I was hopeful that I'd have clear waters come morning.

✳

The dawn—well, not exactly dawn, since the sun only briefly sank below the horizon, just dipping down and up again—brought the clear water I'd hoped for. But it also brought stiff opposing winds that promised to test every ounce of my mettle. I gave it my all, paddling for nearly thirteen hours and battling for every inch.

The winds were relentless now, as I'd reached the middle section of Great Bear, leaving behind the narrower Smith Arm. Here the lake opened up to impossible horizons, with hundreds of kilometres of open water for the wind to gather its full force over. I made sure to stay near the shore, normally not straying anything more than a half-kilometre out from it. This was harder at times than it might seem, given strong winds were often blowing offshore, meaning I had to counteract them with paddling. Otherwise I'd find myself drifting far off into the lake.

There was one place, however, where I debated whether to risk paddling far offshore. I'd arrived at the entrance to a huge bay shaped like an immense paint splatter, with wide inlets extending in different directions. I knew if I could just cut across the mouth of the bay, rather than trace out the shoreline all through its odd shape, it'd save me hours of paddling. But it was a gamble. The mouth was over three kilometres wide—a long way in a little canoe alone on an arctic lake. In calm weather I might have chanced it. But with the wind gusting as strong as it was, and with the icy cold waters all around me, my head said don't risk it.

So instead I rounded the rocky shoreline and turned into the bay, resigning myself to tracing it out and adding considerable distance to my route as a result. The arithmetic was not at all encouraging: instead of a three-kilometre paddle across the bay's mouth, tracing out all of its coastline (except for a narrow bit I was sure I could skip across), it would total over twenty-nine kilometres, which would take at least five hours of hard paddling.

With math like that, I was almost desperate to trim off some of the shoreline with whatever crossing I could manage. Fortunately, just around the rocky peninsula leading into the bay, a bottleneck was formed between the peninsula's protruding rocky shore and the northern coastline. The distance between the two points was less than seven hundred metres, and if I could zip across it I'd saw off a good ten kilometres from the detour.

The wind was raging, with big waves rolling across the channel, but I was primed for the challenge, given what was at stake. I'd been using my bent shaft paddle for the extra power, but to safely navigate the waves I needed my straight paddle.

Taking up my well-loved traditional paddle, I kneeled down in the canoe, and swung the blade deep into the waves, gunning hard for the far shore. The wind was coming straight at me—a perfect headwind. I swung my paddle hard and hard again, fighting the gusting wind with every stroke. The canoe surged up and down on the waves, the bow rising clear in the air on the breaks.

It was rough going. I'd battled my share of big waves before, but never with so heavy a load in the canoe, and my energy was already drained from the long days of paddling I'd been putting in. Determined as I was, not five minutes in I knew I was beaten. I couldn't overcome the howling gusts. It was time to retreat.

I waited for a break between waves to safely pivot. Then I swung the canoe back in the direction of the near shore. There was nothing for it, I'd have to take the long way around, tracing out nearly the whole bay, unless I could pull off a crossing somewhere else.

There's always a silver lining, though. Being forced to take the long way around meant I'd get to see more—and I loved exploring landscapes, especially ones hidden away in the wildest bays. I soaked in the majesty of the place, admiring its endless variety: the hardy tamaracks and spruces, the wiry willows, the ancient rocks heaped and jumbled by glaciers, the clear waters, the different birds, the hidden wildlife. It was a feast for the imagination, the kind of thing I found endlessly fascinating. The natural world is so full of mystery that there's always more to see.

On the other hand, once I reached the bay's inner shore, having taken the long way around to avoid the worst of the wind, my eyes looked longingly across the expanse of open water toward the bay's outlet. It occurred to me that if I were to cut straight across here, making a beeline for the far shore, I'd still be able to save a considerable amount of time and distance by avoiding the northeastern section of the bay. I calculated the distances; if I continued to remain near shore, tracing out the whole bay, there was still another thirteen kilometres to get through. But if I paddled straight across, it was only 3.2 kilometres to the far shore—a significant savings on an expedition where every kilometre counted.

The wind had held steady, blowing hard to the southeast. When I'd first come upon the bay the southeast wind meant it was hitting my canoe broadside, the worst place for waves to hit. If I'd attempted the three-kilometre crossing at the bay's opening, the wind's full force would have been hitting me broadside and pushing me out into the centre of Great Bear's icy expanse. But when I'd turned into the bay and attempted to beeline across it to the south shore, that meant the wind was hitting me head on, driving me back where I'd come with every gust. Now, having traced the bay to its inner shore, if I were to chance this open-water crossing southward I'd have the wind behind me for the first time, giving me a powerful tailwind.

Yet tailwinds can still be risky in a little open canoe: if the waves are too big they can spill into the canoe and sink it. The winds were fierce, but I'd paddled larger waves before—though perhaps not in such an isolated place all alone.

Though canoeing is not normally associated with Great Bear, given that it's ice-covered for nearly nine months out of the year and too northerly for birch trees big enough for traditional canoe-making, I knew of at least five people who'd drowned canoeing on it. There were the two geologists who had drowned in 1960 while canoeing along Great Bear's north shore. Earlier, back in the 1930s, a young trapper by the name of Abe Van Bibber had perished when his canoe overturned in the lake's icy waters. And more recently, in 1987, two men on a fishing trip had drowned when their canoe overturned in big waves.

Once again I got down on my knees in the canoe—it helps concentrate the weight lower, and makes the canoe more stable. If I paddled fast, I might just make it across the more than three-kilometre span before the wind had a chance to shift or pick up. Once committed, there could be no turning back, since that would mean opposing a headwind. One last glance at the thin grey outline of the distant shore and my mind was made up. I gathered up my courage and went for it.

I started paddling quickly but cautiously: I had to navigate the waves just right. Halfway across, a kilometre and a half from either shore, the waves seemed much larger. My canoe rose and fell with each swell. I knew the importance of remaining calm, but it was a white-knuckle affair to see land so far on all sides. Up the canoe rode on the waves, then down again as they passed along.

At last, twenty minutes of hard paddling later, I reached the far shore. Dry land never felt so good. I beached my canoe to rejoice, having saved much time and energy that would have been expended in tracing out the whole bay. I celebrated with a power bar.

My transit of the bay had taken three and a half hours, after which I was once more back out on the waters of Great Bear Lake proper. I pushed on for another thirteen kilometres, bringing my total distance for the day to fifty kilometres. Feeling exhausted, I used my last reserves of energy to haul my canoe up over the rocks to the tundra. There I made camp—setting up my tent, building a driftwood fire, and boiling water to cook a meal.

As I did so, I was surprised to see in the distance moving ice floes, smashing and crashing into each other on the strong wind, and floating down the coastline. It was an ice pack the size of several soccer fields, rushing along on the wind, and drifting right by my little camp. Sitting there on the tundra, it was the oddest feeling witnessing this ice procession moving rapidly along, floe after floe, as if it were an ice parade with me as the sole spectator. A half hour later the parade had passed by, with just a few stragglers, ice slabs the size of kitchen tables, still drifting off after the rest of the pack.

I crawled into my tent and fell into an exhausted sleep.

At the airport bright and early on May 13, ready to fly to the Yukon.

Photo Credit: Aleksia Wiatr.

Hiking through the Richardson Mountains at the start of my journey.

Courtesy Alone Across the Arctic, photo by Martin Wojtunik.

"It wasn't long into my lonely trek before I came across tracks of an unsettling size, sunk deep into the gravel roadway."

A grizzly I crossed paths with while hiking along the Dempster.

Poling up the Mackenzie River under grey skies.

A trio of Sandhill cranes with their distinctive red-bands
around their eyes, along the Mackenzie's sand banks.

It can be somewhat unsettling to find a muskox
staring you down outside your tent at night.

"One beautiful arctic wolf, his white coat streaked with black and grey, was particularly curious about me. He was a big, lanky animal, and followed me along the riverbank for over a kilometre as I paddled along."

Hauling and pushing the canoe through the first of many logjams on the upper reaches of the Hare Indian River.

Camping on the windswept coast of the world's
eighth largest lake, Great Bear.

My route appears to be blocked by ice.

Trying to break a passage through the ice.

After several days stuck in the ice, a dream-like rainbow formed across the ice labyrinth, giving me hope that I might make it through.

Using my pole to force my canoe across more ice.

July 6, 2017, my camp along Great Bear's north shore,
where only a few stunted, hardy spruces and willows manage to grow.
My canoe, gouged and scraped by ice, sits overturned by the tent,
while the two barrels rest near my campfire.

The surreal Dismal Lakes at night. "Across the dark waters the midnight sun, having dipped below the mountains, filled the cloudy sky with an eerie red glow."

Enjoying the (temporary) end of my upriver travel as I race downstream through a canyon on the Kendall River.

Back to exhausting upriver travel as I jump from rock to rock hauling my canoe up the powerful current of the Coppermine River.

A land time forgot, where, amid ancient boulders eons older than even the dinosaurs, a little stream crashes a path down the hillside.

Trying to maintain my balance and not twist an ankle while wading up rapids in a narrow channel connecting two lakes.

"Once I reached the top I had a good view of the river's turbulent, roaring course over the rocks. There were two big, foaming cataracts separated by a rocky island, with large rapids above each one."

In the haze, a pair of shaggy, prehistoric-looking muskox
wander the ancient landscape.

Portaging around the Hanbury River's many dangerous canyons
took four trips per canyon, the first with my backpack, two more
with each barrel, and a final one with my canoe.

Climbing along the cliffs of the Hanbury River while
guiding my canoe below with a rope.

The gusting wind made paddling impossible, so I strapped on my waders,
grabbed the bow rope, and started dragging the canoe behind me,
vast sandy barrens stretching off into the distance.

That look you get when a big wave throws
ice-cold water in your face while paddling rapids.

Thunder clouds mass on the horizon as I huddle in my tent for
another cold, stormy night in late August.

A family of caribou stare at me as they wander the tundra while
snow geese head south for warmer climes.

The moon rises above the ancient hills overlooking the last of
the Thelon's lakes, where I was wind-bound.

September 4, 2017. A herd of muskox graze on the tundra now ablaze with bright fall colours.

Four months later, the end of my journey; looking across the tundra and wondering if we will find the courage and political will to preserve large tracts of wilderness. There's magic in the wild, if allow yourself to feel it.

Courtesy of Alone Across the Arctic, photo by Mike Reid.

× 9 ×

GHOSTS OF THE PAST

J uly brought warmer temperatures, the last of the ice, and fierce winds and storms. Severe winds along the middle stretch of Great Bear's north shore, where the whole mighty expanse of the lake was facing me, required switching to more nocturnal habits. During the rough winds of the day I'd sleep; at night, when the winds had died, I'd paddle under the glow of the midnight sun with everything I had.

Bolts of lightning across the dark water brought me to a halt in the early evening on July 3. A storm was gathering strength in the distance, and it seemed the wind would be bringing it in my direction. I raced to make camp in time, setting up my tent in a low, sandy area back a ways from the water that seemed the safest bet for a thunderstorm. Fortunately, the storm remained distant, and I listened to it thundering across the lake while warm and dry inside my tent.

I slept only a few hours on that lonely beach. By midnight I was on my way again, paddling hard into a thick fog. Following along the wild, rocky shoreline meant taking numerous detours into bays—one of which proved so surprisingly shallow that I actually switched from my paddle to my pole, and ended up poling right across it. This swampy bay stood in sharp contrast to the almost unfathomable, cold depths of the lake proper. In its sheltered reaches I saw pike, flocks of ducks and geese, and even a great bull moose swimming across the water. It was the first moose I'd seen north of the Arctic Circle, since the ones I'd encountered along the Hare Indian River were just short of that latitude.

Except for one particularly frightful day of wind that kept me on shore for much of it, my daily average distance ranged from fifty to fifty-five kilometres. This was better progress than I'd anticipated making, and I'd managed to make up for time lost in the ice. This was good news in more ways than one—the sands of the hourglass before the inclement weather of late summer weren't looking as discouraging anymore. Of more immediate concern, it meant that I could increase my daily rations.

Pretty much from day one of my journey, I'd been hungry. The recommend daily calorie intake for an adult male is 2,500 calories. I'd been consuming more than 3,000 calories a day. That still left me ravenously hungry, and I certainly would have consumed more had it been possible—but there's a limit to how much you can cram into a canoe. And the more I packed, the more I'd have to lug through the trackless swamps, as well as the more deadweight to slow me down when poling up rivers or battling winds.

However, my better than expected progress had yielded me a surplus of food, and I'd now happily increased my allotted daily rations to ten energy/builder/granola bars, a pack of nuts of various kinds, some dried fruit, a bit of low-sodium jerky (some of it goose jerky, a gracious gift from a friend I'd known since grade four), and two freeze-dried meals to be eaten when I stopped for the day. That put my calorie intake at closer to 4,000—enough to keep me going hard all day at distances of up to seventy kilometres—but I was still losing weight—as is virtually inevitable on a journey of this nature.

On the bright side, I figured that as I grew steadily thinner I'd be less appealing to bears, who probably wouldn't find my skeletal figure very appetizing. At least I hoped so.

After a stretch of about a hundred kilometres of rather uninviting shoreline dominated by low-lying willow swamps, the character of Great Bear's landscape changed. I'd entered into the part of the lake known as the Dease Arm, another of its five great arms. As I advanced up the north coast here, I found the willow swamps and tundra gave way to dramatic cliffs. I passed two incredible waterfalls tumbling over cliffs that seemed like something out of an ancient legend. In other places there were pinkish granite rocks with a mix of open tundra and clusters of spruce that looked like a Group of Seven painting come to life—well, aside from the thick clouds of bugs, which don't seem to have made it into any of the Group's paintings.

These changed landscapes were a tell-tale sign I'd reached the Canadian Shield, that gigantic geologic zone covering almost half of Canada's landmass—some eight million square kilometres, if one includes parts outside Canada. The Shield, perhaps the country's most famous landscape, stretches as far south as Muskoka, all the way north to the shores of Ellesmere Island, and east to Labrador. Its western extent is roughly Great Bear Lake itself, right where I'd now arrived. The rocky uplands and millions of lakes within the Shield make it ideal canoeing territory, at least in its more southern reaches.

My last days crossing Great Bear were filled with wildlife. A lone wolf wandered along a marshy section of shoreline as I passed by. When the wolf spotted me she just sat down and stared at me, tilting her head to the side in curiosity as I drifted past in my canoe, staring right back with equal wonder. After a good while she rose and ran off from shore, pausing twice to look back at me, filling me with awe. In the wild, wolves have an average lifespan of about seven years, which means some arctic wolves will likely never encounter humans. This seems to partly explain the differences in how wolves in isolated areas behave compared with ones closer to human settlements. The former react with curiosity; the latter, having learned to fear humans, flee.

Wolves weren't the only carnivores about. At the other end of the size scale, I spotted a lithe little weasel scurrying along a great slab of granite like a character out of a cartoon. Weasels are striking, tough little animals, often taking down prey as much ten times their own size, principally rodents and birds, but sometimes even hares. Pound for pound, they may just be the toughest carnivores on the planet, exceeding even wolverines in their ability to kill prey larger than themselves. They kill with a bite to the base of their prey's skull. In the Arctic there are short-tailed weasels and their smaller cousins, least weasels, both of which are hardy and adaptable enough to survive the harsh conditions. In winter their coats are all white to camouflage with the snows, but in summer they change to brown on their heads and backs.

Soon after spotting the weasel, paddling on calm waters I came across an odd little sight bobbing up and down on the lake, a portly brown lemming swimming valiantly but largely ineffectively. It seemed so slow and helpless as to be almost cartoon-like in its frantic paddling. I wondered what it was doing so far from land, and if perhaps a hawk had dropped it from its talons while flying over the lake. On the other hand, lemmings are known to make great migrations, including even the crossing of large water (not always successfully; they sometimes drown). Their populations follow cyclical fluctuations every few years, much like other arctic prey species, notably hares, which trigger famines among "apex" predators, including wolves, lynx, and, at one time, humans.

Birds were plentiful in the eastern waters of Great Bear. I saw hawks, jaegers, gulls, terns, loons, ducks, geese, and bald eagles. One arctic tern dive-bombed a raucous gull in an impressive display of aerobatic manoeuvres. The terns are elegant flyers with long, sharp beaks, which they don't hesitate to use on any bird, animal, or person getting too close to one of their nests. Gulls will steal and eat other birds' eggs if given the chance.

Once I'd reached the eastern shores of Great Bear Lake I began working my way southward, to seek the mouth of a river draining in from the east. This river, known as the Dease, formed the next link in the hypothetical chain I'd devised to take me across Canada's Arctic. Along this rocky eastern shore were many deeply indented bays several kilometres in width, but I was able to cut across most of them without much trouble, saving me from tracing them out.

One of these big open-water crossings surprised me by the unusual landscape on the opposite shore I was heading toward. It looked nothing like anything I'd yet seen on my journey: rolling hills of open tundra dotted with clusters of spruces and framed by dramatic red cliffs. The whole scene reminded me of Prince Edward Island—the Canadian Arctic astonishing me again with its amazing diversity of landscape. The stereotypical view of the Arctic (some might even say all of Canada) is a place of ice and snow and not much else. During winter, that may be so—but when the snows melt during the brief summers, a delightful complexity is revealed.

On the afternoon of July 7, tracing Great Bear's eastern shores southward, I passed into a channel formed by the mainland and the lee side of an immense island over fifteen kilometres long. It was somewhere up this channel that nearly two centuries ago in 1836, the fur traders Peter Warren Dease and Thomas Simpson and their companions had built a fort to endure the harsh winters, after a long boat journey north from more southern trade posts. Their orders from the Hudson's Bay Company were to chart the unknown coastline of the Arctic Ocean. Dease had selected a crack team of Dene hunters, Canadian voyageurs, and Scottish sailors and craftsmen for the mission.

They built their isolated post, Fort Confidence, here on Great Bear's north shore to serve as a base of operations while they pushed on in summer to map the Arctic coast, hoping to solve the riddle of the Northwest Passage. The older Dease's competence and careful planning, long years of experience in the fur trade, and ability to speak four languages, combined with the younger Simpson's physical prowess and daring, made for a potent combination. Dease, Simpson, and their party spent nearly three years here, departing in 1839. As for Fort Confidence, over the next century it gradually fell into ruin and was forgotten.

Despite the importance of pushing on, I couldn't resist the temptation to pause to search for the remnants of Fort Confidence. Knowing it was somewhere on the northeastern shore, I paddled closer in to keep an eye out for any clues to its whereabouts. There wasn't much to go on, as the shore was screened from view by tall black spruces, willows, and alders, despite being north of the Arctic Circle. (It was precisely the presence of that forest that had attracted the explorers to build Fort Confidence here, as they needed timber for construction and huge quantities of firewood to survive the long winters.) However, I noticed a slight hill where there seemed to be a bit of a clearing, and though nearly two centuries had passed, I figured some scant glade might remain. I also figured the hill would be a logical choice for the establishment of a fort, offering a view of the lake.

There was nowhere to land along the bank, as it was a bit steep and thickly grown over with alders and willows. So instead, with a rope I tied my canoe to a spruce tree, promising the canoe not to worry and that I'd be back soon. Then taking a paddle as a walking stick, I climbed to shore through the thick alder bushes.

Once through the alders, the ground sloped uphill, which was mostly open, grassy land. I scanned around, but couldn't see any artifacts or ruins. So I went a bit farther, rounding a thick cluster of spruces and pushing through some tall willow bushes to see if anything lay hidden behind them.

Then my eyes caught sight of something odd poking up through the thicket of willows and spruces ahead: the ghostly ruins of two stone chimneys. It was Fort Confidence, or rather what was left of it. I pushed through the willows to take a closer look. All that was left of the fort, it seemed, was the masonry associated with the chimneys and their stone and clay hearths. The buildings themselves had long since burned down, with the spruces and willows swallowing up the site over the ages. The chimneys were made of rocks pulled up from the lakeshore, the hearths neatly shaped in half-moons to reflect the heat out—a vital concern in the long, dark, bone-chilling winters. One of the chimneys had toppled over, but the other was still intact and standing upright. I bent down in the hearth, inspecting it, then lay down on my back and gazed up through the chimney at the clouds passing overhead.

Dease and Simpson proved a remarkably effective exploring duo, far more competent than their more famous contemporary, Sir John Franklin. Dease was a native-born Canadian who'd travelled extensively across the country as a fur trader before coming north. He was universally liked and respected, but was noted as being not overly ambitious and, at fifty years of age, inclined not to push things too hard. Simpson couldn't have been more different: he was twenty years younger, a brash, impetuous Scottish Highlander. But they worked well together, and with their expert Dene hunters, Canadian woodsmen, and Scottish carpenters and sailors, they'd mapped huge stretches of the Northwest Passage in small boats, without any loss of life from starvation, accidents, or the elements—more than can be said for Franklin with his vastly larger naval expeditions.

However, things later took a decidedly strange turn for Dease and Simpson. Maybe it was the winters spent isolated in their three log dwellings that were rather grandly called Fort Confidence. Certainly they'd endured numerous dangers on the Arctic Ocean and all the hardships associated with continual darkness during brutal winters. Whatever the reason, while on the return journey south, Simpson, always high-strung, had apparently gone insane, murdering two voyageurs and then shooting himself in the head. Others, however, insisted it was murder made to look like suicide, in order to steal the maps and papers he carried. What truly happened will likely never be known.

There wasn't time, however, to dwell much on the impermanence of things and the ghosts of the past—there'd be time enough for that in the future; for now, I had to be on my way. Turning my back on the crumbled ruins, I returned through the willows to where I'd left my canoe. I was happy to see it, for if by some freak chance my knot had come undone and the canoe had drifted off, my bones might have made a nice addition to the archaeological site.

✳

Once back on the water, I paddled on. Another six kilometres and my journey across North America's fourth largest lake was complete. I'd reached the eastern end of the lake. It was the evening of July 7, meaning it had taken me eleven days to cross Great Bear. That was much faster than I'd expected. I estimated beforehand that, having to assume the worst with winds and ice, it would take at least two weeks, if not three. When planning a solo expedition, it's imperative to always plan for worst-case scenarios.

On all that vast expanse of water, I hadn't seen a soul. Not one soul. In fact, I hadn't seen another person since I'd briefly stopped in at Fort Good Hope nearly a month ago. What's it like to go that long without seeing another human being, alone and isolated? Especially in a world where people increasingly can't go ten minutes without checking their phones?

Personally, I found it relaxing. Of course, I'd spent weeks alone in the wilderness before this, so solitude wasn't new to me. As for life in a major city, that's something I can't fathom. I ask people how they handle living in such massive, sprawling urban environments like Toronto, and although they try to explain it to me, I still can't quite wrap my head around it. I find those crowded, noisy places of concrete, glass, and steel stressful and suffocating, and can't stand to be in them for more than a few hours. But to each their own.

A few more strokes of my paddle and I'd arrived at a place I recognized: it was an island in the mouth of a river draining into Great Bear Lake from the east, an island I'd been to before. A year ago, with my friend Chuck, I'd come to the eastern end of Great Bear Lake specifically to explore the Dease River and its tributaries (named after the same Dease in charge of Fort Confidence). That expedition had helped me plan this one, and so for the next two weeks I figured, I'd be travelling familiar ground that I'd wandered over previously. Chuck and I had dragged, hauled, and paddled a canoe up the Dease River, and then up one of its tributaries; finally, leaving our canoe behind, we'd hiked for miles across tundra and even a sandy desert until at last reaching the Dismal Lakes. At those wild and forlorn lakes set amid mountains we'd turned back, retracing our steps, then paddling all the way down with the current to Great Bear.

We'd begun and ended our journey at the only fly-in point available to us, Plummer's Arctic Lodge, a somewhat rustic fly-in fishing lodge about forty kilometres west of where I was now. At one time, Great Bear's vast waters were home to as many as five different fishing lodges catering to anglers seeking trophy fish, but with the decline of the sport fishing industry, now the lake was home to just two different lodges separated by nearly three hundred kilometres. Plummer's, the oldest, had been established back in 1968; in addition to their fly-in only main lodge, they also operated a handful of smaller satellite camps scattered throughout the lake.

Given that Plummer's lay more than 530 kilometres north of Yellowknife, getting my barrel of rations and batteries on board one of its already scheduled flights had offered me by far the most economical means of a resupply. The lodge had only just opened up a week ago for the season after the ice melt, and I'd pre- arranged for my barrel of fresh rations to be on one of its scheduled flights.

It hadn't been possible to know exactly when I'd reach this point in my journey—if I reached it at all—and so, in order to arrange for the barrel delivery, I needed a satellite phone to communicate. With no cell towers for thousands of kilometres across Canada's vast wilderness, there's no reception for ordinary phones or Wi-Fi. But a satellite phone, unlike an ordinary phone, works with a small antenna that allows it to receive signals from a satellite orbiting the earth. I couldn't afford one, so I'd rented one. The minutes to operate the phone cost extra (without them the phone only works as a paperweight when you need to roll out maps in your tent), and I had to ration out the supply of minutes I figured I'd need to cover my journey.

I followed the instructions that came with the bulky phone to get it operational, folding out the antenna and pointing it at the sky. After a pause, the phone indicated that it had picked up a signal from a satellite. I dialed up a number—it began to ring. It took three attempts, since it kept losing the signal, but eventually I got through to the fishing lodge manager.

He told me some surprising news. The barrel, he said, *had already been delivered*. A fishing guide had taken it on a motorboat the day before and dropped it at the island so that it would be there waiting for me when I arrived.

This news alarmed me a little, since there was no sign of any barrel. In fact, it was the exact scenario I'd been hoping to avoid. Perhaps, if you've ever ordered something important online and then it didn't show up, only to learn that a courier had simply left it sitting on your porch when you weren't home, you'll know the feeling I had. It wasn't that I thought someone had stolen my package—with no one else around for miles, that seemed unlikely—but in the wilderness there's a kind of animal that will happily rip open a barrel left lying around and help itself to any food inside. That's a wolverine.

Wolverines are wonderful animals. A bit like a cross between a bear and a dog, they're capable of killing things much larger themselves, including caribou. Their ability to steal food from traps and cabins is legendary, as is their toughness, including literally chewing through their own legs to escape iron traps. They're elusive, solitary creatures, ranging over vast areas. The males have home ranges that extend over a thousand square kilometres or more. They're seldom seen by humans, even ones who spend their lives outdoors.

In fact, the only time I'd ever seen a wolverine was, coincidentally, on this very river my barrel had apparently been left at. I'd seen two wolverines here the year before. Thus it seemed most unfortunate that a barrel crammed with chocolate-coated energy bars, dried fruits, and jerky should have been left here of all places, with wolverines about. The lodge manager had said the guide had left the barrel on the island in a conspicuous spot, easily visible from the water. But I didn't see any sign of it. The island was close to shore, and a little bit of water is easily swam by a wolverine.

A search revealed no sign of a barrel anywhere. I paddled twice around the island, searching among the alders, willows, tamaracks, and spruces for any hint of it. But if a wolverine, or a grizzly, for that matter, had happened upon my barrel and devoured its contents, I'd expect to see the mangled remains of my supplies strewn about. There was no sign of this either. Indeed, the island looked as though no one had visited it at all since Chuck and I had been here the previous year.

Without fresh rations, things would be difficult. I was more than five hundred kilometres from my next resupply point, and the terrain that separated me from it promised to be more physically gruelling than anything I'd yet encountered. What rations I still had wouldn't last long. I could cut my daily amount to stretch them out, but that would leave me without the calories required to maintain long fourteen- or fifteen-hour days. The other option, to live off the land, was something I'd done before—but time spent procuring food would severely curtail time travelling and would not yield enough calories to sustain me for the route ahead.

Given there was no sign of it, it seemed likely that my barrel had never been delivered. Taking up the satellite phone, I fiddled with it again to get a signal, putting in another call to figure out what had happened to my barrel. I asked, if perhaps, there might have been some chance the guide had been confused or lost, and had dropped it off at the mouth of a different river. This, the lodge manager assured me, was impossible. The guide had deposited the barrel on the exact island. He suggested that I search for it again.

Personally, I've always enjoyed a good game of hide and seek or capture the flag, but now really didn't seem like the best time to be playing it. I felt sure the guide had made a mistake, which I knew was the kind of thing that can happen easily on an inland sea riddled with hundreds of bays, inlets, and islands, especially since fishing guides in their motorboats tend not to stray far from a few favourite fishing spots. My worst fears were always of this sort of thing happening, and partly what had drawn me here the year before with Chuck was to ensure things would go smoothly. We were both astonished, though, to find out that the lodge manager, an amiable fellow, had in all his years on Great Bear never been to the Dease River's mouth. He shrugged and said it was a very large lake. We'd gone there with him that summer specifically to identify a spot for a resupply, and it was this point, with the exact coordinates, that I'd specified for my barrel drop.

Finally, after a tense fifteen-minute wait, I received a satellite text informing me that there'd been a terrible mistake. My barrel, it'd turned out, had been delivered to the wrong river. The error was attributed to a rookie fishing guide, fresh in from Saskatchewan, who'd apparently been entrusted with the delivery the day before. Upon examining a map with the manager back at the lodge, they realized their mistake. Apparently, my barrel was left on an island at the mouth of some unknown creek. I was instructed to sit tight, and a guide would be dispatched in a motorboat after dinner to retrieve the barrel and get it to me within a few hours. Somewhere right about now, I thought ruefully, a wolverine or grizzly was enjoying my chocolate-almond energy bars.

Plummer's Lodge was almost forty kilometres away by boat. Two hours later, just before eleven p.m., the sun still high in the sky, I heard the drone of a boat engine coming from the west. A small boat with an outboard motor materialized, with two men on board. They were powering fast across the bay for the distant shore, about three kilometres from the island I was on. Even with my exact GPS coordinates it wasn't easy to find the correct island—from a distance, its spruces and tamaracks blended into the mainland shoreline. I watched them from the bank as they zoomed back and forth across the bay, evidently searching for the river mouth. Fifteen or twenty minutes later they figured things out and powered back across the bay in the right direction.

As they cruised in close to where I stood on shore, I felt slightly shy at the sight of other humans, though curious, like a wild animal. My barrel was on board, safe and sound.

"Sorry for the mistake. We effed up," said the man at the motor.

"It was my fault," said the younger man at the front of the boat, beside my barrel.

"He's a rookie," resumed the man at the back. "First season on Great Bear and he takes the barrel to the wrong place."

"Sorry," returned the other, looking at me apologetically.

Such excessive conversation felt overwhelming, the noise and all, and I was kind of hoping they'd just deliver my barrel and be gone. But after almost a month without human company, another part of me felt eager to chat. I mustered some words, "Thanks. I never doubted it would arrive safely."

They explained they didn't regularly come to this part of the lake to fish, and so they weren't very familiar with the area. But to make up for the confusion and delay they'd thoughtfully added a six-pack of beer to my rations. I thanked them for the beer, but explained that I didn't drink. I let them keep the beer for themselves, which seemed to make everyone happy.

The barrel they brought I quickly dumped into my nearly empty barrels. I did this because I wanted to keep my original barrels with me, which were slightly smaller than the resupply one; plus, having journeyed so far together, I'd become attached to them. I handed them the empty barrel back and a bit of sealed-up garbage (the empty freeze-dried wrappers).

"Thanks again," I said.

The man at the back nodded and reversed the boat's engine, backing up away from the island's shore as he opened a beer can. They both wished me good luck, then zoomed off across the lake.

I listened to the engine fade away, leaving me in absolute silence, save only for the drone of millions of mosquitoes swarming me, and then, feeling a little worn out from all the socializing, called it a night.

× 10 ×

CROSSING THE DIVIDE

On the morning of July 8 I dipped my paddle into Great Bear's clear waters for the last time, bidding farewell to the most majestic of all lakes. Leaving the lake, I began paddling up a waterway that I found had changed little since Simpson and Dease had described it in 1838: a river inhabited by white wolves and lined with tall spruces and tamaracks along its lower reaches, which thinned out farther up, eventually giving way to windswept tundra.

At its mouth the Dease River is only about two hundred and fifty metres wide, and not far up its twisting, snaking course it narrows to less than sixty. I needed to get over a hundred kilometres up it, against its strong current, to a small tributary flowing in from the north. That little stream would lead me northward, to the spot where I planned to strike overland across the divide separating Great Bear's drainage basin from the Coppermine River's watershed.

The first few kilometres of the river I found I could paddle against the current without too much difficulty, but soon its tortuous course became blocked with rapids. Then I had to wade with the water nearly up to my waist, hauling and dragging the canoe behind or beside me while trying not to lose my footing. The year before, the combined strength of Chuck and me working together had been enough to overcome much of the river's current. Alone, I had no choice but to do more wading and dragging.

This part of my journey had a slightly different feel to it than else-where, as here I was travelling over territory I'd seen twice before—once going upriver and then again going back downriver. I enjoy returning to old haunts as much as the next person, but they don't have quite the same magical allure as unknown places, where every bend in the river brings something new. We tend to think of the world as a fast-shrinking place, where modern technology has bridged dis-tances. That's partly true. But the funny thing is, if you get out on the land in a canoe or on foot, the world remains just as big as it ever was.

When I arrived at a certain sharp bend in the river, not quite five kilometres up from Great Bear Lake, I beached my canoe at the foot of a small rapid. On the far side of the river was a steep bluff, above which stood ancient spruces. This sharp bend, I knew from the prior summer with Chuck, was the site where a 106 years earlier, a Canadian prospector by the name of George Douglas and his two companions had built a small cabin to endure the brutal cold of the long, harsh arctic winter. Chuck and I had a made cursory investigation of the cabin's ruins, measuring its dimensions and photographing it. Douglas had sailed across Great Bear Lake that summer of 1911 on a small boat, before coming upriver here and selecting it as a spot to overwinter.

Perhaps if I were the superstitious sort I probably wouldn't have bothered to stop now and head off into the shadows of the tall black spruces to once more gaze at decaying ruins. There's something a little eerie about abandoned, crumbling cabins in the woods. Such an isolated cabin might be charming enough in summer, but in winter it could quickly feel like a prison.

Here, north of the Arctic Circle, sub-zero temperatures last for nearly nine months. During the worst stretch there are over forty days of unbroken darkness. Shut up inside a tiny, cramped cabin, the walls seem to close in a little tighter, week by week, sometimes driving the occupants mad with "cabin fever." The North is replete with disturbing stories of lone trappers who, isolated for too long during long, dark winters, committed unspeakable deeds. The case of the Mad Trapper is perhaps the most infamous, but there are many others. Shortly before embarking on their expedition, one of Simpson and Dease's men, a certain Anderson, went crazy and ran away in the woods. Simpson himself, after exploring the river I was now venturing up, had apparently become strangely withdrawn, erratic, and paranoid, eventually one night at his campsite murdering two Canadians and then shooting himself in the head. Another explorer who passed over this same ground, Dr. Richardson, Sir John Franklin's trusted companion, once shot a voyageur he suspected of murdering and eating another member of the party (that kind of thing is frowned upon in canoeing circles).

Before Douglas and his two companions had come to this lonely spot to build their cabin, the ruins of which I was now staring at, they'd stumbled upon another cabin on their way to Great Bear Lake. When they entered it they found a scene of horror. Inside the tiny dwelling were the decomposing remains of two men. One of the corpses, in Douglas's own words, had "his head a shapeless mass, blown out of all resemblance to anything human." A note left beside the other body told the tale. Shut up inside the cabin for months in darkness, freezing cold, and increasingly paranoid, one trapper had murdered the other, apparently shooting him in the head while he slept. The murderer, after confessing the deed in writing, had scrawled on the paper, "I am not Crasey" and then ended his own life by drinking poison.

Among the Algonquian-speaking peoples of the subarctic forests, for generations stories were told of individuals who, during unusually hard winters when game became scarce, turned into "windigos" to survive, which meant they ate human flesh. Windigos were believed to be possessed by an evil spirit that gave them superhuman strength. Many of the fur traders and voyageurs who lived in the "fur country" ended up sharing the Ojibwe and Cree beliefs about the existence of windigos.

In the spruce woods, I circled the crumbling ruins of Douglas's cabin. The roof had collapsed and part of the log walls had fallen in. In one corner was an impressively crafted fireplace, made with rocks carefully arranged to shelter the vital heat and chinked with clay taken from the riverbanks. Douglas and his two friends had managed to survive the winter without mishap, departing the area the next summer. They'd come to investigate copper deposits, but nothing ever came of that.

The forest was gradually swallowing the cabin's ruins; aside from its stone hearth, in time there would be nothing left. Slowly it would vanish back into the wilderness. I took one last look at it, then headed back to where I'd left my canoe.

At night as I lay in my tent, the river's rapids rumbling a short distance away, the air thick with the ceaseless buzz of millions of mosquitoes, and occasionally, echoing across untold miles the howls of arctic wolves, thoughts of solitary trappers and windigos would drift into my mind. Then, curled up in my sleeping bag, I'd eventually drift off.

✳

Upstream travel on the Dease I did with a mix of paddling, poling, wading, and dragging. The days were long and exhausting, attacked as I was by hordes of blackflies and increasingly by "bulldog" flies—a type of large biting horsefly that appears around July at these latitudes. When it bites, it feels more like a bee sting and leaves a welt behind.

My legs were daily becoming more scraped and bruised from smashing into unseen rocks while wading in the river. Some of the bruises on my thighs were the result of the canoe hitting me as I hauled with all my strength to pull it toward me against the rapids. My remaining toenails were black from banging against rocks, and I was mindful, as ever, not to lose my footing and slip and smash my head off any number of jagged rocks in the rapids. My feet also had a rash from constant wetness. Despite wearing hip waders, in some places where the river rose higher, or when I stumbled in the current, water would flood into the waders. I'd empty them afterward, but my socks stayed damp.

But as bad as my feet and legs looked, the canoe's hull looked worse. It now sported six or seven bad gashes. There was also a growing patch near the starboard side where the fabric was badly worn with threads visible. The river's frequent shallow, rock-strewn rapids had continued to grind away at the hull, since I had little choice but to scrape and drag the heavily loaded canoe over those jagged rocks. If I were to stop and portage all of the river's dozens of rapids I'd be lucky to get even halfway across the arctic tundra before snows buried me in the fall.

Otherwise, things were going well. Mentally, I was still very much enjoying my journey. My long days of ceaseless upriver travel were yielding about twenty to twenty-five kilometres of progress a day. There weren't many sections suitable for poling—the river was often either too deep for it or too swift—but in certain stretches between rapids, where the current slackened, I was able to do more paddling. In these places the scenery took on an intriguing aspect, with lonely mountains surrounding the river and great sandstone outcrops towering high above it. On some of these crags were gigantic nests of sticks, as large as a small boat: eagle nests, although their astonishing dimensions made them look as though they were home to mythical birds like griffins.

Fish were plentiful in the river, especially arctic graylings, pike, and burbot, a type of freshwater cod. Chuck and I had feasted nearly every day on fish, but alas, on my journey, fishing was a diversion I couldn't afford unless it came down to it as a necessity.

There were also small bird nests along the river's shore, carefully camouflaged in sedges and grasses, but I didn't have the heart to help myself to any of the eggs. My principles are to cause as little disturbance as possible, leaving, as far as I'm able, only footprints. I will admit, though, that I've been mighty tempted at times to throw a rock at the odd ptarmigan or grouse that crosses my path.

Wolves, too, were numerous, and as curious about me as others of their kind had been. A few days upriver, I was in the middle of a very long stretch of wading through rapids, hauling the canoe behind me, and was almost lulled into a daydream by the sounds of the water, the repetitive nature of the work, and the all-encompassing solitude. What snapped me back to attention was a sudden flash of white on the high opposite bank. I glanced up to see something dart behind a clump of willows and then re-emerge a few seconds later. It was an all-white wolf. Such white fur helps arctic wolves blend in with their surroundings in winter when stalking prey. The wolf poked its head out of the willows, staring right at me. Then, drawn by irresistible curiosity, she crept out, sat down, and just watched me passively. Or perhaps I'd merely been misreading all these wolf encounters and they'd been simply contemplating me the whole time as a nice addition to their diet.

In the lower parts of the river there was lots of ice damage along the riverbanks. During the annual breakup the ice rushes downstream on the current, smashing into the spruces overlooking the river and leaving gashes in their trunks high off the ground. These gashes have confused and alarmed a number of newcomers to northern rivers upon first sight of them—wondering what manner of beast could have wrought such destruction. The answer, of course, is ice. (But if you want to terrify the wits out of a group of young campers, tell them it was bears.)

I was often forced to sleep wherever I could find a spot—on rocks, gravel, or wherever else I'd happen to stop, exhausted, for the night. As before, if it had been a question of going downriver, I could afford to be selective, choosing anywhere to sleep that I liked. But with upriver travel, I simply had to force myself to push on for as long as I could.

My second day hauling and paddling upriver I passed through a high, twisting limestone canyon filled with a mix of rapids and deep pools. At the entrance to this canyon, a great rock pillar rose straight out of the river like a lighthouse. Nesting in the sheer cliffs were dozens of swallows that feed on the abundant swarms of insects. The year before, on our return journey, Chuck and I got caught in a July snowstorm in this canyon and were forced to canoe on through the snows, which reduced visibility greatly. Temperature drops of twenty degrees or more can happen over a single day in the Arctic, when frigid masses of air drift down from the Arctic Ocean. I was now only about a hundred and thirty kilometres inland of that icy sea.

Fortunately, this time when I entered the canyon the weather was mild. But the water levels, I noted, were higher than the previous year, probably on account of the later snowmelt. To get through the canyon would require a delicate mix of paddling and wading along the edge of rapids where the current was strong. What I wanted to avoid at all costs was portaging. In the centre of the canyon was a sizable rapid that roared over exposed rocks in a spot where the river narrowed. On its right side was a gravel bar with some willows growing on it. I landed my canoe on that gravel bar, deciding to try hauling it up through the rapids. Grabbing the bow with one hand, I towed it up to the edge of the rapids while trying to stay on shore myself. It took some careful handling to get the canoe up and past the rocks, knowing that if it caught sideways in the current it would flip over.

Once up the initial bit of whitewater I edged into the river knee-deep, in order to drag the canoe farther up to a place where I could safely jump in and resume paddling. The force of the current rushing against my legs caused me to momentarily stumble, but luckily I managed to recover without landing face first in the river. Another few steps and I was able to bring the canoe alongside me and leap back in. I paddled hard against the current, winding around the next bend in the canyon.

A short distance ahead were more rapids and a small but furious waterfall where the river plunged over big boulders. To haul up the thundering cataract would be impossible and dangerous; there was no choice but to portage around it. So I landed my canoe on the left side, just outside the last of the canyon walls, to begin carrying the loads ahead on foot. Getting everything around the cascade required climbing precariously over boulders with my heavy loads, and occasionally leaping across small channels where the torrent of raging water surged through. It wasn't the kind of place where you'd want to slip.

Afterward the river calmed down a bit and I could paddle. In places it flowed past big sandy beaches with thick willow bushes. These sandy beaches made for pleasant campsites, aside from the abundance of "bulldog" flies. My tent, a little worn after nearly two months of travel and use, I discovered had a few small holes through which, alarmingly, blackflies were invading. Fortunately I was able to patch them with some tape.

Four days into journeying up the river I was forced to halt early for the night: a storm was gathering on the horizon. The wind had been fierce all day, which, when combined with the current, had made progress painfully slow. By now the spruces had thinned out almost entirely, leaving only thickets of waist-high willows stretching for miles in all directions. A lone willow-clad mountain with a rocky summit was visible on the horizon.

I hurried to make camp on a bank overlooking the river before the storm was unleashed. After months of camping, my routine had become second nature. Before the skies could open up, I managed to get the tent up, my canoe and barrels secured, a fire going with water gathered and boiled, my thermos filled with tea, and a freeze-dried meal cooked. As I sat finishing my dinner looking out over the winding river, which was now quite small, the skies grew darker and more threatening.

I climbed into my tent just as the first crack of thunder boomed across the land. Rain lashed against my tent as it shook in the fierce winds. But inside I at least felt snug and dry. The storm was perhaps a little too close for comfort, with repeated flashes of lightning and loud bursts of thunder. But I trusted that my little tent was lower to the ground than the hills, mountains, and some scattered spruces, so that lightning shouldn't pose too much of a danger. Eventually the winds carried the storm away and I fell asleep.

※

The wind continued fierce and cold the next day, coming as it did from the Arctic Ocean, but I splashed and waded along against it, reaching by early evening the little tributary I'd been seeking. Known as Sandy Creek, it's a little creek that, as might be guessed, is rather sandy. In places, the stream is surrounded by high vertical banks that make it impossible to see the land beyond them, but on the positive side, they provide shelter from the strong winds.

I towed my canoe with a rope up Sandy Creek, wading through the water ahead, which was easy to do now; there were no longer any rocks to bump into in the clear water. The creek forked and grew steadily smaller, but still I splashed on. It was imperative that I push as far up the stream as possible, tracing it to little more than a trickle. Once I'd left the creek I'd be embarking on the longest portage of my entire expedition—right across the great divide that separates the huge watershed of Great Bear Lake from the Coppermine River, in order to link the chain of waterways I needed to complete my journey. Draining into the Coppermine are the Dismal Lakes, and these wild lakes would be where I needed to get to in order to resume paddling.

It was a portage that I expected to take days to complete, with the total distance, given all my loads, totalling a fearsome amount, perhaps forty or fifty kilometres. Generally, in canoeing terms, anything in excess of five hundred metres is deemed a long portage. And as Bill Mason, the Canadian canoe expert, put it, "Anyone who says they enjoy portaging is either a liar or crazy."

After a few hours of wading up the stream, I came upon a large sandy bar on the creek's eastern bank that I recognized as a place where Chuck and I had camped the previous year. A big rack of caribou antlers lay in the sand, right where I'd left them. No one, it seemed, had been to this lonely stream in the time since. It was here at this beach where we'd left our canoe and barrels behind, before beginning the long, arduous trek overland to the Dismal Lakes with only our backpacks and the bare essentials.

The hike had been long and wearisome, with plagues of blackflies nearly the whole way aside from when the wind was stiff. Chuck, in his considered opinion, had deemed the notion of trying to haul a canoe, two barrels, and a backpack across such a huge stretch as mad. He was wise like that.

One thing perhaps not immediately obvious is just how much more difficult hiking, and especially portaging, becomes when there's no trail to follow. Not only is it a matter of having to simultaneously navigate and lug a heavy canoe over your head or struggle under the weight of a heavy barrel, the real issue is the lack of solid, level ground to hike on. Chuck, having gotten a taste from his travels with me of what portaging without trails is like, once described it this way: "I would say very few people understand how difficult it is to walk from point A to point B without being on a proper trail. It is immeasurably more difficult and dangerous without a hard-packed surface under your feet. You start to wander like a dog, travelling three or four miles just for one mile of forward progress, stepping around obstacles and backtracking. Putting your foot in the wrong place is very likely to cause a twisted ankle or other injury."

Chuck and I, since we'd hadn't been portaging but merely hiking for the sake of exploring, had taken a somewhat indirect route to the lakes. In the process we wandered across a surprising variety of terrains, from flat tundra plains overgrown with dwarf birch shrubs, to snowfields that remained in shaded valleys, to surreal sandy deserts that made us feel as if we'd somehow strayed into the Sahara. Then there were the swampy sphagnum bogs, rolling beautiful hills with spruce groves, and quiet, meadow-filled valleys. Eventually we reached the tip of the Dismal Lakes, which we found windswept and inhospitable, such that canoeing would have been impossible with the waves. After camping a night there we retraced our steps homeward bound to the canoe and barrels.

This time, however, I pressed on farther up the creek, beyond where Chuck and I had left it on our overland trek. Based on what I'd read in Douglas's journals and those of earlier explorers like Simpson and Dease, I hoped it might be possible for me to make it farther up the stream, just as they must have. They'd all come this way on their travels, since they too had crossed the divide to the Coppermine. Simpson and Dease had done so with a party of about fifteen men carrying wooden rowboats, which they'd built to navigate the Coppermine and from there the treacherous waters of the Arctic Ocean. If I could make it farther upstream, it would help reduce the length of the portage needed to reach the Dismal Lakes. Since I had a smaller boat than any of those predecessors, and the water levels seemed higher than they'd been before, I was optimistic about my chances.

Another thing not immediately obvious is that the frequent alternations between paddling or poling and wading—a necessity for up-river travel—cause water to accumulate in the canoe. This is from water running off pant legs and boots once climbing back into the canoe. It might not seem like much water could accumulate in that manner, but it certainly begins to add up quite fast—even when, like me, you take the time to stand on one leg, letting most of the water run off before stepping back in. The accumulating water adds weight to the canoe, not only slowing it down but also drenching any back-packs stowed in the boat. And a waterlogged backpack, with its increased weight, is not a pleasant thing to carry on lengthy portages. Luckily for me, as a boy I'd learned an old woodsman's trick to avoid my backpack getting wet in the canoe. Cut some willow branches, lay them down in the bottom, then put your backpack over them. This inch or so of space the willows (or any other branch) provide is sufficient to keep your gear nice and dry.

Knowing in advance that this gruelling portage would be one of the most difficult parts of my expedition, I'd carefully plotted ahead of time how best to tackle it. With one eye on my budget and the other on my route maps, I'd specifically devised my resupply points to allow me to be travelling as light as possible in this section. Thus, my resupply at the end of Great Bear, and a second one I hoped to obtain a month or so later, when I reached a place on the Coppermine River where a floatplane could safely land. This would allow me to carry rations for only a month over this stretch, a lot less than elsewhere. Indeed, by this point, I'd been steadily eating up all my surplus rations that had been left over when I reached the end of Great Bear, allowing me to further lessen my loads and bulk up at least a little for the gruelling portaging. The cart, too, I hoped, might finally prove useful.

Back in Sudbury I'd also studied the accounts and hand-drawn maps of early explorers like Simpson, Dease, Douglas, and other historic figures who'd been over this terrain—comparing their notes with modern satellite imagery in the hope of pinpointing a route that would minimize portaging by hitting certain small lakes and ponds that appeared scattered like raindrops across the tundra.

Beyond these measures, I had no other tricks to play. Sometimes hard work is the only thing that will succeed. Daunting as such a long portage appeared, my mindset was that simple persistence would pay off. Like the tortoise and the hare again, I just told myself, "Slow and steady wins the race."

The high water levels, it turned out, did allow me to advance up the little sandy creek, and even farther than I'd dared hope. I ventured way beyond the point where Chuck and I had abandoned the creek, managing to make it another twenty kilometres up. This took me past numerous sand hills and up and around a great many S-bends in the river. These repeated S-bends were so extreme as to make the creek resemble a crazy straw, or a giant python.

At night, camped on the creek, I could hear the howls of a pack of wolves echoing out from distant mountains. Wolves were clearly frequent visitors in these parts. I'd often come across their scat on the tundra. From the white hairs in it, it seemed they'd been feeding on caribou.

✳

Early the next morning, after a few more hours of paddling and wading up the tiny, winding stream, I reached a point where I judged it time to begin the dreaded overland trek. It was to be the portage of all portages—nearly forty kilometres in the aggregate, with no trail to follow. I'd arrived at a sand and gravel ridge that appeared to be an esker, formed by the retreat of the glaciers northward about ten thousand years earlier. It ran off to the northwest, the direction where I needed to head. Wolf tracks were faintly visible in its sand. If wolves had gone along the ridge, I figured I'd follow their example.

All of my rations I was able to compress down into a single barrel, leaving the other one empty. This was excellent, as it meant I could simply carry the empty barrel with the canoe, reducing my loads from four to three, and thereby cutting down the total distance by as much as twenty kilometres.

I began by strapping on my backpack. It was my lightest load, weighing no more than fifty pounds. It was also much more comfortable to wear than the barrel. For that reason, I always took it first on portages, as the extra spring in my step let me scout things out more thoroughly, thereby picking out the best ground for the heavier and more difficult loads to follow. (In the wilderness, a straight line between two points is seldom the shortest way—especially if it means making your way across willow thickets, swampy ground, or boulder fields where you can twist an ankle.)

Thus I set off. The sun was beating down, but a brisk wind kept things cool. I wore a mesh bug net to minimize the annoyance of the blood-sucking insects. Navigating was easy enough: I knew which direction to head, and there was a range of high hills as landmarks to guide me.

The sandy, pebble-strewn esker made for good hiking terrain. It curved in an arc around a pond, then took me up a slope and across tundra with low willow bushes. Once over a spruce-clad ridge, I passed on to a great sandy slope. At the end of this sandy stretch, having hiked about a kilometre, I set down my backpack, refuelled with some water and an energy bar, then returned to fetch my next load.

My reason for these short intervals was not wanting to leave any of my packs unattended for too long, which seemed unwise with grizzlies and wolverines wandering about. Plus, regular breaks help make the overall portage seem more manageable.

When it came time to take the canoe, I again experimented with the cart. I strapped the canoe on it and put a number of miscellaneous items inside, such as my waders. It worked well enough across the sand esker, but once I'd passed on to the hilly terrain or over willows, it was much less practical. It was the kind of thing that might have worked effectively with two people—one pulling from the front, the other pushing from the back—allowing even more things, such as the backpack and barrels, to be put inside the canoe. I made a mental note of this for the purpose of future trips. Of course, it didn't do much good to dwell on such things at the time.

Across a valley from this first leg of my portage, I could see a snow-field tucked beneath the bottom of a large ridge. Back in 1911 Douglas had described this very snowfield. Chuck and I had also seen it—and it was encouraging to think that warmer average temperatures hadn't, at least yet, seemed to have changed it much. While all this landscape would be buried in snow most of the year, by June the snows usually melt across most of the low Arctic. However, in this unique spot, as in a few others, the shade of the encircling ridge keeps the ice and snow preserved year-round.

The next leg of the trek took me across vast fields of willow shrubs and dwarf birches. The willows and birches weren't any higher than my knees, so hiking among them wasn't much trouble. In a few places I startled willow ptarmigans. Unlike the grouse in the woods near where I grew up, the ptarmigans startled here didn't fly off very far. They simply flew up a short couple of strides and then landed again in plain sight. Like other animals, birds that haven't been exposed much to human hunting over many generations remain remarkably easy to approach.

This included a mother ptarmigan, with six good-sized chicks that followed her across the tundra. They scurried off as I passed by but they never went far, and I saw them on each trip back and forth with my different loads. They would have made a nice meal, but I didn't have the heart to do it, though I certainly thought about it.

I next headed into a hilly region, passing among hills thinly clad with spruces and an abundance of wild berries, none of which were yet ripe. These sheltered hills seemed to be a favourite haunt of wildlife. Wolf tracks were visible in the sand, and I could easily imagine a grizzly would enjoy the berry buffet when they turned ripe. From the summit of one of these hills I surveyed the route ahead. In the far distance I could see mountains with some snow on their upper slopes. Beneath these lonely mountains was where I needed to get to, the Dismal Lakes.

It was the high-strung Simpson who'd given them that name. In the spring of 1838, when he and his companions came over a high ridge and first caught sight of these narrow, interconnected lakes set amid windswept mountains, Simpson noted, "Never have I seen a land so desolate and dismal as that which stretched before me."

It was precisely that "desolate and dismal" place I was trying so hard to reach.

Luckily, just beneath the hills I'd hiked into were three ponds in a row and then a small lake, allowing me to paddle a bit and refill my empty water bottle. The canoe I went back to simply dragging, which I found faster than fiddling with the cart. The empty barrel I strapped on my back when dragging the canoe, thereby eliminating the need for a fourth trip.

Between each of these ponds, a short portage allowed me to skip ahead to the next one. Then, after crossing the last of the three, I noticed something odd. The ground just beyond the pond was flattened and trampled down, almost as if by vehicles or a stampede of elephants. But there were no roads for hundreds of kilometres, and the last arctic elephants—mastodons and woolly mammoths—had died out millennia ago.

Upon taking a closer look, it hit me what had made these rutted, muddy tracks: thousands of hooves, marching in a great herd. They were from the caribou migration, when the animals form vast herds beyond counting, and march across the tundra for hundreds of miles.

The dwarf birch bushes were all grazed down, and the ground churned up to the width of a three-lane road by marching hooves. The herd must have passed recently, within days it seemed. Perhaps the howling of the wolves I'd heard was from a pack stalking them.

I scanned across the sea of tundra that unfolded before me for any sign of the herd. A white speck was bobbing along on the horizon. I couldn't make out what it was, so I used my camera to zoom in on it. It was a lone caribou, a straggler who must have fallen behind.

I resumed my portage, carrying the canoe and two loads across the rutted-up passage that the herd had passed over. Eventually, just as I was completing the last load, the straggler approached. To my surprise, at the sight of me, the caribou walked right up to me. I informed the caribou that the herd had gone west, and that if she didn't dally she might yet catch up with them. The caribou didn't seem to entirely understand me, but nonetheless she trotted off in the right direction.

A few minutes later, as I was busy launching the canoe into the small lake, two more caribou materialized. These ones paid no attention to me and hurried on their way.

I, too, had to be on my way, north to the Dismal Lakes.

The ponds and the lake raised my spirits greatly, as they cut down on the portaging by allowing me to paddle a little. When I reached the end of the lake, which took only a few minutes, I resumed travel on foot.

The lake brought me to more big sand hills scattered with black spruce. On the far side of these hills I found a great sandy slope that ran down to another beautiful lake. To reach it, I dragged my canoe over the hills and down the slope, then carried my other loads up and over. It'd been about ten hours of solid portaging, but I calculated that I still wasn't even halfway through yet. Exhausted, I camped on the sandy beach for the night. The portage I'd just have to continue in the morning.

In the meantime, after a fire on the beach, I curled up in my tent on what was a cold, windy night. Just as I was getting comfortable, the howling of wolves rang out across the distant hills. I wondered whether the friendly caribou had managed to catch up in time.

THROUGH THE DISMAL LAKES

I woke early, eager for another hard day of portaging. I figured if I could just get this dreaded portage done, it would be a great weight off my shoulders. Coming into the journey I knew it would be one of the most physically demanding aspects of it, and thus if I could pull it off, I'd feel that much closer to reaching my end goal. At this point, despite trekking and paddling nearly fifteen hundred kilometres from the Yukon, that end goal still felt pretty unreachable.

So I tried to focus on the task at hand. (And not dwell too much on all the stories I'd heard—stories about how bad the storms got after mid-August in the barren lands west of Hudson Bay.) In my canoe I was soon paddling hard across the little lake I'd camped on. It was a short paddle to reach the lake's north shore. Here, there was a range of steep, rolling hills covered with short tundra grass and small stones. I landed directly beneath the hills, strapped on my backpack, and began climbing. My legs burned as I ascended the steep slope, but my excitement at what I might see from the summit carried me on.

Coming over the crest of the hill, a magnificent view unfolded before me. The range of steep hills formed a sort of crescent, beneath which lay a sheltered marshy valley and a small, hourglass-shaped lake. Beyond the hills were great ridges, which in places rose up to rocky summits. And just past the lake, tucked behind the hills but below the encircling mountainous ridge, was a small gap. I recognized it from the year before with Chuck—it was where I needed to head.

I cut down the windy, barren hillside toward the valley. It was a little marshy in places, but otherwise not difficult to cross. About seven hundred and fifty metres of hiking brought me to the shores of the hourglass lake. I left my backpack there and retraced my steps across the plain, over the windswept hills, and down the far side where I'd left my canoe and the rest of my gear.

Next I strapped on the big, heavy barrel and, with a paddle to support me, began climbing the hill again. I staggered in the gusts of wind under the weight of the barrel on the steep hillside, but balancing myself with the paddle, I kept climbing. Up on those wild slopes I could see for miles in all directions—there wasn't the slightest hint of any human-made object to be seen anywhere, or another person. It was a remarkably beautiful, soul-filling sight.

When I'd finished that load I took a brunch of cashews and some jerky, drank cold water, and then went back for the canoe. Hauling the canoe up the hillside required a kind of running start, dragging it with one hand while holding the other hand out to maintain my balance in the wind and on the steep slope.

Inside the canoe were, among other things, my empty barrel, waders, fishing rod, and bailer, all of which slid down to the stern of the canoe as I kept hauling it up the hill. Panting heavily, I told myself that this hard work would be rewarded with an easy toboggan ride down the far side.

The summits were a bit rocky, so I lifted the canoe partially up and carried it across the barren hilltop. Once over the top, the canoe did toboggan down nicely, with me jogging alongside after it. When we reached the bottom I took the bow rope, tied it into a harness, and began dragging the assemblage across the tundra like a dogsled. The improvised harness worked well, and I even jogged a bit, excited to reach the hourglass lake.

But these early enthusiasms didn't last long. The lake was only a half-kilometre long, and I was soon across it. On its far side more challenging terrain confronted me: a mix of willow shrubs, dwarf birch, and bog, infested with millions of blackflies, set within a long, narrow gully. This gully ran for nearly five kilometres, terminating at last at the tip of the Dismal Lakes. Of that five kilometres, all would have to be portaged aside from one pond of about five hundred metres that I could paddle across. I strapped on my backpack, and began hiking through willows, up and over a ridge, and then down into the gully.

Swarms of blackflies and mosquitoes attacked me as soon as I dropped into the gully. Their itchy bites on my neck, wrists, and waist-line were maddening, but I pushed on, trying to move as quickly as I could. Down in the gully, however, the ground was wet and boggy. My hiking boots were soon drenched and heavy, slowing me down.

Sinking into this morass with the pack on my back was exhausting, but still I trudged on with clouds of blackflies, mosquitoes, sandflies, and bulldog flies feasting on my flesh as I did so. Eventually, after nearly three kilometres, I reached the edge of the narrow pond and unstrapped my backpack. Then I turned round and hiked back through the boggy lowlands, the bugs still swarming me. When I finally made it back to the hourglass lake, where my other loads were waiting, I flopped down on the soft moss, exhausted.

I rested comfortably in the moss as a cool breeze blew away the swarms of bugs. Needing more energy, I fished out some dried straw-berries, goji berries, and almonds from my barrel. But the breeze soon died, allowing the bugs to resume their assault. So I put away my snacks, lifted the heavy barrel up onto my knee and then onto my back, strap-ping it across my chest. With my other paddle, the bent-shaft one, I set off again through the willows into the gully.

Maybe it was the blood smearing my beard and neck, but the storms of bugs seemed only to get worse on this third trip through the gully. I was wearing gloves, but the blackflies in particular were merci-lessly attacking my exposed wrists. Still I staggered on, knowing that to rest would only allow more bugs to feast on me.

To hike three kilometres with a heavy barrel strapped on your back is perhaps not too difficult on solid ground or with a trail to follow—but the boggy soil made hiking twice as exhausting as would ordinarily be the case. When I at last reached the pond where I'd left my backpack, I set down the barrel and decided I needed some relief.

Normally I use bug spray only sparingly, if it all. Frankly, I don't like spraying chemicals on my skin or clothing. Plus, as I've mentioned, it was my good fortune to have had a family home surrounded by black swamps of foul water that bred great clouds of mosquitoes, granting me a high tolerance as a result. But there are times, such as when portaging multiple loads across boggy lowlands infested with millions of blackflies and other blood-sucking insects, when bug spray comes in handy. I'd packed several containers of it, and fished one out of my backpack now. I knew from past experience in northern swamps that bug spray is of limited effectiveness here, but there are also times when even limited effectiveness seems like a worthwhile improvement. So, I liberally dosed my clothing with the spray.

It seemed to partially diminish the hordes of blackflies and mosquitoes. I then hiked back across the gully for the fourth time in order to fetch my canoe. By the time I reached it the bugs were swarming me as fiercely as ever.

I wasted little time slipping on the harness I'd made and dragging the canoe behind me for the fifth and final trip through the gully. My legs and hips burned, but I kept going. After about a kilometre of dragging, however, I was starting to feel almost woozy from the storms of blackflies biting me—something I'd felt only once before, when one July I'd hiked for days into the heart of muskeg in the Hudson Bay Lowlands. Apparently excessive bites can lead to something called "blackfly fever," which, apart from the fever itself, can bring on symptoms like headache, nausea, and swollen lymph nodes. But I was determined to reach the Dismal Lakes that day, come what may, and so I splashed some refreshing bog water in my face, inhaled deeply, and pushed on.

When I finally reached the pond where my barrel and backpack were waiting, I pushed the canoe in the water, quickly loaded it, and jumped in. The distance from the end of this pond to the tip of the

Dismal Lakes was approximately 1.7 kilometres through willows, spruces, bog, and some hills. With my three separate loads to carry plus two return trips, that meant I actually had five times that amount, eight and a half kilometres, to cover before I could rest easy at the Dismal Lakes.

Having reached the end of the pond, I set off with my backpack, plunging once more into clouds of blackflies that made sure to exact their toll for the passage. The way forward took me first through low-lying boggy ground, then past ancient, stunted spruces as the ground ascended up a long hill.

As I came up a higher ridge, for the first time I caught sight of the Dismal Lakes. They didn't look at all dismal to me: shimmering dark blue water set beneath wild mountain ridges and great green hills with bald rock outcrops. In the far distance, beyond the lake, rose a great mountain barrier with patches of snow on it. Some stunted spruces stood on the nearer side of the lake, but mostly the land was open, windswept tundra. The sight of the Dismal Lakes felt a bit surreal— some effect of the light, water, and distance made the mountains and snow on the far shore seem like a floating mirage. Or perhaps it was just loss of blood from millions of blackfly bites.

The lake was still another seven hundred metres ahead, but the sight of it renewed my energy and I pushed on with my backpack down the ridge to it. The shrieking of an arctic tern, evidently nesting somewhere nearby, greeted me as I dropped my backpack on the tundra just above a small beach. A cold wind was blowing hard across the lake, lapping waves against the shore.

It took several more hours of hard work to finish transporting my other loads. By the time I'd finished it was seven p.m. and I was exhausted.

I celebrated the completion of the portage with a freeze-dried meal and some Labrador tea. Best of all, the fierce winds sweeping across the lake dispelled the clouds of bugs. I could finally breathe easy, removing my mesh bug net. My throat was bloodied with bites.

Flipping the collar up on my jacket, I huddled for warmth by the little blaze of a driftwood fire I'd kindled. I had two other reasons to celebrate. First, I'd reached the most northern part of my journey across Canada's Arctic. The Dismal Lakes are just ninety kilometres south of the Arctic Ocean's Coronation Gulf, which forms part of the Northwest Passage. Second, I'd crossed another major watershed divide, having now succeeded in passing out of Great Bear Lake's drainage basin into the Coppermine River watershed. This meant that for the first significant stretch of my journey I'd actually soon have a river to paddle *with* the current. Before I could do that, though, I'd have to get off this windswept beach.

The Dismal Lakes, a chain of three long, interconnected lakes set amid mountains, are notoriously windy. When Chuck and I had arrived here the previous year, we'd seen nothing at all encouraging to the idea of canoeing. The wind had been fierce the entire time we were at the lakes, and I could easily appreciate historical accounts of past travellers trapped for days here by tremendous gusts that made paddling impossible. On a short journey such a delay wouldn't be too much of a concern, but for me, with thousands of kilometres of paddling still to do across any number of lakes that might leave me windbound, any delays were liable to cause trouble.

I set up my tent in the winds, anchoring it with guy lines. Then I crawled inside. I just had to hope that morning would bring calm weather.

✳

The wind raged that night. My tent poles moaned and nearly buckled from the pressure of the blasts. Sand, whipped up by the gusts as they swept across the beach below, blew all over the tent and even inside through its screen doors. Worried that my little tent would blow away, I crawled out in the night to check on the pegs. Several had lifted right out of the ground, pulled up by the force of the winds sweeping under the tent fly.

I jammed them back down and piled rocks on top to help hold them, shivering as I did so. Back inside I rubbed my arms to keep warm, and burrowed back into my sleeping bag. Sleeping I found difficult in spite of my exhaustion, on account of the racket made by wind gusts rumbling my tent's rain fly and constantly pounding and shaking its nylon walls.

When I woke in the morning the wind sounded as fierce as ever. Sometimes, though, from inside a tent, wind can sound worse than it actually is. Thinking this might be one of those times, I poked my head out the tent to take a look . . . It wasn't one of those times. The wind was as strong as it sounded. It was far too rough to paddle. I'd never make it off the beach in such a powerful headwind.

All day, in fact, the wind never let up. I waited anxiously for any break, but none came. So I tried to make the most of it by resting and recovering my strength. At one point I dug a little pit in the sand to shelter a fire and then boiled water for tea. Rain fell, off and on, but with my knife I shaved off some dry kindling and kept the fire burning long enough for several cups of tea.

I also decided to reduce the wind rushing under my tent. The noise it made was quite distracting, and I didn't much care for the sand sweeping into my tent either. To accomplish this, I stacked up some rocks to form a low wall around the edge of my tent fly facing the wind, which prevented gusts from sweeping underneath. The rock wall made it much quieter inside, and I slept better.

In the cold and fierce wind, the surrounding barren mountains, with their great, ancient rock outcrops, and the distant snows on the far side of the lake, did begin to look a little more dismal and threatening. The skies were filled with dark, low-lying clouds that billowed by on the arctic winds. But then weather can change the mood of any landscape.

I hoped the winds would calm down in the evening. I was starting to feel distinctly anxious, knowing that I'd lost a full day, and could ill afford to lose another. In the Arctic the worst winds are generally in late summer, which in the past have stranded canoeing parties for weeks at a time. It was still only July, which didn't seem to bode well for what I might encounter come August. This was a drawback of solo paddling: one person in a canoe just can't battle winds as effectively as two or more can. In the old days of the fur trade and exploration, there was a reason why canoes typically had between eight and ten paddlers.

The evening brought no respite from the stormy weather, and I huddled inside my tent, just hoping for a calm enough spell to set off. Shortly after one a.m., though, the howling of the wind subsided somewhat. When I went out to investigate I was taken a little aback by the scene. Across the dark waters the midnight sun, having dipped below the mountains, filled the cloudy sky with an eerie red glow. In the faint, unearthly light the mountains stood dark and gloomy, with just patches of white snow standing out against the black slopes. I felt as though I were looking at some portal into another world—I'd never seen anything so hauntingly surreal. The wind was still sharp and cold, but the lake was calmer, with just small waves rippling across it.

I decided to make a break for it. I rushed to get my sleeping bag and extra clothes packed up, the tent down, and my canoe flipped back over and launched into the lake. I packed the barrels and my backpack, zipped up my lifejacket, pulled on the black balaclava and warm gloves, then pushed off, hopping into the canoe.

I paddled hard away from shore under dark skies into the wind, heading toward the eerie red glow of the horizon. The wind, however, proved fiercer out on the water than I had anticipated. My furious paddle strokes could barely edge the canoe forward—the wind kept driving me back toward the bleak shore.

Try as I might I couldn't overcome such strong gusts. All I was doing was exhausting myself for little gain. So, after only a kilometre and a half, I reluctantly put into shore on a gravelly beach. I realized I had no choice but to wait for the wind to die. In the meantime I set up my tent on the gravel, leaving everything else ready to go at a moment's notice should the wind ease up.

I slept some three or four hours, after which the wind didn't appear any better, but anxious as I was, I decided to attempt paddling against it anyway. The northern part of the Dismal Lakes is shaped like a giant T, or, as I thought of it at the time amid such wild and desolate scenery, like Thor's Hammer. The bay I was trapped in formed the hammer-head, the part that looks like it's swinging downward. The fierce south-west wind was funnelling through the mountains and right across the end of the "hammer," which I'd been trying in vain to escape from. I figured if I could just overcome the wind long enough to get out of the hammerhead and around the point into the main section of the T, or handle, the winds shouldn't be as bad there. Tucked away in that narrow section of the lake, the wind wouldn't be hitting head on as it was here, and the mountains would help shelter me.

It was about eight kilometres out of the bay I was trapped in, or six and a half kilometres farther from where I'd stopped on the gravelly beach. All I had to do was paddle with all my strength for that long and it seemed I should be all right.

I put the tent away, did a few stretches to prepare myself, and then once more launched the canoe into the lake. Furiously I paddled; it was some of the hardest, most exhausting paddling I've ever done. Bit by bit, stroke by stroke, I forced the canoe forward. I was glad I had my bent-shaft paddle for the extra efficiency it gave each stroke.

The wind was icy and steady, but regardless I was soon sweating with exertion. There wasn't any chance to rest—for if I did, the wind would immediately drive me back down into the end of the bay. So I kept going. Finally, after several exhausting hours, I rounded the rocky wild shores into the main stem of the Dismal Lakes, the handle of Thor's Hammer.

Here the lake was only a bit more than a kilometre wide, and with the bleak, stony mountains on the far shore sheltering me from the wind's wrath, I could now paddle more easily, pushing on up the lake. The ice had melted here less than two weeks earlier; the Dismal Lakes tend to remain ice-covered right up until July.

The scenery along the Dismal Lakes was wild, majestic, and awe-inspiring. It was true tundra, devoid of trees, with ancient mountains and rolling hills. There wasn't much wildlife about, but the scenery itself kept me enthralled as I paddled all day, not stopping until seven that evening. I'd managed to advance fifty kilometres—through the whole of the first Dismal Lake, and then down through the narrows connecting it to the second of the three lakes. Amid this inconceivably ancient landscape, I pitched my tent on the tundra, and gathered up just enough little willow branches for a fire in the shelter of some rocks. For as long as I was able, I intended to keep making fires, in order to save my precious fuel canister. To travel light, I'd packed only a single mixed butane-propane canister, which I'd need in places where there was scant wood to burn.

＊

The next day I continued paddling through the lakes, feeling almost overwhelmed by the ancient landscape. Some of the world's oldest fossils, containing primitive life forms dating back over a billion years, have been discovered in the area around the Dismal Lakes by geologists. And to the south of these magical lakes, just east of Great Bear on the Canadian Shield, are possibly the oldest rocks ever discovered on the planet, dating back an astonishing four billion years to when the earth was a lifeless wasteland.

After passing through a weedy, sandy channel, I came to the last of the three Dismal Lakes. The wind was roaring as I reached it. This time, however, the wind was blowing in my favour, creating big waves rolling across the lake. It had been over a month since I'd used my sail, not since the Mackenzie River had I had a chance to unfurl it. Poling and hauling up the smaller, rapid-filled rivers hadn't afforded any opportunities for it, and Great Bear Lake had been either too calm, too icy, or too dangerous for it. But now conditions seemed ideal for me to test it out again. I pulled the knots holding the sail to my canoe's centre thwart, and like an old friend it sprang up as if happy to see me, catching the wind.

As it did the canoe suddenly leapt forward, speeding ahead across the lake. With my straight-shaft paddle I steered over the big waves. After over a month of painstaking travel I'd almost forgotten how exhilarating it felt to sail a canoe.

We seemed to practically fly, and when the wind really gusted the sail shook then folded over almost double as the wind struck it forcefully. With breaking surf and the canoe flying along I felt a little nervous, given the size of the waves. The cautious thing to do would probably have been not to sail in such high winds alone in a canoe, but I just couldn't resist the temptation—it felt incredible to move so fast, especially after such wearisome portaging and stiff headwinds. The canoe's speed I estimated at over ten kilometres an hour, based on clocking time on my watch and measuring it against distances along the lake. In less than thirty minutes I'd crossed the last of the Dismal Lakes.

Draining the Dismal Lakes is the Kendall River, a fast-flowing, rapid-filled stream of about thirty kilometres length that empties into the Coppermine River, which in turn flows out to the Arctic Ocean. Once I'd reached the river's outlet from the lake, I quickly reefed my sail and switched back to paddling. Seeing how it was the first significant water I'd paddled on since my trek began where the current was actually in my favour, it felt almost like a holiday to travel without having to wade, haul, drag, and pole against a current.

The river was full of small rock-strewn rapids, which I plunged through in the canoe, dodging the rocks and enjoying the speed of the current. Most of these rapids would have been easy to navigate were it not for the same strong winds that had driven me across the lake. The wind, in places where the river curved, now hit me broadside, which made steering the canoe trickier than normal. Still, my progress was swift and I soon reached a canyon that marked the end of the short river.

This high-walled, red limestone canyon had some bigger rapids inside of it, one of which saw fit to fling my canoe at the canyon wall after I'd plunged through its foaming water. Fortunately with my paddle I was able to brace myself from slamming into the cliffs, and continue downstream. By evening I'd made it through the whole of the Kendall River and reached its outlet into a far larger, more powerful river—one steeped in history and fable, where a half-billion years ago volcanoes roared over the land. The Coppermine.

No aspect of my journey across the Arctic was more fraught with danger, uncertainty, and hardship than what this storied river promised to unleash upon me. Somehow, against all conventional logic, I had to find a way to canoe the Coppermine River *in reverse*—a river whose current made the Mackenzie's seem tame in comparison. Its formidable, roaring current, packed as it was with thunderous whitewater rapids, treacherous cliffs, and deep canyons, I knew, would take everything I had.

✱ 12 ✱

THE SERPENT'S COIL

Back on those acid rain–scarred hills above Sudbury I'd visualized my entire route, brooding over its every aspect, and how best to approach its various obstacles. I'd come up with different stratagems for different sections, planning everything as carefully as I could. But there was one section of my route that always filled me with doubt. That was the Coppermine River.

If trying to canoe up the Mackenzie alone was regarded as absurd by experienced canoeists, trying to canoe the Coppermine in reverse— a river whose current was perhaps three times stronger than even the Mackenzie's, was seen by veteran northern travellers as utterly delusional, if not a case of actual self-harm. The river's tortuous course was filled with innumerable obstacles: thundering whitewater rapids, sheer cliffs, canyons, and a powerful, rip-roaring current that extended for hundreds of kilometres. My task was to figure out a way to navigate my canoe upriver, against the fearsome current and foaming rapids, with what amounted to about hundred and twenty pounds of gear and provision inside the canoe, slowing it down.

In 1770, when the explorer Samuel Hearne and renowned Chipewyan leader Matonabbee reached the river's rugged valley, seeing the falls, canyons, and rapids, they at once deemed it unnavigable for birchbark canoes, instead opting to travel on foot. They were smart like that.

Where I came upon the Coppermine River, it was certainly an impressive sight—a noisy, fast-flowing waterway over a half-kilometre wide. To the north were strange-looking mountains formed of long slabs of stacked pinkish rock, which looked vaguely like the Egyptian step pyramid of Djoser. They'd been formed by ancient lava flows piling up one on top of the other hundreds of millions of years ago.

In the middle of the river lay a couple of big, flat, meadow-like islands sprinkled with bright clusters of purplish pink fireweed and yellow cinquefoil. I paddled a short distance against the current to land on the nearer of these islands. By now it was late evening, and a light rain had begun to fall. So I made camp and gathered driftwood for a fire. I needed a good night's sleep to prepare for what promised to be a gruelling, exhausting upriver battle that would exceed anything I'd yet attempted.

Lying in my tent, listening to the noise of the nearby river, I thought over what I had to do if I were to succeed in getting up the Coppermine. Against a current that powerful, brute strength would count for little. My only chance was to rely on agility, careful decision making, and, above all, determination. Now more than ever the idea of the tortoise racing the hare was my guiding philosophy. Only with a great deal of patience and persistence could I overcome the river's seemingly impossible current.

I got an early start in the morning, packing my canoe with a sense of dread as I listened to the rumble and roar of distant rapids. There was no kidding myself: I was in for the challenge of my life. I began by paddling away from the island, against the current, over to the river's western bank. It was strewn with rocks and steep slopes, not at all ideal for wading and hauling. Worse yet, my wading boots were starting to fall apart, the left one having been ripped open on some sharp underwater rocks. The waders themselves had several punctures in them. I'd become used to wet feet, but it wasn't great for the agility needed for scrambling about on rocks.

With my hip waders on, I began wading while pulling the canoe behind me. This kind of wading is typically shunned by canoeists because it's dangerous. As the wise Bill Mason put it, when wading, if you "jam your foot between rocks when in waist-deep water [and] if you fell downstream, the current could hold you from getting back up without help." That's probably why wading alone on arctic rivers isn't often encouraged. In 1979 the federal government published a manual for canoeists seeking to paddle "barrenland" rivers in the Canadian North. In the chapter on the Coppermine a helpful warning was included in bold type: "The Coppermine is a river that should be attempted only by canoeists experienced in whitewater. The region is totally isolated; the water is fast and cold and serious mistakes can be fatal."

Canoeing parties of six to twelve are the norm for safety, and some northern outfitters refuse to rent canoes or equipment to parties of less than four, on the grounds anything smaller is reckless. Even travelling in a group of two in a single canoe—as Chuck and I did, and as my friend Travis and I were also in the habit of doing—is seen by many northern canoeists as risky. As for travelling upriver, alone, that was simply not done.

I thought back to the days I'd spent poling up the Mackenzie, and how, in comparison, that now seemed almost easy. Here the current was too powerful even for poling, let alone wading and dragging the canoe like I'd done on other rivers. My only options were either to hike along the shore with a rope pulling the canoe in the water, or else to keep one foot on dry land and the other on the water's edge, grasping the canoe's bow directly in my hands and hauling it upriver that way.

The shoreline was steeply sloped, with jumbles of skull-sized rocks that were easy to trip over, especially when having to keep an eye on the canoe as I either hauled it with rope or else directly with my hand on the bow. It proved hard, difficult work, but I kept at it, putting one foot in front of the other, choosing my spots among the rocks with care. In some places, where the river ran over shallower stretches, I had to climb down into the water to pull the canoe forward.

It was a sunny day, and the glare off the fast-flowing water, coupled with the mesh bug net I wore, limited my vision. The clouds of blackflies were extreme, attacking any flesh they could get at. Before long I came to a large, roaring rapid that I had to very carefully line my canoe up with rope.

Lining, also called tracking, is a delicate business. It consists of guiding your canoe up rapids with a rope while standing on shore. I'd been doing it for thirteen years and fortunately had never had a mishap. But there's little margin for error; if the canoe catches the current wrong, it can take only seconds for it to tip, fill with water, and get swept away. Truly, there's something very unsettling about watching your canoe—loaded with all your essentials, including emergency means of communication—out in the swirling, turbulent waters tethered to yourself with just a thin rope. As such, I only use this method when I have little choice, which on the Coppermine looked like it was going to be most of the time.

Hours passed without much progress. The current remained riproaring, with dangerous eddies, whirlpools, and rapids nearly everywhere I looked. The steeply sloped shoreline, filled with rocks perfect for twisting an ankle on, further complicated things. Whenever conditions were slightly less daunting I tried to hike as fast as I could, as I was ever conscious that time was ticking on my journey, and that at the rate I was going I'd still be stuck on the Coppermine when the snows of September came.

After about five kilometres of difficult wading and lining, the river began to rapidly narrow, forcing all that roaring water into a channel less than two hundred metres wide. This increased the current's velocity as a result. Now the river was racing past at a terrifying speed.

I soon came to large boulders on shore, which ran straight down into the river, forming small cliffs. Given the boulders, I couldn't continue hiking while pulling the canoe in the water beside me. Nor could I avoid the boulders by wading; the river was too deep for that.

I'd have to climb over the boulders, while letting out rope to guide the canoe in the water around them.

I took a moment to visualize things. I had to be sure. There was definitely no margin for error here.

I coiled up the rope in my right hand, pulling the canoe in a back eddy close to shore, where it could rest for a moment out of the main current. Ahead were the giant boulders, first I'd have to climb them, then I'd carefully tug the canoe out into the river, before pulling in the rope to advance the canoe up the current. Then I'd skip to the next boulder, keeping ahead of the boat, and repeat the manoeuvre. It was important to move fast so that I'd stay ahead of the canoe to control it; if I let it get too far from shore, or if I wasn't precise with the rope, it could catch the current, pull sideways, and overturn—leaving me stranded.

My palms were sweating as I executed my moves: scampering ahead as agilely as I could in ungainly waders, climbing from boulder to boulder, reeling the canoe up almost parallel to me, darting ahead again. To ease the tension I talked a little to the canoe as I went, reassuring it, telling it that I'd reel it back in safely.

So far, so good. Then high red cliffs loomed up ahead, running straight down into the river and blocking the way forward. I pulled the canoe into a low spot on shore before the cliffs, securing it there. I'd have to go ahead on foot to scout out how to get around these cliffs.

It was dicey work, edging up the cliffs, climbing carefully over steep rocks. One slip and I could fall into the river below or bash my head on a rock. I was thankful for all the indoor rock climbing I'd done; the training helped me move with more confidence. After scouting things out, it seemed it was possible to line around the cliff if I was careful.

I returned to the canoe, towing it into a calm spot just below the start of the cliff. It could rest there while I climbed as far ahead as I could, leaving just a bit of slack rope. Once up on the cliff, I stood near the edge and looked back at my little canoe bobbing in the turbulent river below as waves rippled out to the rocky shoreline from the rapids in the middle.

All right, I said to myself, here it goes. I tugged gently on the rope, nudging the canoe's bow away from the calm water and into the main current. The current caught it, but I moved rapidly to reel it in, pulling fast to safely control the canoe and bring it alongside the cliff. When I'd coiled in almost all the slack rope, I darted ahead along the cliff, keeping the rope tense to hold the canoe steady in the current.

Next I climbed down to a steep, cobble-strewn bank where I could reel in the canoe the rest of the way along the edge of the rock wall. A few more pulls brought the canoe safely up alongside me. I breathed a sigh of relief to have the canoe in my hands again.

This feeling proved short-lived. Just a short distance ahead I came to more cliffs, only these were much larger, again rising straight out of the water. They were far too big for me to climb—my rope wasn't nearly long enough. And even if I had more rope, it would be too risky to chance tracking a canoe from such a height.

I looked around trying figure to out what to do. Clearly, I couldn't go over the cliffs, nor could I pole or paddle ahead: the fast-flowing river was too powerful. I thought of portaging, but even that seemed doubtful, as the rocky cliff promised to be difficult to get around. And even if I did succeed in getting around this cliff, what if there were more ahead? I couldn't see beyond these cliffs, but from what I'd so far encountered, this side of the river seemed like it was going to have a lot more cliffs, and the contour lines on my maps weren't encouraging.

I looked across the surging water to the far bank. That side of the river had steep slopes filled with rocks of the sort I'd been hiking along before coming to the big boulders and cliffs on this side. But there weren't any cliffs that I could see on that side. If I could get across to it, I might have more luck there.

I decided to try crossing the river. It wouldn't be easy; the current's velocity here was tremendous, ripping by at great speed. Downriver was a big rapid, which I'd lined up along the shore, and I didn't want to be swept down into it. I could probably run it if I had to, but that'd mean getting spit out far downriver, causing me to lose precious, hard-worn progress. Covering just five kilometres had taken me nearly three hours.

To ferry across the river against the current to the far side would require some careful manoeuvring and hard paddling. I coiled up the rope, stashed it in the bow, then fetched my straight shaft paddle, which I needed for the greater control it would allow me in the current. To get across, I'd essentially have to paddle upriver, which would put me in a sort of treadmill on the current, but in the process that would allow me to shift the canoe across sideways without yielding distance.

I braced the canoe along shore, took a last glance at the river above and below, then hopped in and shoved off. On my knees I paddled hard upriver; fortunately the current wasn't as strong near the shore and I shot ahead a bit before catching the main force of the water. This pushed me back a little, but hard strokes held me steady in the current. I began to edge across, paddling as if trying to go upriver but angling my canoe slightly to ferry or shuffle it across. The whole operation went quite fast, and I landed on the opposite rocky bank more or less where I'd intended.

This side of the river was cliff-free, but still a challenge to make headway on. The current remained fierce, and the jumble of small rocks everywhere on the sloping banks made walking tricky, as I could lose my footing just about anywhere. Slow and steady, I told myself and kept going.

Hours of hard effort later I came to a place where the river widened, forking around a couple of low gravel islands before curving sharply out of view. The near side of the islands was easily navigated; the water was shallow and the current less strong, allowing me to wade.

Beyond these islands, I encountered a spectacular sight: a towering, steep-walled canyon through which the river roared. Securing my canoe on shore, I went ahead on foot to scout it out. There was a small beach just below the stupendous cliffs that marked the canyon's entrance, or rather, the end of it, as it only seemed like the entrance to me since I was travelling upriver. The canyon walls towered some sixty metres high. Along the cliff edge grew spruces and willows while inside the narrow walls swirled massive rapids and dangerous whirlpools. From a theoretical point of view, the canyon was beautiful. From a practical point of view, it was a nightmare. How was I to get up it?

It seemed unlikely that I'd be able to continue through the canyon, but anything that might reduce portaging was worth investigating. I began by climbing up the rocks near the canyon's start, picking my way carefully up to a rugged peak. These rocks weren't part of the main canyon but rather formed a sort of spur, or peninsula, that jutted out into the river. Here the river narrowed to about fifty metres, with furious whitewater roaring in the main channel, but on the inside of the rocky spur I'd climbed there was a little tranquil cove.

However, from atop the rocks, I could see that the canyon walls rose much higher farther up, the whole force of the river squeezing through it and forming violent rapids. I climbed down to the cove and then moved up the shoreline, deeper into the shadows of the canyon, until I came to vertical walls that prevented me from advancing any farther along the water.

Between these vertical cliffs was a narrow slope, a sort of rock and gravel slide with some willow bushes where I could climb up. Huffing and puffing, I scrambled my way up the cliff here to the canyon's rim. When I reached the top and stood up to look around, my eyes met with an unexpected sight—a large stone monument about six feet high perched near the cliff edge. After months travelling alone in the wilderness, stumbling across human-made objects felt a bit startling, accustomed as I'd grown to uninterrupted rocks, trees, tundra, plants, or water.

I walked around the monument and saw on its face a finely cut stone inscription above a concrete base. It read:

DAVID

AND

CAROL JONES

WHO LOVED THE NORTH

AND ITS PEOPLE

WERE DROWNED IN THESE RAPIDS

ON AUGUST 14TH 1972

THEY RESPECTED

HONESTY AND TRUTH

This inscription discouraged me a little. I took a few steps away from it over to the cliff edge and looked down two hundred feet at the swirling, thundering water below. That didn't seem very encouraging either, so I turned back from the edge.

Beside the monument was a faint trail. This must be, I realized, from parties of canoeists coming downriver when they portage around the canyon. The Coppermine, due to its wild rapids, attracts parties of whitewater paddling enthusiasts willing to pay the hefty fees for an air charter by floatplane to get dropped off on the river. Such canoeists can paddle down with the current, usually taking two or three weeks, then fly out again at the river's mouth. Since I was here at just about the right time, midsummer, this part of my route offered me my best chance of crossing paths with fellow canoe campers, something I hadn't seen any of since my journey began thousands of kilometres away in the Yukon.

I followed the trail in the direction I'd come, until it petered out and I picked my own way down a rocky hill and over some willows to where I'd left my canoe and gear. "Well," I said to the canoe, "there's no way we can make it up that canyon; we'll have to portage. But don't worry, there's a bit of a trail we can follow."

I strapped on my backpack, took some water, then set off. The portage, it turned out, was about half a kilometre long, snaking up over the cliffs and along the canyon edge. The trail was distinct along the top part but toward the end faded away on the rocks and I found my own way back down a steep, rock-strewn slope to the river's edge. When I reached the monument, I paused for a moment's silence.

Four more trips back and forth were required to transport my two barrels and the canoe, which I carried over my head, as I didn't wish to drag it on the rocks and hard ground. However, when I reached the top, near the canyon's rim, I set the canoe down. Instead of carrying it here, I dragged it through the willows, knowing that if I tripped on a rock or if the wind were to gust and knock me off balance, I'd topple two hundred feet into the river below. The sunny weather seemed to make the blackflies particularly vicious while my hands were full with the canoe.

Once I'd transported everything across I carefully repacked the canoe alongside the river and then edged it out into the water, which was still swirling along with tremendous velocity. Glancing at the narrow entrance to the canyon, I thought how bad it would be for a canoeist coming downriver who failed to stop and was sucked into the canyon, not having realized the danger. I wondered if that's what had happened to David and Carol Jones.

With the canoe ready, I turned away from the canyon and began slogging ahead on foot once more, pulling the canoe beside me. The portage had meant a lengthy delay, and my heart sank at how little progress I'd so far made upriver. The banks remained steeply sloped and difficult to walk along without twisting an ankle, due to the piles of rocks everywhere. I was feeling exhausted and a little discouraged, but I forced myself to keep going.

It was late in the day, and suitable campsites were few and far between. The river's steep banks, beyond which were high hills, meant a lack of level ground anywhere to sleep on. I pushed on, inching forward step by step, hauling the canoe against the powerful current. In vain I looked for any flat ground to sleep on. At last, wearied and hungry, I settled for a tiny, partially sloped bit of gravel beneath high, steep banks near the water's edge. It wasn't by any means a nice place to sleep, but I was too exhausted to much mind. Inside my tent I studied my maps. With despair, I calculated that despite having put in eleven hours of my hardest efforts, I'd made it just twelve kilometres upriver. Such pitiful progress was demoralizing. At no point on my journey had I felt so low. Even my worst days on the Mackenzie I'd still done twenty kilometres, and that was over a shorter day. At this rate, I knew, I'd never complete my journey.

Difficult as it was, I had to dispel these doubts, and try to encourage myself for what tomorrow would hold—another brutally hard day of upriver travel in which somehow I'd have to do better. Lying in my tent on the cold, hard ground, I tried to prepare myself for the morning. I consoled myself with the thought that, on balance, I was probably doing what I loved most.

× 13 ×

GIFTS FROM ABOVE

The next morning I was underway early, hauling my canoe upriver while hopping along the rocks beside it. Then came more rapids, which required a combination of strenuous effort and careful precision to overcome, as I knew all too well what might happen if I slipped in the current and fell over, or lodged my foot in an unseen crevice beneath the water, twisting an ankle.

As I pushed on, sections of the river improved greatly, widening enough so that I could actually stand in the canoe and pole off the bottom near shore. To switch back to poling was a great relief. I made the most of it, poling as hard as I possibly could. Some of the smaller rapids, or swifts, I even managed to pole up, by sticking close to the high banks and choosing my spots just right.

At the edge of the rapids were often large grey boulders sticking up like the back of a hippopotamus, which created a calm spot directly behind by diverting water. As I approached these I'd spring off the bottom with my pole and, once behind them, hop out onto the boulder, pull the canoe around it, and then jump back in on the far side, poling ahead to the calmer water. In some of the smaller swifts, however, I found that with great effort I could fling myself out from behind the boulder with the pole into the main current and, poling hard, make it up through the swifts. (Once or twice, though, the current proved too strong when I tried, spinning the canoe around and forcing it downriver. I'd have to steer back into shore and try again, this time reverting to my safer hopping-out-on-the-boulder approach.)

In a few sections the river widened enough that I could actually paddle, as long as I kept close to shore and out of the reach of the main current. And in places where high sloped banks towered above me I could jab at them with my pole, propelling myself along; this was even faster than poling through the water, but it only worked in places with the right steep banks for it. Finally, in a precious few spots few and far between, but encouraging all the same, the surging current would create back eddies close to the high banks, where the water rushed back upstream. When I caught these currents the canoe would seem to fly along, cheering my spirits, though they lasted only a few seconds. Mostly, however, I had to haul the canoe as I waded through the rushing water.

When I halted after twelve hours travel to make camp, I found my progress had much improved: I'd managed to make it twenty-five kilometres. Still, I didn't want to get overconfident. My route entailed travelling some two hundred kilometres upriver on the Coppermine before I could cross into the lakes of the central Arctic, so there was still a long way to go.

My third day battling up the Coppermine I navigated more difficult rapids, but my dread of them faded as I rounded a sharp bend and came to a place where the river widened and the current slackened. A great rugged range of hills—or more accurately, small mountains—rose up on the eastern side of the river in successive waves, stretching beyond the horizon. Along their lower slopes grew black spruce, which survive along sheltered river valleys, though a short distance beyond them the trees give way to vast open plains of seemingly limitless extent.

I was happy to see this wide bit of river not only because it meant an easier current, but because it was the spot I'd selected, based on satellite imagery, for my next resupply. There are few places on the Coppermine River where a floatplane can safely land, given the rocks and rapids, but this wide part, with its more subdued current, was one of them. I paddled up the middle of it, checking the water levels and looking for any hidden shoals that could cause trouble for a plane.

Having pushed myself as hard as I could, I'd again exceeded my estimates, and it'd taken me only two weeks to arrive here from the end of Great Bear instead of the three I had to cautiously figure on.

It was with economy in mind, and the need to minimize the amount of heavy food rations that I was carrying during such arduous upriver travel and portaging, that I'd resolved for a resupply at this point. That wasn't all: to save money and cut down on the weight of my loads up the remainder of the Coppermine, I'd decided on a gamble. The pilot was going to give me only half my rations, keeping the other half with him on the plane. On his return to Yellowknife, he would land on a lake to leave the rest of the supplies for me inside a wooden crate. There was a chance, of course, that a wolverine or grizzly might find the crate and break it open for the rations, but that's why I'd asked for it to be put on a remote island far offshore. It was a risk, but knowing what I did of the Coppermine, and what I'd seen so far of it, the prospect of allowing me to travel lighter up the remainder of it, since I wouldn't have to haul all the extra supplies with me, was worth taking.

Once I'd found a suitable spot with deep, unobstructed water where the plane could land, I made camp. Since I'd be expecting visitors, I figured I ought to try something I hadn't done in weeks—what's known as "bathing." Bracing myself, I took a swim in the river's frigid waters. It felt chilling, but refreshing all the same (aside from the blackflies swarming my head).

Afterward I unpacked the satellite phone from its waterproof case and called the pilot in distant Yellowknife to confirm the resupply. When I got through to the pilot, over the staticky line, I also asked a favour. My waders had become hopelessly punctured from bumping against sharp rocks while wading upriver, and I asked if he could get me a new pair from the store—the cheapest ones would do, I said, as I was still on a budget. Luckily, the pilot indicated that conditions on the radar looked decent enough for him to attempt the flight early the next morning. It would be a long flight for a little single-engine bush plane to make—about a thousand kilometre round trip, over uninhabited forest and arctic tundra.

In the meantime, while arctic terns soared gracefully over the river, I sorted through my gear. The long portages and strenuous upriver travel had made me obsess over ways to travel lighter by eliminating anything I could. The canoe cart, which hadn't been effective and had been a pain to lug all this way, would definitely be a gift for the pilot. Also included on the to-go list were my trekking poles (which I hadn't used since the Dempster), the ripped hip waders (I'd be getting a new pair in my resupply barrel), as well as the chest waders (which I'd worn only once and figured I could do without), the broken water purifier (I hadn't gotten sick at all and no longer had any worry on that account), a harness with ropes that I'd also worn only once on the Mackenzie while walking on shore (it didn't weigh much, but I figured that the improvised harness I made out of ordinary rope was good enough), as well as small miscellaneous items such as carabiners and dead batteries. On the flip side, I'd have additional weight coming in from the new waders as well as several canisters of camp-stove fuel that I'd included in my next resupply barrel. Wood was becoming scarce, and especially on the tundra, during storms, it would be nice to be able to boil water beside my tent to warm up.

The morning dawned cold and rainy, delaying the flight in. Finally, by noon I heard the drone of an engine, and then out of the overcast sky a plane materialized, looking in my imagination like a machine from another world. The little floatplane sliced through the grey clouds, and flew in low over the wide stretch of river. Twice the pilot circled, scouting out the water below before attempting a landing. I'd verified from my canoe that there was no rocks, but one can't be too careful when landing planes on isolated northern rivers.

Finally the pilot executed a perfect landing, skimming along the water on the plane's pontoons. I'd never met this pilot before—I'd been communicating only with his boss beforehand down in Yellowknife. A young man of about my age emerged from the cockpit, jumping down on the plane's left pontoon and waving to me. I waved back (it seemed the appropriate thing to do). With him were two passengers—Francis and Pablo—who'd come along for the ride.

These were the first people I'd seen since my brief interaction with the two fishing guides on Great Bear—who in turn were the only humans I'd seen over the last forty-one days since my brief stop in Fort Good Hope.

The pilot, whose name was Michael, handed me the barrel I'd carefully packed before the journey. As before, I emptied it into my existing barrel then handed it back to him, only this time I left half of the supplies in it. He also handed me the new hip waders. Then we discussed the logistics of where he'd leave the food drop for me on an island. It was impossible to say precisely; bush-plane flying has its own set of rules, and he couldn't know in advance where it would be safe to land (water levels shift frequently, exposing rocks), but we'd agreed on an approximate location.

Francis, who'd seen me set off on the Dempster, said he'd never fully realized the vastness of the land until he saw it from high above in a tiny bush plane. Flying for hours, they'd passed no signs of any human-made object below—just thousands of lakes, rivers, ponds, and mountains appearing to go on forever in all directions.

I was anxious to get on my way, regretting the time I'd already lost that morning. And again I felt a little overwhelmed with socializing, especially compared to the relaxing simplicity of navigating canoes up whitewater rivers. When everything was settled, the plane's engines roared back to life. They waved goodbye and I was already off. The day was getting on, after all.

I listened to the floatplane as it faded away into silence—leaving me with just the sounds of water swirling from my paddle strokes as I headed upriver, enjoying the slacker current and the sight of the wild mountains framing the land.

That night I camped on an overgrown island on a small hill in the rain. Lying outstretched in my tent, a mattress of soft moss and lichens beneath me, I felt content and even serene, feeling like I'd overcome the worst of the Coppermine.

✳

For nearly a week the weather stayed cold and rainy. Meanwhile the river's character changed dramatically as I continued my upriver journey. It widened out to more than a kilometre across in marshy lowlands surrounded by mist-shrouded mountains. They were great, green crags with dark, rocky summits that, in the fog and rain, appeared gloomy and forlorn, much like the Scottish Highlands. Or, at least, much like what I imagine the Scottish Highlands look like.

The river's current had slackened such that I was actually paddling my canoe upriver most of the time, alternating with poling in stretches where it narrowed. My days were long, but with the wind occasionally in my favour, I even managed to sail a little. I was now averaging about forty kilometres a day. And it was always with a feeling of contentment that at the end of a long, tiring day, wet from the rain, I'd climb into my tent to get warm. The weather didn't bother me too much— I was able to scrounge up enough wood to keep making fires, and there was something about the rain and wild, romantic scenery that helped lull me into daydreams as I paddled. This whole section of the river had a lazy, dreamlike air to it, with its fog and mountains, and its marshy shorelines of sedges and willows. It was a welcome change from the fury and roar of where I'd first entered the Coppermine.

The more subdued river brought a return to wildlife. Robins, bald eagles, terns, swans, loons, sandpipers, ducks of various kinds, including ones I hadn't seen before, and even a beautiful little red-coloured pine grosbeak. Muskrats were also about. Caribou and white wolves wandered the riverbanks. I startled a big bull moose that was busy munching on some weeds in the water; in response, he startled me too. In a wider, more tranquil stretch that I could paddle, the sight of a white wolf along the banks stirred my sense of awe. The wolf was more timid than others I'd seen, but still very curious as it watched me paddling along.

The only wildlife that wasn't very friendly were the nesting arctic terns. These elegant birds make their annual migrations from the Arctic all the way to Antarctica—the longest migration of any animal on the planet. I'd always admired the tern's beauty and amazing flying abilities, though I was rather less enthusiastic about their insistence on trying to dive-bomb me with their razor-sharp beaks as I navigated upriver. Paddling downriver, I could travel fast enough to escape from their aerial assaults, but going upriver is another story, and I found myself repeatedly experiencing the sensation that Alfred Hitchcock's film *The Birds* had been adapted to 3-D. To protect myself, I had to switch from my broad-brimmed hat into my helmet, which I'd actually only packed for running whitewater rapids later in the trip, not bird attacks.

On July 24, while making camp in a marshy area, I found my first ripe blueberries. They were a bit tart but I regarded such a find as a great treasure. And I eagerly looked forward to more becoming ripe soon, as well as all the other berries that I'd been eyeing for weeks with anticipation.

One decidedly unexpected thing was what I uncovered one night in the crooked branch of an ancient, twisted black spruce near my camp: the white-feathered claw of a small animal. Evidently, it had been severed from its body—for there was no sign of the rest of the creature. Turning it over in my hand, I realized it was the talon of a snowy owl. What could have killed it? Owls are sometimes hunted and killed by foxes, as well as by lynx, which pounce on them unseen. It seemed likely that this particular owl had fallen victim to one or the other, its talon and some feathers were all that was left of it. For a while I thought of keeping it as a good luck charm, like a white rabbit's foot, but then it occurred to me that an owl that had been killed in such a manner probably wasn't very lucky. So I tossed it away.

*

After five days of relatively pleasant travel, conditions became more difficult. I awoke the morning of July 26 to find frost blanketing the ground. And just as the weather had turned cold the Coppermine turned rough again, with swift currents and huge rapids.

That frosty morning I was frequently reduced to painstaking wading, harder than anything I'd yet experienced. My feet took a beating among the sharp, jagged rocks along the river bottom in those spots where I had to wade almost up to my waist against the powerful current. In most places, though, the shoreline was a chaotic jumble of rocks and boulders, such that I could usually, holding on to the canoe's bow for balance, half wade and half jump along these rocks to make progress.

The chilly morning turned into a cold day. At one point I stumbled in the current, allowing waves to come over my hip waders, flooding them. I inhaled at the shock of the cold. Then I pulled my canoe into shore, climbed up onto a flat rock, and emptied the waders. My pants and socks were drenched, but there wasn't time to dry things out. I just wrung out the socks, put them back on, and kept going. Discouraging as having your waders flood with frigid waters can be, I always found that there was some little thing to cheer me up: the sight of robins hopping along the banks, or a lone wolf wandering the shoreline, or an eagle soaring overhead. Sometimes it's the little things that make all the difference.

Since wading was proving increasingly punishing on my shins and feet, I tried to line, or track, the canoe with rope wherever possible. In a few stretches the bank, with its low boulders, wasn't too difficult; I could jump from one to another with relative ease. My progress was pretty good. Then, up ahead, I saw a couple of big rocks extending from shore out into the turbulent water. These kind of rocks always made me a little nervous, as they are often the hardest and most dangerous to navigate around.

Still, it looked possible. So with the canoe in the water and me on shore holding it with rope, I went beyond where the two rocks protruded from the river. Then I began to pull the canoe upstream toward me. I had to extend my right arm out from shore, tugging the canoe so it would nudge around the boulders. But the canoe's bow edged just an inch too far, catching the current on its side.

Fear shot through me. The force of the water began to tip the canoe as it pivoted sideways in the current. Water began lapping in; I had only seconds to act. If the canoe flooded it would be swept downriver through the rapids and lost. I had to do the opposite of what instinct suggested—instead of holding on tightly my only option was to ease up, letting the rope go slack in my hand.

Doing so allowed the half-flooded canoe to right itself as it spun back to a straight position out of the rapid. Then I dashed downstream, pulling it in toward a tranquil pool where I could safely haul it ashore.

My heart was pounding—had I reacted a second slower my canoe would have been lost, the current's force carrying it and all my gear far away downstream. I stepped into the water beside the canoe and began to unload it on the bank. I had to empty the water out of it before I could continue. I wasn't going to risk a second attempt lining with rope around the rocks—instead I portaged.

After such a close shave, my reaction is generally to get back in the saddle as fast as possible. Dwelling on what might have been, I don't think is helpful, but pushing on helps restore confidence. So, once I'd portaged around the boulders, I was back to tracking the canoe with a rope along the shore and in some places wading, as the swift current continued for miles.

Then I came across something else on shore—a destroyed canoe. It was an old aluminum boat, apparently crushed and mangled by the rapids when it had pinned on a rock, the force of the current folding it in half. Evidently, whomever had been paddling it never made it downriver—at least not in that canoe. It looked several decades old at least and was a reminder of what a single mistake in powerful rapids can do.

That afternoon, after hauling, wading, and lining up a succession of large-scale rapids alternating with calmer sections, I came to the wildest rapid I'd ever seen—a tremendous, roaring affair over a kilometre wide. Normally rapids occur in narrow sections of river, so such a wide, tumbling rapid that went on for as far as I could make out upriver was an impressive sight (and also a little demoralizing). Beneath this massive cataract of rushing water and boulders was a wide calm stretch, allowing me to paddle in toward the start of it. I canoed toward its roaring fury, trying to determine if one side might be better than the other to struggle up it. Neither looked promising, but I opted for the left.

It took all my reserves of willpower and strength to get the canoe up this great rapid—wading, hauling, dashing between rocks, doing everything I could to overcome the current. Then, amid the endless sharp rocks, my new waders, fresh in from the resupply, punctured. The frigid waters of the Coppermine flooded right into my boot. There was nothing to be done about it; I had to push on for another two hours before I could call it a night and make camp.

Once I had the tent up and a fire going, my priority was to repair the wader. From the bark of a nearby black spruce I gathered some sap, or spruce gum. The sticky resin I heated on a rock in my fire until it melted to a honey-like consistency. Then with a stick as a ladle, I applied it to the small puncture in my wader. Overtop the pitch I laid down some tape (the tape on its own won't stay, even when you heat it beforehand). This done, the waders were as good as new. I just had to hope they didn't puncture again, as I knew the spruces were thinning out and that soon there'd be none at all.

✳

My belief that I'd overcome the worst of the Coppermine's rapids proved a bit optimistic. It took another two and a half days of gruelling travel to battle my way through endless swifts and many more large

rapids—some of them as much as Class IV or V on the paddlers' difficulty scale. In the midst of one fast section of river with high sandy
banks, I was standing in the canoe poling along when I looked up and
suddenly saw other canoes coming downriver. At last, in two months of
travelling, these were the first other campers I'd encountered.

To my eyes, there seemed to be unbelievable multitude of them—
fully eight people. It was the biggest crowd I'd seen in months. They
were men in their early or mid-twenties, divided between four canoes,
each of them wearing a helmet. The current was strong, with swirls
and eddies everywhere, and it was carrying them along at a fast pace.

The sight of me, long-haired, heavily bearded, standing upright in
a canoe while poling off the river bottom, seemed to surprise them.
They stared at me in apparent bewilderment as they drifted rapidly by
on the current. At last, when they were almost past, one of the eight
in the rear canoe mustered a shouted hello. I responded with "hi," as
I jabbed my long pole through the rushing waters, driving the canoe
forward. As quickly as they'd come, the river carried them out of
sight, and I saw no more of them. I supposed it would only be logical
for them to have assumed I was some sort of crazy hermit of the kind
that's best prudently avoided, as doubtless they thought, as everyone
I'd spoken to about the matter beforehand had, that travelling upriver
on the Coppermine was an act of insanity. Or perhaps they figured I
was only poling upriver a short distance for some odd reason—and
would soon set aside the pole and follow after them.

In any case, I kept going upriver. Fortunately, after passing another
roaring rapid, I came to a short stretch that was a bit less fierce, and
here I met a friendlier group of river travellers: a family of seven
Canada geese. Five goslings followed their watchful parents, paddling
along near the grassy shoreline, the little ones seeming to regard me
with curiosity. They were a much more communicative bunch, honk-
ing at me cheerfully. The geese come here to raise their young; then
by late August, once the goslings are big enough to fly, they make their
own great journey south to warmer climes.

The following day I wearily continued upriver. After some eleven hours of exhausting travel I stopped and made camp at a narrow section where a massive rapid thundered ferociously. I camped by the rapid, though the blackflies were atrocious, on account of the fact I was just too tired to press on farther. I'd made it twenty-eight kilometres upriver during the day, and there was now a decent crop of ripened blueberries for me to feast on.

With July nearing its close, the bugs were worse than ever. Each night, inside my tent I performed a little ritual, it consisted of killing every last blackfly that had made its way in. No matter what I tried— wiping them off, standing near the suffocating smoke of my fire— about a hundred of them managed to get inside during the seconds it took me to unzip and rezip the tent door. Not only were there always intense swarms of them outside my tent, but many would also be hidden in my clothing, hair, beard, and anywhere else they could get at. There's nothing worse than blackflies buzzing around inside your tent at the end of a long, hard day. Fortunately, they tend to fly up to the top, where they can be easily squished against the ceiling. My once beautiful tent had become utterly streaked with bloodstains from squishing bugs.

Lying inside my tent, the mid-summer arctic sun still shining, I cast a glance out the screen door at the river and was surprised to see bright objects moving on it. I sat up and looked closer: it was a second party of canoeists, some half-dozen of them! My goodness, I thought, this river is getting altogether too crowded, I need to get off it soon.

The canoeists landed above the rapid on the side of the river I was camped on, evidently intending to scout out the whitewater. They hadn't seen my camp yet, so I lay quiet inside my tent, making notes in my journal. The proper thing to do was probably to have gone and introduced myself, but having just worked so hard to make my tent blackfly free, I really didn't wish to unzip the door and allow another invasion. At any rate, one of them, having spotted my camp, headed in my direction.

"Hello," she announced as she approached. "Anyone home?"

I thought for a moment, then said, "Hi." I added, from still inside my tent, "Sorry, since the bugs are bad I'm just going to stay inside if you don't mind. But you can come over to the door, if you like."

"Oh," she replied. "Yeah, they're awful." She swatted at the horde of blackflies and mosquitoes swarming round her head as she approached.

"How many of you are in there?" she asked.

"Only one," I said.

"Where's the rest of your party?"

"I'm it."

"*Just you?*"

"My canoe, too."

"You're going solo *down this river?*" She seemed surprised at the notion, as if travelling alone in the arctic wilderness was strange or something.

"No," I said.

"Oh," she replied, nodding.

"I'm going solo *up this river.*"

"*What?*" She crouched down to look through my screen door. She appeared to be about the same age as me.

"I'm Adam, by the way," I said from inside. "Sorry, I don't mean to be unsocial, it's just that I've only just got my tent bug-free and don't want more to come in."

"Oh, no worries, I understand. I'm Erica." She waved a hand. "I thought for a second there you said you're going upriver," she laughed.

"I am."

Her eyebrows raised and her mouth opened, staring at me as if I'd said something crazy. After a moment she seemed to realize I was serious. "But how's that even possible?"

I briefly summarized my methods.

"Wow," she said slowly, "that's kind of impressive, but also kind of insane." Then, evidently deeming me either an object of great curiosity, or else not dangerous to the group, she called to the rest of her party to come over and join her. There were five of them—an all-women's group from a canoe camp in northern Minnesota. They'd been dropped by a floatplane some weeks earlier on a lake, and now they were descending the Coppermine to complete their trip. Erica was the camp leader; the others were younger.

I told them about some nicer sites I'd seen farther downriver that they might make it to within an hour or so that were good for camping, with some nice beaches, and a bit about what rapids they could expect. They seemed shocked when I spoke of the Boundary Waters in Minnesota, apparently having assumed I was some lone wanderer who must know nothing of the outside world, let alone anything of their home state. It seemed to reassure them that I wasn't as crazy as I first appeared.

They wished me well, and I did the same for them, and fifteen minutes after our conversation had begun, they left and continued downriver. Such extensive socializing had quite worn me out, and I half-hoped that would be the last of it for at least another month or so.

× 14 ×

LAKES BEYOND COUNT

nother hard day of battling rapids—some whose edges I could wade along, others so large I had no choice but to portage around them—brought me to the Coppermine River's outflow from a beautiful lake. I'd come to Rocknest Lake, a maze-like lake with a huge tabletop mountain overlooking it. To escape from the river's fury and be back on calm water was a great relief. I could paddle easily once more. I happily pulled off my waders, which had flooded again as I struggled in the current, and went barefoot in the canoe, my socks drying on the reefed sail.

It was somewhere on this lake that the pilot Michael had promised to drop off the remainder of my resupply. I wasn't sure of the precise location, but it was supposed to be on a remote island, easy to spot. Fortunately, the bush pilot was as good as his word: I found the stash without any trouble. No wolverines, bears, or Minnesotans had touched it.

I decided to make camp on the little island my resupply crate was left on. It commanded a charming view of the wonderful surroundings— sparklingly clear waters and big green hills, with granite cliffs and boulders scattered about the land as if by giants long ago. Even nicer was the island itself—catching the sun as it did, the multitude of berries growing on it had ripened nicely. I could fill myself with arctic blueberries, crowberries, bearberries, and lingonberries, the last of which were still a bit tart but perfectly acceptable to me. There was also dwarf Labrador tea for a warming drink, caribou lichens (a decent emergency food if you boil it first), and sphagnum moss, which is useful for treating cuts as it has naturally occurring iodine in it. With the berries finally ripening, it felt like having a supermarket right next to my camp.

The character of my journey had now shifted again: I'd left the furious Coppermine River proper behind, and was entering into a long series of interconnected lakes. Technically I was still within the Coppermine River system, but now it was made up of almost all lakes connected by just a few narrow channels. Some of these channels did have powerful rapids, which I'd still have no choice but to battle up, but other than that, I was now turning the corner on my route's exhausting upriver travel.

Most of these lakes lie beyond the trees, surrounded by nothing but apparently limitless tundra that in summer resembles vast fields, some of them boulder-strewn. To many people it's a desolate, eerie-looking landscape, at least compared to the more hospitable forests to the south. On maps these wild lakes appear as a virtually indecipherable maze of byzantine complexity, featuring hundreds of bays, channels, islands, and peninsulas that can easily confuse travellers and make getting lost extremely easy. It was on these large lakes that I was now paddling that almost two centuries earlier John Franklin led twenty men to horror and death on his first doomed quest for the Northwest Passage.

Unlike his later, more famous naval expeditions in the High Arctic, on this first Arctic foray in 1821 Franklin had opted to travel by birch-bark canoe with four British naval compatriots, a party of Canadian voyageurs, and two Inuit interpreters. Their expedition didn't turn out all that well. Although they managed to make it down the Coppermine River to the Arctic Ocean, and even travelled along its dangerous coast in canoes, on their return trek things unravelled. Their food supplies ran out, the canoes were destroyed, one of their interpreters became lost, and finally, ragged and starving, they grew increasingly paranoid about one another. It seems some of them began to look at the others as meat. As they huddled around their tiny willow-twig fires, whispers of cannibalism could be heard.

One by one the party dwindled, men falling behind and perishing alone on the tundra. The survivors eventually reached the very lakes I was paddling, but without canoes they were unable to cross them, at least until winter froze them solid. For days they wandered, desperate and destitute, along the barren shorelines. Of the twenty-one men who set off, only ten returned.

It was also this same landscape that a half-century before Franklin, back in 1770, the young sailor Samuel Hearne and his friend Matonabbee had made an epic journey on foot across thousands of kilometres. They'd set out from Churchill and wandered all the way to the mouth of the Coppermine River and back again. Matonabbee and Hearne, upon first sight of the river, with the sort of wisdom one gets from living in these places, immediately judged it far too treacherous to be navigable. Their journey, however, was marred by the tragedy of Bloody Falls, when Matonabbee's Dene followers ambushed and massacred an unsuspecting Inuit camp. The attack was part of a larger, centuries-old conflict between the Inuit, who lived near the seacoast, and the Dene, who lived to the south within the spruce forests. Between them lay the vast no man's land of the "barrens," where battles tended to happen if wandering hunting parties ever crossed paths.

✳

A long day of steady paddling took me through Rocknest Lake's snaking bays and channels. By midday I'd reached a narrow section with rapids where I had to put away my paddle and pole hard off the bottom. This brought me into a new body of water, Red Rock Lake, which I found surrounded by rocky hills and, most prominently, a gigantic towering cliff over a hundred metres high composed of red rock. I figured that this was probably the origin of the lake's name.

I'd been paddling steady, dealing with wind that was alternatingly hitting my canoe broadside, head on, or from behind, the direction changing based on the zigzagging pattern of the lakes' maze-like shape. A light rain dissipated as I completed a necessary crossing from the lake's northern to southern shore over a large stretch of open water with big waves. Then I spotted something farther up the opposite shore: a collection of little white and brown rectangular specks that clearly indicated something human-made. It was, I guessed, mostly likely some fly-in fishing lodge, although I'd never heard of one existing on this lake, which seemed odd.

A small open motorboat materialized near the white and brown specks, a lone figure on board. The boat moved back and forth along the distant shoreline, evidently the person on board was trolling, likely for lake trout.

My little speck of red moving alone up the far shore eventually attracted the notice of the figure in the motorboat that had issued out from the mysterious encampment, and the boat now powered across the lake in my direction. When the boat neared I saw on board a young man, seemingly not much older than twenty. He switched off his engine and coasted in toward me.

"Hello," he called, waving.

"Hi," I said.

"Where did you come from?" he asked.

"The Yukon."

"What?" He looked puzzled.

"I'm paddling across the Arctic."

"All by yourself?!"

"Yeah."

"My God." He stared at me.

"That's a nice-looking fishing lodge," I said, pointing across the lake. I could see it a bit better now, and compared to any other fly-in fishing camp I'd ever seen, this one looked rather more elaborately constructed. "I didn't know there was one on this lake."

"Oh, that's not a lodge," he said.

Catching my intrigued look, he launched into an explanation. He said the compound belonged to a mega-wealthy airline tycoon who'd had it built as an ultra-private fishing escape for his family and friends, with a whole lake to themselves, miles from anywhere. The owner, who was 95 years old, was at the compound this very moment, having recently arrived on one of his floatplanes.

"He'd love to meet you and have you stay," said the young man enthusiastically. "Do you want a hot shower? You can stay the night. We can feed you too. We've got plenty of spare beds. It'll be great!"

"Hmm . . ." I hovered on the waves. "Do you have any orange juice?"

"We've got loads of orange juice!" he exclaimed.

"Well," I said, mulling it over, "I'm afraid I have to be on my way. I'm on a tight schedule. Maybe next time I'm here. Thanks, though!"

The young man looked a little downcast, but seeing my resolve to keep paddling, he wished me well with real warmth.

The truth was, I'd become so accustomed to my routine of long days that I didn't wish to deviate from it. More importantly, the winds were at the moment pretty good so I couldn't afford not to make the most of them, fearing as I did what the storms of August would bring.

I paddled hard, wanting to put as much distance as I could between me and the compound of more than a half-dozen small buildings. To me it had been a bizarre sight—jarringly incongruous after passing thousands of kilometres of natural landscapes. To suddenly see buildings perched on rocks in the middle of nowhere felt like stumbling upon the set of a science fiction movie. I thought how it must have cost a fortune to have built such a place—all the construction materials, furniture, solar panels, motorboats, and other stuff would've had to have been flown in by helicopter or bush plane from far away. But, I guess that's the kind of thing that's easier if you own an airline.

I pushed on another four hours, paddling up the lake's snaking bays past islands and barren hills. Appealing camping sites were scarce, as the lake's shoreline was high banks cloaked with willow thickets. Hauling all my gear up such steep banks wasn't a pleasing prospect, especially since sleeping inland like that would mean enduring appalling clouds of bugs. Whenever possible on lakes I try to camp near an open shoreline, where a breeze can help keep the bugs to an acceptable minimum. But after passing kilometres of shoreline with just high, willow-thicketed banks, I realized I had no choice. I pulled in to a steep, fifteen-foot-high bank and wearily began hauling my three loads, and then the canoe, up to the top to make camp.

The bugs were as bad as I'd feared: masses of them assaulted me, making eating my freeze-dried mac and cheese joyless. Just pulling up my mesh bug net a little to take a bite caused suffocating clouds to swarm my face. How many I swallowed with the food I'll never know. I just tried to eat as fast as possible so I could escape into my tent.

✳

Glancing at a satellite image of northern Canada you'll see that there are three million lakes, creeks, ponds, and rivers. (In your spare time, I suggest counting them.) Most of which are of recent vintage, having been gouged out during the retreat of the massive, mile-high Laurentide Ice Sheet ten thousand years ago or less, depending on their location.

With that many different waterways, the amount of resulting route combinations are *infinite*. You could live a thousand lifetimes and not even begin to scratch the surface of paddling all the possibilities. To devise my particular route, I examined satellite imagery: looking at what at first glance appeared an incomprehensible labyrinth. Then I measured distances between points to create the most efficient route I could, while taking into account whatever else seemed important. In those first few weeks of planning, though, every time I'd look at the satellite images or topographic maps laid out on my desk and posted on my walls it was difficult to make heads or tails of them all. With such a puzzle of lakes and ponds, it's hard not to confuse one bay or inlet for any of the thousands of others.

But once I'd committed it to memory, I could pick out at a glance on any large topo map or satellite image my exact route, and what day I ought to be at any nameless bay or point. As a kid I'd always enjoyed puzzles and memory games, but it didn't seem like it would ever amount to much career-wise. Then I realized I could put it to good use doing these sorts of journeys. A GPS built into your brain is a huge asset; one that's easy to overlook how advantageous it is when travelling, as checking a map or GPS screen is time-consuming (it's not like checking a phone at home with the swipe of a finger, in the wilderness, the GPS has to first power up, load the satellite imagery, and then, on a small screen, fiddle with it for a bit to see what you need.) These memory and spatial skills—the ability to transfer a two-dimensional map image into a real three-dimensional lake—were exactly what I needed now to navigate these lakes quickly without fiddling every ten minutes with maps or a GPS.

My route from the end of the Coppermine River proper would next take me through a complex maze of different lakes across the central Arctic—more than three dozen in all. The distance I'd have to cover through these often dangerously windy lakes, plus a bit of river travel and portaging for good measure, totalled roughly 883 kilometres, or more than double the distance I'd crossed on Great Bear Lake. Of course the actual distance, when factoring in the multiple trips required to complete the many portages between lakes and around dangerous rapids, was considerably greater.

On the last day of July I paddled into a new lake, Point Lake, which is over a hundred kilometres long and punctuated by numerous, bays, islands, and peninsulas. The lake seemed almost unnaturally quiet. There was barely a hint of wind; the skies had turned blue without a speck of cloud; there weren't even sounds of birds or any sign of wildlife. I'd paddled far offshore, so even the bugs had vanished. There was nothing to be seen in all directions except rocks, cliffs, hills, and tundra.

It was a strange, empty, quiet place—so calm that it felt as if I were paddling in a landscape painting.

The dead calm allowed me to make excellent progress, in part because I was able to cut across the largest open-water crossings I'd ever attempted solo in the Arctic—in some places exceeding three kilometres between points. To be that far from land, surrounded by nothing but blue water on all sides, alone in my heavily packed canoe, could make me slightly uneasy, but I felt the calm conditions more than justified it. The result was excellent progress, allowing me to make it over sixty-five kilometres that day.

To add to such agreeable weather, when I made camp I found my first ripe lingonberries of the season, though the bugs were extreme onshore. Interestingly, I calculated after repeated experiments that it took an average of five minutes after landing for the full onslaught of millions of bugs to materialize. This meant that I had a few minutes of relative peace to gather berries before the bugs passed along the word that human flesh was to be had for the taking. The only wood available now were little bits of dwarf birch, typically no larger than finger-sized, and these I burned just for the smoke to help drive off the insect swarms. For boiling water I now relied on my little camp stove.

The eerie, perfect calm lasted for several days as July passed into August. I continued paddling eleven or twelve hours each day, tripling the daily distances I'd managed when travelling upstream on rivers. My route took me past great towering cliffs, jumbles of immense boulders as old as time, and vast grassy fields without a tree in sight. In other places, some of the great grey cliffs were so cracked with fault lines as to give the suggestion of ancient masonry, as if they were crumbling castle ruins. On one of these vertical cliffs overlooking the lake, raspy little cries rang out as I paddled below. Looking up, I spotted in a crack on the cliff face two baby peregrine falcons. They were hungry, calling for their parents to serve lunch.

I was hungry, too, and that night when I landed on a rocky, hilly shore to make camp I could barely contain my excitement at what I found—the first ripe batch of cloudberries! These are my favourite of all berries: they're big, juicy orange berries, a bit sour but wonderfully delicious (perhaps especially if you've taken the trouble to spend several months eating only energy bars). I ate multitudes of the cloudberries, finding a veritable jackpot of them on a hillside. Cloudberries occur all across northern Canada, but in Newfoundland they're known as "bake-apples" on account of tasting something like a baked apple (and also because Newfoundlanders like making up their own names for things).

The thought of baked apples while I sat alone on the hillside eating cloudberries reminded me of a childhood memory. My father had spent the better part of two years building our house with his own hands. My brother and I at the time were only seven, and while he worked long hours on the house, we were turned loose in the encircling woods to amuse ourselves. One late summer day, having made a fire with a magnifying glass, we were naturally keen to roast marshmallows over it. My father, however, who was busy working on the house alone, said we had none. To get us out of his hair, he told us that when he was a boy he used to roast apples, telling us these made a wonderful treat, and he fetched us some from an old overgrown tree on the edge of the woods. I was so excited at the thought of this delicious treat that I picked the best apple I could find among the bunch he brought. With a cut green stick for a spit, I patiently roasted mine with care, my mouth watering. When the apple was good and roasted, I bit into it with excitement, only to scowl—it didn't taste good at all, just sour! As I busied myself setting up my tent on a level patch of moss and lichens, still snacking on the abundant cloudberries, I thought to myself that the taste of bake-apples was the finest thing in the world.

*

I awoke the next morning to a strange haze hanging over the land. At first I thought it might be fog, but as I packed up my gear I realized it was something else. The haze had a faint smell of smoke about it, which told me that somewhere far off to the south, in the land of the trees, there must be forest fires. The winds had carried the haze north across the tundra, perhaps from hundreds of miles away.

This thick haze combined with the absence of wind gave the glassy lakes and silent, rock-strewn hills an odd feel, almost as if I'd drifted into some timeless world. The calm weather and eerie haze lasted for days. These windless days were also unnaturally hot, which made the clouds of blackflies extreme whenever I landed on shore. My wrists were badly swollen from numerous itchy bites; even my eyelids had red sores on them. Lying inside my tent beneath the surreal haze and midnight sun, strange cries would pierce the silence—young gulls along the lake, which make the oddest cries.

When the haze dissipated on the wind, it would reveal what looked increasingly to my mind like a fairy-tale landscape: vivid green hills with ancient grey rocks and boulders beyond counting scattered about, with the odd little stream crashing a path down the rocky hillsides. I could picture dinosaurs walking about amid the lichen-covered rocks that were eons older than even those giant reptiles. More and more, it seemed like a land time forgot.

The unnaturally calm weather I knew was but a brief interlude from the terrifying high winds of the arctic tundra. I knew full well the power of those winds sweeping off Hudson Bay in late summer— that they'd been clocked at nearly two hundred kilometres an hour, that they had trapped canoeing parties for ten days or more on the barrens with relentless gusts that made paddling impossible. I'd heard stories of bush pilots and search-and-rescue aircraft whose planes were grounded for weeks by the power of the gales. Nothing filled me with greater dread than the thought of those great gusting winds as I paddled across icy lakes. But while the dead calm reigned, I intended to make the most of it. I pushed myself twelve hours a day to try to get as far across the tundra as I could before the weather turned bad, as inevitably it would.

On August 3 I passed through a narrow, rapid-filled channel connecting Point Lake to Lake Providence, wading the rapids and leaping from boulder to boulder. The next day I was at it again, paddling through the haze across more lakes and confronting more rapids in the narrow connecting channels.

The first of these rapids was large and came in two sets. I managed to wade up both of them cautiously, sparing me a lengthy portage over rock-strewn terrain. A third rapid followed soon after; this, too, I waded through along the edge. But a fourth stretch of long, powerful rapids defeated my efforts to wade it. I concluded I'd have to make a painstaking portage of about a half-kilometre over rough terrain of willow thickets, boulders, steep hills, and finally soggy marshes to get around it.

This portage was extremely exhausting, given the intensity of the blackfly attacks combined with the unusually warm weather (about nineteen degrees Celsius). So when it came time for my fourth load, the canoe, I had a mind to try getting it up the rapids with a combination of wading and lining, which I figured I could do now that it was empty. Anything, it seemed, was worth it to avoid the nightmarish string of obstacles in the long, pathless portage.

In this roaring, dangerous rapid, I banged my shin hard against a rock ledge concealed beneath the swirling, foaming water. Wedged in a crevice formed by the ledge, I struggled to free my leg and get out of the rushing torrent back to safer ground, ignoring the pain. Pulling back and forth on my boot, holding on to the canoe, and struggling to maintain my balance in the rapids, I finally got free and made it to the safety of the bank. "Well," I said to the canoe, "that one's really going to leave a mark."

Exhausted, I reached the end of the rapids, repacked the canoe, and paddled across the nameless lake I'd arrived on, passing by a grizzly on shore that ran off at the sight of me. Then I made camp near a willow thicket, my body aching from the labours of the day, my shin swollen, and myself utterly exhausted.

× 15 ×

ON ROCKY SHORES

The week of hot, hazy, windless weather ended abruptly on August 5. Frigid air came over the land, bringing with it rain and strong winds. The sudden cold weather seemed to miraculously dissolve the clouds of bugs, leaving the air clear and letting me breathe freely without a bug net. I could hardly believe it. On the downside, the stiff winds could make travel hazardous.

Fortunately I was setting out on a series of smaller lakes, so for now anyway I'd be more or less protected from any big waves. My plan was to paddle through the chain of lakes—some were small enough that I could cross them in mere minutes—and then portage to the next one, totalling several dozen in all. This would eventually take me out of the Arctic Ocean's watershed and into the Hudson Bay drainage basin, after which all the rivers would be flowing eastward, the direction I was headed, allowing me to travel much faster—exactly what I needed if I were to complete my journey before the weather rendered canoe travel impossible.

To get to the Hudson Bay watershed, however, was easier said than done. I had a long way to go, with no trails to follow and topographic maps that left something to be desired. The maps showed many of these lakes as connected by streams, whereas in reality there was nothing but impassable boulder fields linking them.

On August 5 I managed to complete four separate portages, passing through a total of six different lakes—each similar to the one before, surrounded as they were by rocky, hilly tundra. The strong winds were mostly blowing southwest, which actually helped propel me rapidly across the lakes. My feet, though, were drenched from portaging over sodden moss and rain-soaked dwarf birch, as I'd switched back to my hiking boots now that I was done with wading. I wanted the extra ankle support for the rugged portages.

The uneven ground made portaging vastly more difficult than would be the case on a hard-packed surface with a trail to follow. But I was simply grateful that the cold and windy weather had driven off the bugs, and for the bounty of delicious wild berries that allowed me to snack anywhere I liked now. Through the steady rain I transported each of my four loads across dense willow thickets—a favourite haunt of grizzlies—and around rocks to the next body of water. Some portages required different methods: one marshy section I wore my waders through; others, I changed into my hiking boots to better jump from rock to rock across dried-up creek beds filled with big grey boulders.

Another day brought me across another eight lakes and another eight portages separating them. My barrels were getting a little emptier, such that I actually began to carry the lighter of the two simultaneously with my backpack. This cut the number of loads from three to four, and trips back and forth over the rocky hills and marshy valleys from seven to five. In other words, a one-kilometre portage was now no longer a seven-kilometre ordeal, merely a five-kilometre one.

Crossing one little nameless lake I saw two heads moving across the choppy waters. I assumed they were caribou, which regularly swim across lakes and rivers. But as I paddled closer I realized it was actually a cow moose with a young calf. I wondered what were they doing north of the treeline. Moose don't normally roam about on the arctic tundra like caribou do. Then it occurred to me that these moose were likely driven north by the forest fires that had been raging somewhere to the south. Hopefully the rainy weather would allow them to return home soon.

By early afternoon I'd reached Starfish Lake, the first lake large enough to have a name on my maps for some days. It was not quite ten kilometres long, and I battled stiff winds all the way up it. From Starfish Lake I hoped to advance into a much larger body of water over sixty kilometres long known as Courageous Lake. Connecting these two lakes was a hypothetical stream drawn on my topographical map. I wasn't so naive as to believe such a stream actually existed in anything like a navigable state, but on some level, everyone has hopes and dreams—and mine were now principally that such streams might really exist, like unicorns or leprechauns. Otherwise, I'd be in for yet another long and arduous portage.

The winds were fierce as I approached Starfish Lake's southern shores to search for any hint of a stream. The choppy waters complicated my paddling efforts, since to pivot and paddle along the shore meant allowing waves to hit the canoe broadside. A spill into icy water here would test my fire-making skills to the utmost. Cautiously I angled my canoe diagonally as I weaved in toward the rocky coastline. The "stream," I could see, was just a dried-up, boulder-filled creek bed. I'd have to portage.

But where and how to land the canoe? Waves were pounding into the rocky shoreline, with no sand beaches or soft soil visible anywhere for me to glide into. The last thing I wanted was to drive the canoe into the masses of jagged rocks along the lakeshore, smashing the canoe and tossing me into frigid waters. I looked in vain for anywhere to safely land. There was nothing. So that settled it: I had to take my chances. To execute a landing in waves onto a shoreline composed of great jumbles of jagged rock would take perfect timing and manoeuvring. I wasn't sure I could pull it off, but sometimes you just have to go for it.

I edged closer to the rocks, letting the waves carry me in. It was critical that I time my landing between waves. When I was as close as I could safely get, I let a final wave pass by and then made my move: drawing a stroke of my paddle to first drive the canoe forward and then two more to sharply spin it parallel to the rocks.

I had only seconds to jump out before the next wave rolled in and slammed the canoe against the rocks. I made my dash, getting both feet onto the rocks, which were slick from the rain and waves. Then I grabbed the heavily loaded canoe to hold it steady, but a wave jostled it into the rocks. Fortunately it was the side that took the impact, and its tough design was in little danger of any damage there—it was the underside that worried me, where the ice and rocks had been by degrees grinding it thinner.

Moving as fast as I could, I pulled out my barrels and backpack, then lifted the canoe up onto the rocks. Finally, after I'd secured everything, I turned around to consider where I'd landed. Tall shrubs of leafy green willows screened my view of what lay inland, so I took the pole as a staff and set off to scout which way to head for my portage. So far the portages hadn't been too bad. I felt optimistic.

Pushing through the willows, my heart sank: what I saw looked like a nightmare. A vast boulder field—its enormous slabs heaped and tumbled every which way like rubble after an earthquake—stretched as far as I could see in the direction I had to head. To hike across it without a heavy pack would be hard enough—to do it with four loads in high winds seemed rather hazardous. It was the perfect place to twist an ankle, or fall and smash my face off a boulder. Outside the chaotic boulder field, things were scarcely any better. The uneven ground was cloaked in almost impenetrable dwarf birch thickets at least chest high. Neither option was a good one, but I opted for the birches. It was already early evening and I didn't have time to delay.

With my backpack strapped on, I slung my lighter barrel over one shoulder and set off into the thicket. It was my fourth portage of the day, so I was at least suitably warmed up for it. The cold wind also ensured that there were no bugs to torment me.

It took a few dozen steps before I gave up on the idea of making it through the thicket. The bushes were too easy to trip over, and concealed beneath them were more boulders. Back I went into the piles of rubble—ancient Precambrian rocks, billions of years old, covered in lichens. By comparison they seemed easier, as long as I made sure of my footing. I stepped across yawning cracks between the great slabs, jumping from one oddly rectangular-shaped boulder to another, climbing up and down, enjoying the full cardio workout.

I had about a kilometre of this to do before I'd reach the next lake— or rather, more than that, since the obstacle course meant I couldn't travel in a straight line. After a while I tired of climbing boulders; plus, the birch shrubs seemed to have thinned somewhat, so I veered back into them. They didn't prove much thinner, but I decided to try my luck in them anyway. I plowed through the tall bushes, pushing them aside with one hand as I trudged along ground that sloped up then down, with deep pockets strewn all about. The thickets made navigation trickier, since I couldn't see much in them, but I knew which direction to head and kept a steady course.

When I grew tired of struggling through tangled birches I crossed back into the great boulders and then back again to the birches, as my fancy dictated. Sometimes, I find, simple variety is encouraging when portaging.

Eventually, lying beyond haphazard piles of rocks and boulders every-where, I caught sight of blue water ahead. I pushed on over the last stretch and was delighted to discover, amid a wilderness of desolate rock, a patch of moss, crowberries, and dwarf Labrador tea just big enough for my tent. It'd make a nice soft bed for the night. I set down my two loads beside it and turned around to fetch my next one, the heavy barrel.

Zigzagging around the various obstacles, coupled with the thickets and the uneven ground, made hiking back and forth time-consuming and physically draining. By the time I headed back for my final load, the canoe, it was getting late, but I hoped with hard effort to get it across, so as to be fresh and ready for an early start come morning. Given the obstacles, I'd have to carry the canoe over my head. But that would restrict my vision, which is not a thing to be lightly dismissed when there are no trails to follow. I needed to be able to look up to pick out a path of least resistance among the rubble and shrubs. Further complicating things were the gusting winds. Still, I began gamely, lifting the canoe up to my knee and then tossing it over my head. I made it five steps before a wind gust caught the canoe and threw me into a boulder. Clearly jumping from rock to rock with a canoe over my head in high winds would be more difficult than it seemed.

I unclipped the water bottle from my belt, took some sips, and rested for a bit. Then I ate a granola bar that I'd stuffed into my pocket. Feeling fortified, I lifted the canoe again, gripped it tightly, and moved forward as best as I could. I headed for the colossal rubble fields. I figured I'd rather climb among the rocks, where I could at least see my feet, than plow into birch shrubs that concealed everything below the waist and made tripping easy.

After a few hundred metres of weaving amid the boulders my energy and strength were too drained for it. Sooner or later, another gust would knock me over, and I might topple five or six feet off a rock slab, smashing my head off a boulder. Thus, I decided to cut back into the pathless birches, in the hopes of simply dragging the canoe behind me among them. Dragging was painstaking slow and exhausting, as the thicket was, it turned out, not easy to plow through with a canoe. Frequently I had to rest; it'd been eleven hours so far of paddling and portaging, and as much as I disliked the thought, I realized my canoe and I were going to have to spend the night apart. I laid it beside a big willow bush and tucked it in as comfortably as I could, promising to return first thing in the morning.

On the far side of the portage, I settled in for the night on my little patch of soft moss amid the ancient boulders. It was a fine campsite, surely one of life's greatest pleasures.

Since the tundra is riddled with hummocks and holes, there'd been many nights when I had to sleep on uneven ground. In other places it was difficult just to climb back down to the shore to fetch water for boiling or driftwood for burning. Filling a pot with water, too, could be easier said than done when the water was difficult to access due to immense jumbles of rocks that extend far out from shore, with just little pockets of water—too small to scoop from—in between the rocks. In less desirable sites, too, I might sleep in willow thickets that made it easy to lose anything I'd unpacked. But here everything was perfect. The tundra was covered in short little plants and mosses, wonderful for spreading things out on and looking over my gear, and there were nice slabs of flat rocks for cooking on. My pole, meanwhile, I converted into a clothesline by jabbing it into some rock crevices, and I'd strung my wet clothing up on it. (My rain-jacket, the lighter of my two jackets I'd brought, was clearly becoming old and worn, as it was no longer keeping me very dry.)

Still, I was as content as could be, admiring the beauty and solitude of this rock-filled landscape. It was a little surreal how, nine or ten thousand years ago, the glaciers had arranged the great boulders in their present position. Nearby, one giant rock had come to rest precariously on top of another, a bit like a giant booby trap. In the crevice of another rock I found a spider's web. This interested me greatly, as spiders reach their northern distribution in the southern Arctic, where they can tolerate the extreme cold and feed on the abundant bugs during brief summers. I hadn't seen many of them on my journey. I find patterns in nature—like a spider's intricate web or the colossal heaps of rubble left by a melting glacier thousands of years ago, or the ancient cliffs weathered and shaped by the elements for eons into resembling masonry—can keep a person engrossed for hours.

✳

I retrieved my canoe early the next morning and completed the portage in good time. The rain had subsided, but it remained cold and windy. Reaching Courageous Lake, I'd crossed another watershed divide, though not the coveted Hudson Bay one that I was after. Hard paddling battling side winds took me south through Courageous Lake, where I passed a giant sand peninsula before coming to the lake's big eastern bay. The scenery was gorgeous, with sandy beaches, dunes, and rolling grassy fields. Once I'd rounded the giant peninsula, the wind was in my favour and I could travel much faster, weaving between islands.

Tucked in a sandy bay I spotted some ruins. It was an abandoned fly-in fishing lodge consisting of little plywood cabins. There are a few of these scattered across the North; back in the 1990s, sport fishing was a bigger draw, and it was possible for quite a few of these remote camps to operate. There are still some in business, but this one had clearly been left to rot away. All of these lakes, I knew well, were home to delicious lake trout and other cold-water species that can survive in their icy, nutrient-poor depths.

As I completed my crossing of the lake I noticed a few other signs of humans. Appearing as tiny specks on the horizon I made out some radio towers; these, I knew, were associated with mining operations in the area. Indeed, I saw in the far distance inland across the tundra some sort of mining encampment—a few little cabins or something. In a land of rocks, willows, tundra, and lakes that seemed to go on forever, the sight of these objects felt very bizarre, like looking at something that belonged in another world. Approximately sixty kilometres northeast of me were major open-pit mining operations for diamonds. Those massive mines functioned as off-the-grid operations, supplied by aircraft and resembling a sort of lunar colony.

That night I slept on a wonderful bit of mossy tundra, luxuriously comfortable despite the sandflies that showed up to disturb my peace. But inside my tent I was happy. I could see a full moon rising over the pale sky—there were now a few hours of partial darkness each night. The season was getting on. As I drifted off to sleep, the words *winter is coming* were at the back of my mind.

× 16 ×

OF WIND AND WAVES

Mid-August was supposed to be the date after which the winds became increasingly unmanageable for canoeing on the arctic tundra. It was now August 8, so I figured I had only a week of decent weather left. I had to make the most of it, especially now that the biggest lakes I'd seen since Great Bear lay in front of me. It was thus discouraging to awake to high winds that morning, which promised to make paddling extremely difficult. Under ordinary circumstances, it was the kind of wind that would prompt a day off to rest, but that was no longer an option for me.

Fierce as the wind was, I had to push on. After all, I told myself, if I can't handle this wind, what chance would I have in another couple of weeks when it got really bad?

Eleven hours of hard, exhausting paddling saw me advance only thirty kilometres. The wind had constantly been hitting the canoe broadside, so that the majority of my strokes were merely to keep the canoe from crashing into shore rather than propelling it forward. I passed rapidly down a small river, known as the Snake River, the first river I'd paddled on with the current for almost three weeks, since the Kendall River. It was a short river with some small rapids and ledges that were easily navigated; the only difficulty arising from the powerful wind gusts that I had to counteract by paddling while simultaneously zigzagging around rocks. The Snake River spit me out into a large body of water known as MacKay Lake. In rough weather, if I had to trace out its shoreline to where I needed to get to, that'd total a sixty-six-kilometre paddle. But I hoped for a calm spell that would allow me to make a large open-water crossing, "island-hopping" across the centre of the lake, and thereby greatly reducing the distance to its northeast tip, where I needed to end up.

I camped on the lake's western shore, my little tent and canoe looking very lonesome against a backdrop of miles of grassy tundra with hardly a feature on it other than some small hills. The tundra here was almost entirely devoid of rocks, resembling more of an overgrown soccer field.

The wind stayed cold and strong—I had to use my canoe and two barrels as a windbreak just to boil water over the camp stove. As I waited for it to boil, I took the opportunity to eat as many cloudberries, crowberries, lingonberries, and blueberries as I could.

While searching out these berries I'd made an unexpected find: a clump of thick white fur lying on the tundra. At first it looked uncomfortably like polar bear fur. But I was still too far inland for polar bears, which stay near the seacoast hunting seals. So I told myself it couldn't be from a bear. It seemed more likely to be the fur of an arctic wolf or even arctic fox, though I favoured a wolf as it felt too coarse for a fox, and anyway a fox would still have its grey summer coat at this time of year.

After dinner I bundled up to stay warm and crawled into my tent. The full moon rose over the lake with a pale orange glow against a purple sky. The nights were growing almost dark now.

My gear was starting to feel the effects of continuous use and the elements. The tent was patched in a few places with duct tape and its main support pole had stripped where it attached at the joint, due to the pressure of the winds. My canoe was a more serious concern; the gouges were really accumulating and getting deeper from all the grinding over endless rocky rapids. Both my paddles were chipped up along their blades from jabbing at rocks. My legs were pretty bruised up too, from wading and bumping into rocks in the rapids.

I fell asleep, wondering what the dawn would bring. If I were to cross the lake's big open water, I'd need fair weather.

*

The morning of August 9 broke in my favour: the skies were clear and the lake calm, with just a pleasant breeze. I was determined to take full advantage of the conditions. In the high winds and dangerous waves, I'd never risk crossing the lake. But in this calm weather it was no problem. I cut across a two-kilometre open stretch to some grassy islands, followed along this archipelago for some way, then made another two-kilometre crossing to a big point. And from there another open-water crossing to the lake's end that I needed to reach.

Among those islands I saw mergansers swimming in the water and on the rocky shore a great bald eagle looking regal and majestic. There were also some rocks.

Living outdoors, you quickly become attuned to the weather in a way indoor life makes impossible. Every change, no matter how slight, in the weather's mood demands attention, and you begin to realize just how variable weather can be. Every shift in the wind, which it did frequently, would directly affect my travelling, like which side of a lake to follow or which side of my canoe to paddle on. And these changing moods of the weather increasingly influenced my own—high winds demoralized me, cold weather made me forlorn, and clear skies and calm conditions left me carefree.

I made camp early that evening, selecting a site near deep water along a small beach. This was to be the site of my third and final resupply. A resupply by necessity caused me to lose a precious day, as it would take that long to arrange things and wait for a pilot. It was a shame to lose the time, but to press on any farther would drive up the cost of the resupply flight, as the pilots charged by the kilometre for how far they flew; and with the increasing winds, the likelihood of delayed flights was increasing. Besides, my rations wouldn't last the more than thousand kilometres of travel that still lay ahead. How long that would take to traverse was difficult to forecast, considering how heavily it depended on weather—on a calm day I might make a hundred kilometres; on a windy day, zero.

I knew of a pair of paddlers who, almost twenty years earlier, had completed the trip from here to Baker Lake in just thirty-three days. But there had been two of them paddling together, and only one of me—and they'd done it in mid-summer during the best wind conditions, not late in the season. They'd also taken exceptional risks to make such time: cutting across big lakes far from shore and running dangerous whitewater rapids. Still, I had the advantage of youth over them, and whereas they'd started cold after a floatplane dropped them off on the lake, my body was already conditioned from thousands of kilometres of journeying. If I could, on my own, equal the two of them together, even with the worst weather, that'd put me in Baker Lake to end my journey by September 15—late in the year for Arctic canoeing. If I couldn't match their pace, or if the wind held me back further, I'd be looking at the onset of winter. These were the kinds of calculations I had to ponder as I sat on the tundra overlooking the water, trying to decide how much extra weight in the form of rations and propane fuel canisters to carry from here on out. It was a double-edged sword: more food would give me a larger cushion; more weight would slow my paddling and compound the many long, arduous portages around dangerous canyons I knew lay ahead of me.

If my rations ran out, I couldn't get more resupplies. My budget for flights was used up; and the farther I went, the more expensive any hypothetical flight would become. In terms of paddling speed, I probably couldn't equal what the combined efforts of two paddlers could do together, but I could exceed them, I figured, in the length of the days I put in—more like the tortoise and hare than ever. Ultimately, I resolved on five weeks' worth of supplies on the basis that I hoped to equal the two paddlers who had it done it in mid-summer; if I had to go a little hungry toward the end, I figured I could manage it.

In the meantime, the weather just now was glorious, and since I was stuck waiting for the floatplane, I figured I'd go for a swim while it was still possible. Catching my reflection in the water, I realized how thin I'd become. I guessed I'd shed about twenty pounds since I'd started the journey.

After a brief dip in the frigid water, I let the sun dry me as I sat on the tundra, watching bold little arctic ground squirrels scurrying about on the sand, chirping and standing up like prairie dogs to look around. That night I slept soundly on a nice bed of lichens.

The next morning dawned with overcast skies. A thunderstorm rolled in over the lake but rolled out just as quickly, narrowly missing me. A tent pitched on flat tundra isn't the most carefree place during lightning strikes, but I always selected my sites with care, away from high points or big rocks, in lower-lying areas wherever possible.

The resupply flight was delayed (they always seem to be) and it wasn't until late afternoon through a cloud patch that I saw the small plane materialize. The pilot circled round, spotted my tent and over-turned canoe, then skidded down across the water. It wasn't possible for the plane to come in toward shore, due to some rocks that extended far out. So I had to paddle out to the plane to get my supplies.

This was a different pilot from the one who'd resupplied me back on the Coppermine almost three weeks earlier. Things went quickly. He stood on the plane's aluminum float and handed me my barrel; I sorted through it, then gave it back to him empty. He wished me well, made an encouraging comment about the gale-force winds coming in the weeks ahead and how he sure was glad he wouldn't be out here during that time, then revved his engine back to life, wished me well again, and departed for the long flight back.

His was the last face I'd see for a while.

It was only four p.m., so I decided to press on. I'd already lost a full day's worth of travel waiting for the resupply since reaching the end of MacKay Lake, and I couldn't afford to waste a minute more. The winds were light, so I set off.

Draining MacKay Lake is the Lockhart River, a short river but one with serious whitewater, the kind you wouldn't want to make the slightest mistake in. I was paddling with the current, and would be for the remainder of my journey. That meant much faster travel, but also the need for caution around dangerous rapids.

The first rapid I came to was a big roaring affair, more than a half-kilometre long, where the river descended steeply through a narrow stretch. It was the kind of thing I might possibly have run on a warm summer's day in a less remote locale with an empty canoe. Here, alone, on the arctic tundra, any mistake could be fatal. The safe option would be to portage. But that would be time-consuming and exhausting. As an alternative, I could try to wade down the edge of it, hopping from rock to rock, and guide my canoe down with ropes, keeping it safely out of the big waves in the centre.

For months I'd become accustomed to wading up rapids, so it felt a little strange to now be wading down them. This wasn't actually any easier, as going downstream the canoe is more difficult to control when lining or wading, and like with upstream travel, the force of the roaring current is always threatening to tear the canoe away. I had to combine caution and force to get it through safely. Sometimes this meant letting out the rope and allowing the canoe to drift ahead on the current and around the rocks, where I could then catch up to it.

Once through the rapids I resumed paddling, pushing on for a few more hours before making camp on a high bank. That night I had to say a solemn goodbye to an old friend: my pole. It had been with me since early on, back on the Mackenzie River. Shaped by a beaver from balsam poplar, it had served me well—never breaking, and helping me get up rapids beyond counting. I was sad to part with it—much like the feeling one gets with losing a walking stick you've come to know. But from here on out all my travel would be downstream, across lakes or on foot, and in those scenarios the pole could be of no further use. And where I was headed every extra ounce mattered. So I turned it over one last time in my hands, said goodbye, and set it gently down among some willows.

＊

I crawled out of my tent the next morning to find the wind gusting fiercely across the land. The little knee-high willows shook with each burst, and ripples appeared along the river's surface where the powerful gusts raced across—like a kind of ghost imprint, as I could see the outline of the air current as it moved rapidly over the water.

It wasn't exactly good weather for paddling. But I had the current in my favour and I had to press on. So I pulled on my hat. The wind knocked it off into the willows. I fetched it back and decided I'd go hatless for the day.

With the canoe loaded, I set off paddling downriver. It should have been easy but it was anything but. The howling gusts made steering the canoe difficult; they knocked and jostled it about, at times even overwhelming both the current and my paddle strokes to drive the canoe into the banks. Trying to steer through small rapids and avoid rocks with such tremendous gusts proved frustratingly difficult. The canoe felt as though it were under someone else's control, careening wildly across the river wherever the crazy gusts took it. It was all I could do, battling with all my strength against both current and wind, to avoid smashing it into the rocks in the rapids.

I tried to escape the brunt of the gusts by tucking in under the high banks whenever I could. It wasn't much help, but it did at least allow me to continue working my way downriver. After about thirteen kilometres of difficult paddling, I spotted something up ahead that made my heart beat faster. Thin curls of mist rose, and over the roar of the wind I could hear a distinct crashing sound of falling water.

The far side of the river looked better for approaching this hazard, so I waited for a break in the gusts and then paddled with all my strength for the far shore. When I reached it, I had a clearer view of what lay downriver: it looked like a vertical drop. I'd have to approach it very carefully. If the wind or the current caught me I might reach a point of no return and plunge right over it—which isn't half as fun as it sounds.

The gusts were too steady and too fierce for me to proceed by water, so instead I took the canoe by the bow rope and splashed ahead on foot, towing it behind me until the stream carried it past me. Then I followed behind it. In the far distance ran great blue ridges; nearer toward me were hills partially covered in dwarf birch. It was a very windswept, empty-looking place. As I cautiously edged along the shore, I saw where the river appeared to vanish into thin air, the white-water splashing up before it tumbled out of view.

I hauled my canoe onshore and secured it so that I could go ahead on foot. I can't recommend enough the need to haul the canoe fully onto the land when doing anything like this. If I'd merely pulled the bow only partway up on some rocks and left it there, disaster could follow if the gusting wind dislodged it and swept it over the falls. I hiked ahead along the curving course of the river, climbing up a steep, high ridge that overlooked it. The winds were fierce as I ascended, and I made sure to keep away from the edge.

Once I reached the top I had a good view of the river's turbulent, roaring course over the rocks. There were two big, foaming cataracts separated by a rocky island, with large rapids above each one. Clearly, I wasn't going to be able to navigate that. A portage was necessary, which, from what I could see, was going to be a long, drawn-out effort. I'd have to haul each of my loads and the canoe a long way to get around the rapids, and then to get back to the water's edge would require a steep climb.

In the middle of all this surveying from high above on the ridge, I did pause and think to myself that the vast panorama of open tundra and crashing water looked remarkably beautiful from afar. Scrutinizing the landscape, I began to wonder how I could shorten the lengthy, difficult portage.

It appeared that if I could manage to cross the river above the falls to the far side, its mostly flat rocks would mean a much shorter and easier portage than having to climb the steep ridge on this side. But given the rapids and especially the powerful wind gusts, to cross the river would be tricky. I'd have to haul my canoe back upriver some

ways to be safe, then cut across with hard paddling against the combined force of the wind and current to the far shore. Still, this extra
effort seemed worth it, as the portage promised to be much easier on
the opposite side.

So I returned to my canoe, splashed back down into the river, and
towed it to what seemed like a safe distance up from the thundering
cataracts. The wind was still howling, making it hard to hear much of
anything between wind and falls. I took a deep breath, pushed my canoe
away from shore, leapt in, and began paddling across. Wind gusts
almost immediately drove me diagonally in the direction of the waterfalls, which didn't seem desirable. But the canoe I actually turned slightly
into the current, as if to run the falls, but this I merely did to aid steering,
so that the current would help get me across against the wind.

I aimed the bow as close as I dared toward where the cascading
water began. Several strong strokes brought me to the rocky shore,
safely above the start of the turbulent water. I hopped out, grabbing
hold of the gunwales as I did so to keep the wind from tearing the
canoe away.

A short hike convinced me that the portage was indeed relatively
easy. Past the flat rock was just a steep, somewhat tricky climb over
boulders and ledges to get back to the water's edge at the end. The
only serious part would be getting the canoe across. I couldn't drag it
over the rocks, and carrying it over my head in the gusting wind promised to be difficult. But there was no other way.

I waited for a break in the howling gusts, then quickly lifted the
canoe and tossed it over my head. Gripping the gunwales as tightly as
I could, I started moving over the rocks. The wind was blowing across
my path from the southwest, which meant hitting the canoe broadside. When the really powerful gusts came I'd totter, but rather than
trying to stand against the gusts I'd allow them to pivot me. Since I
couldn't hope to hold the canoe against them without falling, I'd just
spin with the wind so that the canoe was aerodynamic—the stern end
facing into the wind. Then, in the relative lull between gusts, I could

safely continue. I climbed down the rocks with the canoe over my head, but when I reached the last steep bit I had to set it down. This final stretch was too steep to climb in the wind with the canoe over my head, so I half-carried it, half-pushed it down the rocks.

Immediately ahead lay more small rapids and boulder fields to canoe through. In calm weather they'd be fun to plunge through; in the high winds, a bit of a nightmare. Still, I pushed off into the current, paddling as well as I was able and choosing the widest, deepest spots between the protruding rocks in the rushing waters to snake through. The last thing I wanted was for the wind to hurl the canoe into a big rock, capsizing and pinning it there as the current flooded it. When you see destroyed canoes along rapids (certain popular paddling rivers have veritable graveyards of them), that's normally what did them in—becoming pinned on rocks where they get bent round like horse-shoes by the tremendous force of the water. The ruined, abandoned canoe I'd seen along the Coppermine had been such a case.

When I got through these obstacles, the river brought me to a rectangular-shaped lake not quite eleven kilometres long and about three or four kilometres wide. Along its southern shores was a long escarpment, or ridge; if not for the winds, I would have admired it. As it was, the gusting wind, which was bad enough on a closed-in, narrow river, was almost impossible on a long lake. To cross it, ideally I needed to be on the south shore, where I'd be more sheltered from the pre-vailing winds by the hills. The problem was the river flowed into the northern part of the lake, and to get over to the south shore would mean paddling into headwinds for some three kilometres, an impos-sible prospect. So I had no choice but to try the exposed north shore, where the full force of the wind, sweeping across the open water, would be hitting the canoe almost broadside.

With hard, furious paddle strokes I drove the canoe slowly for-ward, all the while carefully navigating the waves, the bow riding over them as they rolled into shore. Progress was slow, and I kept thinking that it was only August 11 and that the *really* powerful winds hadn't even arrived yet. Worse, this was just a small lake—ahead lay two vastly larger ones that I'd have to cross, and still others beyond that.

As I continued deeper into the lake, waves began to spill into the canoe, lapping against its side with a thud and splashing up into the air, some of the water landing on my gear and soaking it. My heart sank: to push on in these waves was to risk swamping. I'd have to head to shore.

Cautiously I turned the canoe with the waves, paddling into a grassy peninsula to wait things out. On shore, I tried to make myself as comfortable as possible, telling myself this would be a temporary delay, and that getting windbound for an afternoon, even several days, was to be fully expected on the arctic tundra. But try as I may, I found it difficult to relax with the wind roaring. I couldn't help fretting over what this wind boded for the weeks ahead. Time was critical. I had to do alone, in deteriorating weather, what it had taken those two paddlers longer to accomplish earlier in the season twenty years earlier. Right now it was difficult to see how that was possible, given I was sitting on shore rather than canoeing, staring at frightful waves.

There was some slight consolation nearby when I noticed earth and rocks had been dug up in five or six places—these, I knew, were from a grizzly digging up the burrows of arctic ground squirrels. Those adorable little squirrels are the favourite hors d'oeuvre of the arctic grizzly. Two and a half centuries ago, the explorer Samuel Hearne, who wandered on foot across much of the barrens that I was now passing over, described his astonishment at the size of the rocks the grizzlies were able to lift out of the way in their quest to dig up ground squirrels. The bear's sheer strength is indeed astonishing, and getting to inspect the evidence of it helped keep me occupied while the wind roared.

Several hours elapsed with me still sitting on shore, the wind howling away while I ate cloudberries and lingonberries. Finally, wind or no wind, I resolved to relaunch my canoe and push on. I was just too anxious to wait any longer.

On the theory that confidence is half the battle, I decided to give myself a little bit of a morale boost by first portaging my canoe and gear across the narrow peninsula I'd come to shore on. By portaging across it, that would let me relaunch the canoe into the water on the lee side of the peninsula, sheltering me from the worst of the wind and waves. Of course, I'd have to face the wind and those waves soon enough, but this would at least allow me to ease into them, rather than starting off with the most difficult and hazardous part, which would be trying to round the tip of the peninsula in the waves. By portaging, I'd avoid that. With an action plan in place I immediately felt better. Frequently I find that there's nothing worse than indecision, and that any plan is better than sitting idle and letting worry eat away at you. Feeling better I completed the portage quickly, as I now felt I had an extra spring in my step from the rest. I was prepared to give it my all.

The canoe I pushed into the water, then I jumped in, paddling hard. Sheltered behind the peninsula, things were much easier starting off, and I built up some speed and confidence. Within a few minutes I was once more facing the wrath of the waves. The first ones splashed against my bow, spilling a little water in. But I steered my canoe carefully, angling into the waves, avoiding any more of them lapping into the canoe.

Some canoeists favour spray covers—a modern innovation that in effect transforms an open canoe into a closed-in kayak by putting a cover across the boat. This prevents water from lapping in when in big waves. I find them useful for downriver trips, or on lakes, without much portaging. But I dislike spray covers for more complex journeys, when anything extra is a pain on a portage, and the covers have to be removed and put back on each time you need to lift the canoe or switch to poling. More than that, on extended journeys, when long days of twelve-hour travelling are the norm, I like to be able to access my cameras, food, maps, and anything else I need easily and fast, which a cover can prevent. A cover can also be potentially dangerous if it lulls the paddler into a false sense of security, making them risk bigger waves alone than would be prudent. I figure if you can't handle the waves in an open canoe, you probably shouldn't be risking them at all. Last but not least, if my canoe were to swamp or tip, I don't want a spray cover obstructing or entangling me—I want to be able to swim free. I also need my gear to be able to fall out, as if my canoe were pinned in the middle of a rapid, alone there would be scant hope of recovering it. But by allowing my barrels and pack to float free, I have a better chance of retrieving them downriver.

Several hours of hard paddling brought me across the lake. The trickiest parts were rounding the points that jutted out into the water; here I had to turn into the waves, paddling into headwinds. But after I rounded the peninsulas, then I had the reward of easier paddling on the far side as I cruised back in toward shore.

Once through the lake I passed through some narrow channels, zigzagging around a maze of islands and bays, and into more lakes. By evening the weather had calmed; I pushed on to take advantage of it.

I finally halted for the night at an attractive bit of tundra above a small rocky beach. A blood-red sun cast its fading rays across the water as I made camp. The sight of the red sky gave me hope, as I remembered the old sailor's proverb: "Red sky at night, sailor's delight/Red sky in morning, sailors take warning."

In the morning I'd find out if the rhyme held true.

IN THE LAND OF THE MUSKOX

The old sailor's rhyme didn't disappoint —the morning dawned calm. I was up early to get underway, pushing off for thirteen hours of paddling that saw me cover about seventy kilometres. Around midday the wind increased, blowing from the south and bringing with it a smoky haze—which I knew must be from forest fires still burning somewhere far away.

Under that surreal haze I'd entered into a large expanse of water known as Aylmer Lake. This vast body of water has giant bays radiating off in different directions like a lopsided star, each filled with rocky islands. In the middle of the lake's southern shore appears a great square-shaped peninsula that is very nearly an island, with only a narrow isthmus joining it to the mainland. This giant almost-island covers about seventy square kilometres, and within its wind-ravaged confines are nearly fifty smaller lakes and ponds, all contained within the larger lake I was crossing.

Besides being merely a curious bit of geography formed by a glacier thousands of years ago, the square almost-island presented a navigational dilemma to me as I canoed across the lake. The lake's north shore was carved up with very deep bays and long peninsulas that I wished to avoid, and it was also more exposed to the wind and waves. So I'd resolved to take the south shore, which, besides its own share of bays and peninsulas, has that peculiar almost-island joined by the isthmus to the mainland. Paddling around it would add more kilometres to my route. Instead, my plan was to try portaging across the isthmus—if I could pull this off, it'd save a lot of extra time.

The isthmus was only five hundred metres wide, which I calculated would take less time and effort to portage across than the additional paddling to get around it. There was only one slight catch to the plan: I wasn't sure what the terrain was like across the isthmus, as my maps were too limited to give that kind of detail. If it turned out to be, say, impossibly thick willows, or some other difficult terrain, a portage there might turn out to be more trouble than it was worth. At any rate, once I'd committed to it, there was no going back, as to paddle all the way back around the square peninsula would take nearly five hours, depending on the wind.

Through hazy weather I paddled down a steadily narrowing bay, passing rocks and willows and tundra. When I reached the end I'd come to a little bit of sand, above which rose eroded banks covered in willows, moss, lichens, and other arctic plants. It looked promising. I strapped on my backpack and set off across the pathless tundra.

The plan worked out better than I could have hoped: it proved an easy portage over flat ground that was a bit marshy in places, but otherwise no problem. There was even a pond in the middle to break up the trek, which I paddled across. The only downside was that the wind had faded, allowing an unbelievable number of black-flies to viciously attack my neck, wrists, face, and anywhere else they could get at.

While the flies were swarming me, there was something else I noticed while making the multiple trips across the isthmus. The willow shrubs had been grazed down; an indication of muskox, and sure enough I found some of their big hooved tracks in the moss. I needed to refill my water bottle, but I was reluctant to do it anywhere near where herds of muskox were about. Months of drinking untreated water had so far had no ill effect on me. Consuming as I did lots of water every day, I'd long since ceased to worry about it.

However, given the signs of muskox in the area, I decided to play it safe and wait until I made camp, when I could boil up several pots of water to purify it. It had been a long, hard day, and by the time I'd finished the portage, riddled with blackfly bites, I was eager to halt for the night. My camp, too, I selected with more than usual care. While the tracks indicated there were muskox about, by this point in my various arctic wanderings I'd seen over a hundred of them, and they didn't seem like anything more than gentle giants. The only trouble one had ever given me was the big bull that had woken me up a couple months earlier on the Mackenzie River. And even that big bull had run away at the crack of a bear-banger. Still, when I can, I prefer to err on the side of caution. So I decided to make my camp a little less exposed to muskox.

One thing I'd noticed about muskox, from regular run-ins with them, was that they were strangely unobservant. It often seemed they didn't notice me at all until they were ten feet away; with their head down grazing, they seemed almost dopey, or poor-sighted. Sometimes they would almost stumble into me before noticing my presence.

So, to avoid startling any muskox that might wander by, I decided to make my camp more easily visible. Normally, I was reluctant to sleep on any kind of hill, preferring to camp in low-lying areas to minimize lightning hazards. But, scanning the skies, I saw no hint of thunder-storms, so I figured I'd put my tent on a small sand hill near the water's edge. That would make it readily visible, and hopefully help grazing muskox avoid stumbling into it. I also carried my canoe up the hill, flipping it over beside my tent, and I put the two barrels on the other side, to form a sort of perimeter fence. With the brightly coloured barrels, overturned canoe, and a smoky willow fire to help drive off the bugs, I figured the camp was secure.

I crawled into my tent, feeling as comfortable as I'd been in days, and soon drifted off to sleep.

✳

Probably the most horrifying noise I've ever heard was the one that awoke me around four a.m. sleeping on that sand hill. A thundering half-roar, half-snort erupted from immediately outside my tent, jarring me wide awake. I knew there was only one animal that could have made such a powerful snort: a muskox. I'd heard bulls bellow in farmer's fields before, but compared to the snorting roar outside my tent, those bulls sounded like mere frogs.

Still, I wasn't too alarmed. I'd been sleeping alone in the wilderness for months, and I'd seen little to make me think muskox were aggressive. So I unzipped the tent door a few inches to peek out, expecting to see a muskox gently grazing on the tundra, its back to me.

Only that's not what I saw. Instead, through the unzipped opening, I saw a huge muskox ten feet away, horns curved, nostrils flaring, glaring with its huge eyes right at my tent.

Now, if you've read survival manuals, you'll know they'll often say never make eye contact with a big wild animal, because that's apparently triggering something in its brain to see you as challenging its dominance and will supposedly encourage it to respond aggressively.

But I'm not sure how you're supposed to avoid making eye contact when you just peep out through a crack in a tent door and you see glaring right back at you a giant muskox. The big muskox suddenly snorted again and pawed at the ground, taking up what looked unmistakably like an attack pose. In response, I quickly zipped up the tent.

Unfortunately, it didn't seem at all structurally possible that the tent door would withstand a muskox charge. So I looked frantically around my tent for some means of protection. There was no way I was going to fire off a bear banger, not with the beast that close. Nor did it seem wise to attempt using bear spray on a muskox of such enormous proportions.

My eyes scanned the tent for anything that might be of help. Then I saw my lifejacket, half-buried under my spare clothes as an extra pillow. "Ah ha!" I thought, and snatched up the lifejacket. Hurriedly I threw it on and zipped it up. "Now I've at least got some padding on my body," I thought to myself. "If the muskox charges into my tent and tramples it, this padding will help shield me."

Of course, the rational side of my brain was immediately dismissing this as nonsense that wouldn't do any good to protect me from a half-ton creature trampling over my internal organs. But just now, I was disinclined to listen to that side of my brain, and instead let the non-rational side have its say.

Anything it seemed was a comfort in those tense seconds that I expected a charge to come. I made myself as small as possible, huddling and pulling my knees up to my chest—when the bull plowed through I didn't want to be caught lying down. Maybe with luck I could jump aside before one of his horns caught me.

Just then another snort erupted from outside the tent; it sounded mercilessly close. I think the creature was actually sniffing around the edges of the tent—though I didn't dare unzip the door again to peek. Next I heard its hooves stomp as it trotted around to the other side of my tent.

This was at least an improvement, as that was the side my canoe was overturned on. Now at least there was some barrier between us, even if the canoe wasn't much of one.

When the sounds of hooves hitting the ground and grunting ceased, an unnerving silence followed. I chanced a slight unzipping of the door on the side nearest the canoe, only to zip it right back up again. The muskox was still right outside, just beyond the canoe, still glaring straight at the tent. I tried to guess what it was thinking—maybe it's an old bull with bad eyesight, that's mistaken my grey tent for a fellow male muskox, and now he thinks the tent is here to challenge his dominance of the herd?

I sat still, not daring to make a sound. In other encounters with animals outside my tent, I'd shout to scare them off, but that was always under the assumption they were skittish and had just timidly wandered into my camp, whereas there was no mistaking this muskox. It had come right up the hill, aggressively snorting. I sat there for what felt like an eternity (but I think was probably much less), preparing myself to jump out of the way the second the tent began to collapse from the muskox's charge.

A second later I heard galloping hooves and loud snorting—*the charge had begun.*

Only it sounded like it was going the other way. Quickly I unzipped the door to see: there was the muskox, galloping noisily off in the opposite direction, down the hill toward the lake. Then he splashed into the water, making what seemed to me like a very ostentatious shaking of his head, before charging off down the lakeshore and out of view.

For some reason I had a sudden urge to break camp immediately, having decided not to sleep in any later. I wasted no time in doing so, and was soon paddling as far away up the lake as I could.

✳

Two long, hard days of paddling brought me across the huge expanses of Aylmer Lake and then Clinton-Colden Lake. There were some large and somewhat stressful open-water crossings that I had to make, but the relatively light wind allowed me to manage it. Meanwhile, except at midday when the north winds picked up, the strange haze from the distant forest fires remained. It felt like paddling through a kind of twilight zone—during the worst of the haze, the sun was only a faint orange orb, dimly visible.

What caused me somewhat more consternation than the haze was the no-less-than fourteen different muskox I counted wandering the shorelines. In the haze, their great curved horns, shaggy coats, and odd appearance was accentuated, making them seem as though they'd wandered out of some fantasy land. I kind of half wished they'd wander back into it, for the time being at least, so that I might sleep easier. I found it difficult to sleep as peacefully as I was accustomed to after the experience of the night before. Still, it wasn't the night that held real terror; it was the day. Nothing scared me as much as the high winds and whitecaps on the exposed lakes. These posed a far greater danger than any wildlife did.

Bird life was becoming scarcer now; although I saw mergansers, arctic terns, loons, and Canada geese, many of the songbirds and shorebirds had already sensed the change in the weather and begun their migration south. The result was a much quieter land than what the cheerful singing of the birds had made for in the spring. The caribou, or reindeer, for they're the same species (reindeer is what the animals are called in Europe), seemed curious about me, sometimes pausing to stare at me as I paddled by.

By August 15 I'd reached the last of the big lakes and begun a series of four portages across a collection of smaller lakes, which would take me across the great divide of Canada's North—the last watershed divide of my journey. You wouldn't know it to look at it: there's no dramatic mountain range, no roaring torrent. It's just a flat spit of tundra with boulders and rocks and a little willow-choked stream. On one side of the divide all the water drains north to the Arctic Ocean; on the other the water flows east, to Hudson Bay. And it was east I had to go.

The four separate portages between various small lakes totalled only about a kilometre, but with my four loads (I was back to four after the resupply) the actual distance I had to cover on foot was, again, seven times that—after which, I'd have crossed the great divide of the North. (These portages are known as "Hanbury's portage" after David Hanbury, the naturalist and explorer who'd passed this way in 1899.)

Aside from the jumbles of rocks and some uneven ground, I found most of the terrain easily navigated. When I'd finished my last load across the final portage, sweaty and bug-bitten, it did feel like a watershed moment in my journey. I'd begun nearly three months before in the Bering Sea watershed, and now I was on my way to the tides of Hudson Bay. There were still, at minimum, another eight hundred kilometres in front of me before I could reach the end, but I took heart in the knowledge that it would all be downriver from here.

✕ 18 ✕

CANYON COUNTRY

By August 16 the change in the seasons had become clear. The caribou were heading south to the trees; the geese and most other birds would soon follow. The leaves of the bearberries had begun to turn red, and the willows were fast fading to yellow. Soon the whole tundra would be a blaze of autumn colours, with chilling frosts, shorter days, and bitterly cold winds. Looking at the crimson and yellow hills outside my tent, I thought to myself, "It's all very beautiful." Then I thought, "I really need to get a move on."

I was perched on a small rocky ledge overlooking a little river where I'd camped the night before. I'd almost reached Sifton Lake, a star-like labyrinth of long, twisting bays easy to get lost in. In my backpack I had a photocopied government report of a canoe journey that had started from Sifton Lake and ended at the little community of Baker Lake, my own end point. A floatplane had dropped the party at Sifton Lake on August 2, 1972. It had taken them forty days to reach Baker Lake, arriving on September 11.

If I could equal their pace I'd finish my journey by September 25. Again, though, there were two of them per canoe and only one of me; plus they'd started two weeks earlier in the season. And if bad winds held me up I might not arrive until October—at which point winter would have also arrived, and with it blinding snows, gale-force winds, hand-numbing temperatures, and lakes icing up.

The details in their report weren't all that encouraging about the winds after mid-August:

> It is advisable to plan the trip for July ending during the first two weeks in August to assure the best weather. After mid-August, the weather can be very unpredictable and the party may be forced to abandon any schedule to wait out stormy days. Winds are the biggest factor to contend with on the Barrens. Without the trees as a wind break and over the wide expanses of the 193 km of open lake a party may be windbound up to 10 days at a stretch.

In other words, since I was only just beginning the route and it was already August 16, I could expect dangerous winds the whole way. Their report had also helpfully noted that:

> Winds can build up very rough waters . . . swamping in heavy waves or violent rapids could prove fatal. With little wood fuel for a fire to dry out wet clothes canoeists must be very cautious in their movements.

Now more than ever I thought of the tortoise and the hare as my guiding philosophy. The late season and bad winds were beyond my control. But, I reasoned, I would put in longer days, slow and steady, cutting down on sleep if need be.

Hard paddling brought me clear across the spidery bays of Sifton Lake, which was surrounded by rock-strewn boulder fields in many places. Beyond that, in all directions, lay thousands of lakes gouged out by ancient glaciers.

Leaving Sifton Lake, I arrived on the Hanbury River (named for the same Hanbury alluded to earlier): a river with violent whitewater, numerous deep canyons, falls, and cliffs. It's a dangerous river, and one perhaps not best attempted alone and late in the season. The river's fast-flowing, turbulent narrow stretches alternate with many sections of big, wide-open lakes where wind would be an issue.

Thunderstorms and overcast skies marked much of the first part of my advance through these maze-like lakes of the upper Hanbury. Fortunately, the storms occurred mostly overnight when I was warm and dry inside my tent. I avoided camping on any high rocky areas, of which there were many, setting up my tent in low-lying, willowy areas whenever I could find them.

The route next took me toward violent rapids and dangerous waterfalls. These required multiple portages to evade. The last of these portages was a long and difficult one; the total distance I had to trek on foot to avoid impassable rapids and falls was about a kilometre and a half, which, as usual, took four loads and seven trips to complete. The trek alternated between high, windswept rocky outcrops, which often involved careful scrambling to climb and descend (especially with a canoe in the high winds), and low-lying, swampy areas where blackflies still reigned.

But there were cloudberries scattered across the still-green tundra like little yellow-orange jewels, which I feasted on happily. The crop of these berries is brief; soon they'd begin to fade away.

More windy lakes followed, and more big rapids. When I'd crossed another big, round lake and arrived at the start of a second narrow stretch of turbulent river, I saw my first opportunity to save some time and get a leg up on things. (I thought I'd been too cautious the day before when I'd first come to rapids and falls, and probably could have shortened the lengthy, gruelling portage with some wading, lining, and paddling between the worst parts of the rapids.) At first it looked like I was in for another kilometre-and-a-half long portage, to avoid dangerous, unnavigable rapids. I'd strapped on my backpack and hiked for about a kilometre along willow-covered hills, keeping an eye on the roaring river below. But then I noticed that, between two major sections of violent whitewater, the river didn't look too bad: just minor rapids, swifts, and rocky sections. I figured I could paddle these parts or else line and wade them, and thereby greatly lessen the length of the portage. So I scampered down a steep hillside to the river below, scouted things out again, assured myself it could be done, then left my backpack on shore. I'd pick it up in the canoe when I came down through the swifts and boulder fields above. The only catch was to make sure I didn't paddle too far and get swept down into the massive, foaming cauldron of water below.

It was a little tricky in sections, given the extensive rocks and currents, but I zigzagged around them and cut across to the opposite shore above the dangerous, seething stretch of water. Here I portaged over a steep hill to get around the thundering rapids, resuming my travels safely beyond them.

Now the river passed through more variously narrow and wider parts, the latter more like lakes where the wind gave me some stiff opposition. But I paddled hard, and aided by the current, continued downriver through rocky rapids, coming eventually to the most startling sandy hills and deserts I'd ever seen—looking more like the Sahara than northern Canada. It was a strange landscape, with windswept sandy barrens that extended for kilometres.

But the river's course was highly variable; beyond the sand barrens were green hills rapidly changing to red and yellow with the fall colours, and ancient, weathered rock outcrops. With the shorebirds gone it sounded strangely quiet, adding to the sense of desolation within the river sections that were dominated by sand barrens. As hours passed in silence, I'd feel less lonely whenever I spotted some lingering ducks or tundra swans. The sight of a bald eagle soaring overhead cheered me up, as did the return of vegetation along the river.

The cloudberries were nearly done now; their bright orange berries quickly fade to sickly yellow and turn to mush. But there were still plenty of arctic blueberries, and these I ate as much as I could. I made camp on a small lake the river passed through, on what I considered a very attractive little tundra site above some rocks. A warm cup of tea was my reward after what had been a long, hard day of portaging and paddling.

✳

The following morning I awoke to fierce, cold winds of the sort that would normally rule out any kind of canoeing. Given the circumstances, I resolved to push on as best I could. A very exhausting paddle brought me across a three-kilometre-long lake-like section of the river I'd camped on. But given the extreme winds, it felt more like a thirty-kilometre paddle. Fortunately this wide section emptied into a canyon that helped shelter me from the howling winds. The canyon had nothing but minor rapids in it, allowing me to travel quickly down through it with no trouble.

Perched nearby this canyon were two little metal-sided cabins. These had been there for some time, as they were mentioned in the 1972 report as belonging to federal government water scientists (who accessed the river by floatplane). I had neither time nor inclination to investigate them as I whizzed by below in the canyon on the swift current. The fast-moving water brought me to a big, windy, and wave-tossed expanse known as Hoare Lake. This was the last significant lake I'd pass through for some time; afterward the river narrowed for a long way. As such, I was eager to get through it as quickly as I could, to escape from the big whitecaps that had been a constant cause of anxiety to me while crossing dozens of exposed, windy lakes over the past several weeks.

When I entered its waters a gusting northwest wind was sending big waves rolling across its expanse. It's always hard to judge the size of waves—frequently I find they turn out to be bigger than they looked from a distance. Seated in my canoe, paddling near shore where the river emptied into the lake, my eyes searched the water, trying to determine which way to head and whether I could safely cross in such fierce winds and waves. Hoare Lake is shaped like an upside-down T; I had to get across it and down the stem of the T. Crossing the open lake would mean having the waves hit my canoe broadside, which didn't sound too encouraging. There was a good chance, too, that the wind would overpower my paddling efforts and carry me down to the far end of the lake, away from where I needed to reach. But if I didn't cross, instead tracing out the shoreline, that would mean paddling into powerful headwinds, draining my energy, and eating up valuable time.

The best plan, it seemed, was to paddle into the headwinds only a short way and then pivot, allowing the force of the waves to do the work for me—carrying me across the lake until I could peel off and head for the stem of the T. It would be much safer than trying to bee-line straight across.

My plan set, I devoured some jerky and dried fruit, drank some water, and tightened the Velcro straps on my gloves. To steer in the waves, I was using my straight-shaft paddle, as I found the bent-shaft one was effective only on calm water. Setting off against the howling winds I began by using the land to my advantage. There was a long island in the lake whose lee side blocked me from the worst of the big waves, so I set my course diagonally up the island's shore. Once past it, I was into the whitecaps.

"Here we go," I said to the canoe, drawing powerful strokes to launch it forward into the waves. The canoe's bow rode over them, reaching into the air, then back down as we plowed through each swell. It was exhausting, but I didn't have to make it far—a few more strokes and I made my move. Timing it between surges, I executed a quick pivot, turning to ride the waves. Now I could paddle easier, letting the wind carry me swiftly across the lake with me steering.

The final bit would be the hardest: I'd have to temporarily turn broadside into the waves to make the dash up into the north bay (the stem of the T). The waves jostled me a bit but I paddled hard and steady, stroke after stroke, until I was out of the heart of the lake and well up into the safety of the bay where the waves were smaller. A few more minutes of hard paddling and I'd left the lake behind and was heading back down the Hanbury River's narrow confines.

It was a relief to be back on a closed-in river. I zoomed along as fast as I could, running rapids whenever they appeared. But the wind was not to be placated. It grew stronger and stronger, roaring across the rocky hills and wide-open tundra. The wind was so fierce it soon overpowered the river's current and my paddling, to the point where I was actually just spinning round and round in the river, like a corkscrew, as even the combined force of the current and my paddling could no longer make headway against the wind.

This called for a new strategy. I landed on shore to rest and rethink things. To overcome the wind I'd need to shift everything I could up to the bow of the canoe, concentrating the weight near the front. This would help the bow sit lower in the water, thus catching less of the wind, and the extra weight front-loaded would make it easier for me to propel the canoe downriver against the wind. At least, visualizing it on the bank, that's how I figured it'd work.

I shifted everything I could to the front, and shoved off from shore. This proved the difference I needed, and I was able to keep paddling despite the tremendous gusts. But hard paddling, even with the strong current, was necessary just to keep the boat going downriver. If I tried to drift, the wind would just push me back upriver or into the banks.

The river's course eventually brought me to a desolate scene of expansive sand barrens, where the sand swirled on the force of the winds. In the distance loomed great sand and rock hills, which looked in my imagination like some stark post-apocalyptic landscape. The grey, dismal skies only added to the effect of these sandy deserts that stretched as far as the eye could see. From the satellite imagery I knew one of the sandy plains extended nearly four kilometres, with still other desert wastes lying beyond it. The permafrost in these regions, I figured, prevent trees from growing while the relentless winds strip away any thin topsoil, exposing the sand.

The winds had grown fiercer yet, to the point where, even with my canoe reloaded, paddling became impossible. Still, I couldn't afford to stop, knowing as I did that summer was over, and that fall had come to the tundra. So I beached the canoe, put away my paddle, and grabbed the bow rope. With my waders on I continued on foot, splashing along in the shallows and dragging the canoe behind me. The winds were cold, and by now I was wearing my wool toque, gloves, and had the collar of my jacket flipped up to protect my face from the blowing sands.

Staggering on like this was slow progress, but advancing even a few kilometres an hour was better than nothing. Yet the weather continued to deteriorate. The winds were so loud I couldn't hear myself think. On shore was a small patch of green willows. Farther ahead I could see nothing but miles of sandy desert, which didn't seem an encouraging place to camp in high winds. So I took advantage of this last patch of soil to halt early for the night.

I staked my tent down in the securest place I could find, which on the tundra really wasn't all that secure. I'd had storms blow down my tents before, but this one, once it was staked down and secured with guy lines, was marvellously strong. The wind shook it violently but it held steady. Even boiling water on the camp stove was difficult; I had to use my canoe and barrels to shelter it from the winds. After a bit of tea and a freeze-dried dinner, I hunkered down in my tent for a stormy night.

※

In the early morning I woke to lashing rain and screaming gales shaking my tent. It didn't seem like very good canoeing weather. So I slept in a bit, as I didn't want to take down the tent in such a downpour, since doing so would mean getting the inside wet. And the wind was too extreme for paddling. Hours passed with no letup in the rain and wind, and I noticed with some disappointment that water was beginning to pool inside my tent in a corner. This was from the sheer force of the wind, which was pressing down the outer rain fly, buckling the tent poles and forcing the drenched fly to press against the tent itself, causing rain to soak through and drip in. The tent, on the whole, was admirably well designed—rain alone couldn't get in, nor could the winds knock it down—but the combination of continuous heavy rain and fierce winds is something no tent can withstand indefinitely.

But fortunately, I'd spent my teenage years camping and tramping across wilderness with a twenty-dollar Canadian Tire tent, so I'd become somewhat accustomed to putting up with a little water inside a tent, and always made light of it. Some of my fondest memories were of my friend Wes and I stranded on miserable islands on far-flung lakes, enduring terrible thunderstorms in that ragged, threadbare little tent. When I reached my twenties I went through a phase in which I didn't bother with tents anymore, preferring to sleep in the open or in shelters I'd fix up on the spot (it's a phase I imagine everyone goes through at some point). This, too, I associated with all sorts of fond memories of adventures far and wide. Eventually, I don't know if I went a little soft, but I invested in higher-quality tents and rode out countless storms in them.

So, on the whole, I judged my tent's performance excellent and didn't too much mind the bit of water that had pooled inside it. I was still warm and dry, and my sleeping bag was dry too, which was the main thing to be concerned about. I also had an emergency blanket that I kept specifically for spreading out inside my tent if the water became problematic.

By mid-morning the rain had slackened enough that I decided to make a dash for it—breaking camp, getting the tent rolled up and secured, and my canoe packed. The wind was still too fierce for paddling, so I took the bow rope in hand and waded ahead, towing the canoe behind me. The desolate sand flats continued for miles.

Wading was painfully slow, not only because of the fierce winds, but because I sank into the soft sand with every step. In one place, because of steadily deepening water that I couldn't wade through, I had no choice but to paddle across in the high winds to the river's opposite side. This allowed me to continue wading and towing the canoe. The landscape was dominated by immense ridges made of fine white sand, dunes, and vast windswept desert plains. In places, distant mountains loomed on the horizon. When I made it through the last of the sand barrens I found I could paddle again with hard effort, as some hills helped partially shelter the river from the winds.

It was necessary to run a couple of rapids, which in calm weather would have been a simple matter, but in the high winds required considerably more determined paddling to avoid slamming into protruding rocks. Not far beyond these I came to a small canyon with a roaring waterfall that halted my progress. Here the river squeezed between narrow jagged rocks, crashing loudly over a three-metre, or ten-foot, fall into a pool, then on to smaller cascades over boulders below.

A short portage of a few hundred metres enabled me to safely bypass the falls and cascades, and also gave me time to snack on blueberries. In high winds, one thing I always made sure to do, before setting off with my various loads, was to secure the canoe well onshore. If a wind gust caught it, the canoe might easily flip over and tumble into the river, getting swept over the falls and destroyed. The portage was fairly easy, aside from carrying the canoe over my head in the wind. The gusts made me stagger back and forth with it, but the ground was mostly free of obstacles and I completed it in good time. Just a short distance ahead, however, I knew was a much longer and more difficult canyon.

Less than a kilometre of paddling and wading across a wide pool, with sandy beaches and a few clumps of stunted black spruce tucked in valleys out of the winds, brought me to the start of another jagged canyon. I had to approach it cautiously, as the current was strong immediately above it, but I wanted to get as close as I safely could before beginning what promised to be a long and arduous portage to bypass it.

Where I landed the canoe the entire river was funnelling into a narrow chasm cut through sharp, jagged rocks that looked like something from another planet. The whole scene seemed frightfully apocalyptic. A waterfall marked the start of the chasm, which continued beneath the narrow canyon walls for several hundred metres until it disappeared around an S-bend. I knew from my maps that the canyon was nearly three kilometres long, punctuated with numerous violent rapids, waterfalls, and more S-bends. To portage around it, I figured I could cut diagonally across some of the river's snaking course, but that would still necessitate a more than two-kilometre portage over rough terrain. And with my four loads, the total distance I'd have to cover would come out to about sixteen kilometres. Such a long portage would have to be broken into stages, and I suspected I'd have to break it up over a day.

I strapped on my backpack, setting off on the first leg. My trek began with some scrambling over rocks and boulders before reaching more hospitable ground that had enough soil for dwarf birch and berries to grow; this level tundra then led me to a steep, rugged range of green hills. I climbed up the first slope, picking my way carefully in the wind. When I reached the rocky summit I had a better view of the snaking course of the nearby canyon.

It had an utterly wild aspect about it—like something primordial, from the very dawn of the earth. Seething, violent rapids raged beneath its jagged walls that twisted through repeated S-bends. Inside the shadows of the upper canyon, amid the swirling, surging dark waters, rose a towering pillar of ancient rock.

I continued my trek down the hill and along the rim of the canyon, hiking as near to the edge as I dared. It was amazingly narrow, just a deep chasm cut into the earth; whitewater frothed and roared some thirty metres below where I stood. When I became worn out with trekking, I rested to drink water and snack on the last of the fading cloudberries along with some blueberries, crowberries, and lingonberries. The skies had stayed dark; rain fell intermittently. I hiked on through willows, up and down ridges, cutting away from the snaking course of the canyon on a diagonal at times to shorten the total distance.

When I reached a flat plain with short grasses, opposite the canyon's third S-bend—this one concealing a large roaring waterfall tossing mist high up in the air—I set down my backpack. That was far enough for one stage of this long portage. It would take the remainder of the day just to transport the two barrels and the canoe to this spot—although that last was doubtful. It seemed that once more my friend and I might have to spend the night apart.

I managed to get my two barrels across, trekking back and forth four more times after my initial trip with the backpack. My first trip had purposefully been more meandering, as my curiosity about the canyon had led me along it rather than veering off on a more direct route.

I set up my tent on the tundra, made another quick dinner, and then dove inside just before more rain fell. On cold, stormy nights, my tent seemed more homelike than ever. Feeling a little sore and weary from the repeated portaging of the day, I stretched out comfortably in my sleeping bag and drifted off listening to the hypnotic-sounding roar of the distant waterfalls.

✳

In the rain the next morning I carried my canoe over the high rocky hills and across the plains to my camp. Up in the high country, it was a struggle to hold it tight and maintain my balance in the gusting wind. It made me think of a passage in the explorer John Franklin's journal in which he described one of his Canadian voyageurs portaging their canoe on the tundra only to lose his balance in a wind gust, smashing the canoe off rocks as he fell. Things hadn't ended very well for any of them after that.

Fortunately, my portage went better. Once I reached my camp I set the canoe down, taking up my backpack in its place to scout out the rest of the way forward. It proved another meandering kilometre of travel: across a mix of level tundra, over high, windswept ridges, then down up to my knees in swampy lowlands and alder thickets over my head. This was followed by sandy plains and dunes, then finally another stretch of rock-strewn tundra to a steep eroded bank where I could resume paddling. When I'd finished transporting all my loads across this kaleidoscope of landscapes, I was underway paddling again.

But this lasted only a few minutes before I came to another wild, dangerous canyon that couldn't be navigated. To make the arduous portage as short as possible, I paddled as close to the start of the turbulent water as I dared, snaking between great boulder slabs and cliffs. When it felt unsafe to go any farther by water, I climbed onto the rocky cliffs and, holding on to the bow rope, escorted my canoe along in the swift current below. Just before the start of the violent cascading rapids, I pulled into a little cove.

But portaging up and out of the cove proved an exhausting struggle. This sheltered valley hid a small grove of black spruce, alders, and willows, which required some difficult climbing up steep slopes to get through. The canoe I had to haul up from the bow, heaving and pulling to get it up the slope through the thicket. The terrain was thick with spruces and willows; strangely, the wind died just at this moment, allowing bugs to magically rematerialize and attack my face.

I ended this difficult portage by descending another steep slope to a rocky beach. There was still a half-kilometre more of boulder-strewn rapids I hadn't bypassed, but with the wind down they didn't pose too much trouble. So I reloaded the canoe and carefully paddled my way through the rapids, passing huge boulders of red sandstone as I went.

It wasn't long before I reached yet another canyon—this one concealed a considerable plunging waterfall of some forty feet, and demanded yet another strenuous portage. It was late and rainy, so I decided to save this portage for the morning. I figured I'd used up my portage quota for the day.

When morning arrived I was up early—hauling my canoe and three other loads around this last canyon, passing a plunging waterfall tossing spray into the air. Nesting peregrine falcons along the canyon flew up to yap at me with their shrill calls, telling me to be on my way. I told them I was moving as fast as I could.

The portage was a long one, about two kilometres (or fourteen kilometres total with all the trips). The problem was that after bypassing the falls I couldn't get back down into the canyon easily. The water below was tranquil, but steep rock cliffs meant there was no easy way down to it.

Eventually I came to a less steep gravel slope; although still precipitous, it seemed safe enough. The trickiest load was the canoe, which I had to balance over my head. Angling sideways, I picked my way carefully among the loose stones and gravel, descending the slope to great slabs of rock that jutted into the river.

Here I happened upon an unexpected sight—a pile of abandoned gear. It included three large backpacks crammed full, a plastic canoe barrel, some old, rusted empty fuel cans, and a bag of garbage. From what I could tell, the stuff looked as though it had been sitting there for years. Had someone simply littered in a place like this?

The story the gear told seemed clear: a party of canoeists coming downriver apparently hadn't been prepared for just how lengthy and gruelling the many portages around the river's canyons were, and dumped their gear here to lighten their loads. If this conjecture was true, it was ironic: this was the Hanbury River's final canyon, meaning they'd needlessly littered (and tossed away valuable gear) to no purpose.

The only alternative that seemed possible was that something had gone badly wrong, and the party had needed an emergency evacuation, abandoning their gear in haste. Given the dangerous falls upriver, it didn't require too much imagination to guess what that might have involved, or else the steep cliffs were perfect for breaking an ankle on. Still other possibilities could have been a different sort of medical emergency, like an allergic reaction to a bee sting. One of the worst accidents I'd heard of involved a party of canoeists on the Coppermine River that had left their propane-butane fuel canisters too close to a campfire. The resulting explosion had caused severe injuries that required an emergency airlift.

An acquaintance of mine, an air force pilot, once told me about the search-and-rescue missions that are part of his job in the Arctic. I was surprised when he told me that the majority didn't involve canoe expeditions at all, but rather locals from the scattered little towns, who, out for a day trip hunting or fishing by snowmobile or motorboat, became lost or stranded. It's a reminder of how easy it is for anyone to get lost or turned around in such a vast landscape.

In any case, I concluded that my first theory was the most likely one and that this abandoned assortment of a barrel, backpacks, and fuel cans was simply from litterbugs. (There were no canoes or paddles left behind, and the pile looked deliberately left at the end of a portage rather than hastily ditched.) As such, I couldn't help but feel a bit of annoyance at whomever had littered in a place like this. I try to tread as lightly as I can: even that unwieldy and ineffective cart I lugged for miles so I could put it on the floatplane rather than abandon it somewhere, and my barrels included my sealed-up wrappers.

My canoe reloaded, I set off downriver, passing cliffs, sand bars, and eroded rock pillars rising along the banks like castle turrets. Paddling the remainder of the river was easily done, with only a few smaller swifts to get through. I pushed on, taking advantage of the calm conditions, until I came to an impressive sight: the Hanbury River's confluence with a much larger waterway, the last of my journey—the storied Thelon.

× 19 ×

DOWN THE THELON

The Thelon River, at about nine hundred kilometres long, is one of the largest rivers draining into Hudson Bay. Where I entered it the Thelon was over a half-kilometre wide, with impressive white sandstone cliffs on its far shore. It was the biggest river I'd seen since the Mackenzie. I paddled for some thirty kilometres down it, before making camp for the night on its western bank. Just beyond the river were high hills and ridges, which gave it a closed-in feel, as though it was somehow its own little world in the midst of thousands of kilometres of northern wilderness.

I slept soundly, more so than usual, except that I dreamed I'd fallen into some water.

Sometime later I awoke to water pooling on my head. My lifejacket was soaked; my hair was wet; the sides of the tent were drenched. But I heard no rain. Had the river risen in the night? I sat up and unzipped the tent door to see what was going on.

What I saw was nothing at all—an impenetrably thick mist had smothered everything. It was the thickest mist I'd ever seen, so thick as to seem less a mist than an actual raincloud that had fallen to the earth. The mist had drenched my tent until, heavy with the weight of water, it began dripping from the ceiling and soaking my head.

Breaking camp proved a little more difficult than normal, as I couldn't see more than a few feet in any direction. I'd camped inland from the riverbank, and had to carefully wander down through the mist with each of my loads to the water's edge.

When I pushed off into the water, my only option was to hug the shoreline, as with the mist I couldn't see anything. It felt a bit eerie, alone in the wild, paddling a canoe inside what felt like a cloud, unable to see the sky, across the river, or ahead or behind. At least there wasn't any wind.

Eventually the mist cleared, or actually, it didn't—I simply passed beyond it, as once I'd come out of the cloud, I could look back along the river and see the edge of the mist from which I'd emerged. It was an odd feeling, as if a magician had cast some spell on that part of the river, shrouding it in thick mist that abruptly ended at an exact point.

Now that I was in the open, immediately beyond the mist, I realized that it was actually a sunny day with glorious blue skies. With the fair weather, my progress was rapid. I paddled steadily downriver, passing two bull moose standing together—which was unusual, as normally moose are solitary animals. I also met with a handsome caribou swimming across the river, and another on the bank with glossy, velvet-like fur and impressive antlers. There were still large numbers of waterfowl: mergansers, Canada geese, tundra swans, and, most common of all, white snow geese. But in a few weeks they'd all be heading south.

The river snaked through numerous islands, presenting a choice of channels to take. I generally stuck to the east. For my first several days along it, the Thelon flowed in a northerly course before trending eastward then north again. That second night, as I was making camp, I was delighted to find a perfectly shaped slab of rock: it served as a wonderful kitchen table. Cooking with my stove was easier, and the rock table allowed me to spread my things out nicely. It was as fine a table as I'd ever seen.

The winds, however, soon returned. A misty morning the following day turned into a blustery afternoon, with roaring headwinds that eliminated any sense of travelling downriver. Instead I had to paddle with all my strength just to make progress. The wind was so bad that it actually created reverse whitecaps in the river, a bizarre experience that required me to run rapids kindled solely by the wind. The canoe's bow crashed over them, cresting into the air before plowing back down into the waves.

Back in 1927 the Thelon was the scene of a famous tragedy. An eccentric trapper from an upper-class background named Jack Hornby had made plans to canoe the Thelon and overwinter there. Hornby was a veteran of the Western Front's trenches and seemed almost to have a death wish, confessing as much in some of his letters. The year before, while portaging through a canyon on the Hanbury River, he was nearly killed by a landslide. And now he was ignoring conventional wisdom by seeking to overwinter on the isolated Thelon rather than in the more hospitable forested lands to the southwest, where other trappers made their cabins.

There's a notable grove of spruces on the Thelon's bank, a natural oasis where black spruce are able to take root, surrounded by windswept plains in all directions. It was this grove where Hornby planned to survive the harsh winter. With him were two companions: another war veteran, twenty-seven-year-old Harold Adlard, and Hornby's eighteen-year-old nephew, Edgar Christian.

The record of what befell them is told through the faded pages of Christian's diary, which was discovered years later stashed away in their crude cabin's iron stove. The trio canoed north through Great Slave Lake, eventually arriving at the remote spruce grove on the Thelon. Here, in the fall of 1926, they built a small cabin. They planned to survive the winter on caribou and anything else they could hunt or trap—a dangerous plan, since living off the land usually requires a nomadic lifestyle in order to follow the caribou herds. But unlike most trappers, the three didn't have a dogsled team, and as a result were tethered to a small radius around their cabin.

By April they were mere skeletal figures, surviving off scraps of hide and discarded bones they dug up in the snow from their earlier hunts. By April 10 Hornby, the only one with much experience in the

North, was dead from starvation. The others, too weak to do anything else, wrapped his body in blankets and left it just outside the cabin. Eighteen days later, Adlard followed Hornby's fate. Christian continued to struggle on, living off bones and hides. Then he made his final, half-coherent diary entry: "June 1st, Got out too weak and all in now. Left Things Late." He died in the cabin.

A year later, in the summer of 1928, a four-person prospecting party was exploring the Thelon by canoe when they spotted the crude cabin set back from the river's edge. One member of the party, Ken Dewar, a McGill University graduate student, recalled what happened next: "There was no immediate signs of life and the place looked as though it had been deserted for some time . . . To the right of the cabin door were two objects all wrapped up, lying on the ground . . . From the shape they appeared to be skeletons . . . There was one way to be sure of this so I took a knife and made a slit in both objects and revealed the two skulls. They had been dead a long time."

Next Dewar and his three companions entered the musty cabin. It appeared deserted, but with the crack of light from the doorway Dewar went over to the bunks. He recalled: "The right-hand bunk appeared to have something under the blanket so I gave the blanket a slight pull . . . the bones of two feet fell off the foot of the bunk and the skull rolled off to the side." The bones terrified the men. "When the bones fell off the bed we were of one mind: *Let's get the hell out of here.*" They set off paddling downriver, putting as many miles between themselves and the haunted cabin as they could.

Not until the following year did a party of RCMP officers, after months of canoeing from Great Slave Lake, arrive at the isolated site. The officers found the skeletons and buried them in shallow graves beside the cabin. Inside, the officers noted something Dewar's group had missed: on top of the cast-iron stove was a scrap of paper with the weak, faintly scrawled words "WHO . . . LOOK IN STOVE." This turned out to be, apparently, a dying note from young Christian. Inside the stove the officers found his diary telling the tragic tale.

✳

I didn't have time to stop and investigate the remnants of the cabin or the graves, although I liked the idea that their ghosts still haunted the grove. My thoughts were on the fierce winds and the notoriously stormy lakes of large size that lay toward the end of the Thelon's course that I'd have to get through.

On August 25 I put in a thirteen-hour day of paddling, passing many sandy beaches and one giant island, all while battling headwinds and side winds. In the afternoon the wind shifted in my favour, and for one glorious hour I actually sailed, flying along at great speed. The wind soon shifted though, and back I went to paddling. But the sail had certainly cheered me.

But what really excited me was approaching a bend and seeing a lone wolf standing sentinel on a ridge, apparently keeping a watchful eye on me as I paddled along below. This wolf had a creamy, blondish-white coat, differing from the purer white ones I'd become accustomed to seeing. This wolf also seemed more alert and watchful, as if it had encountered humans before. This was probable, since in midsummer the Thelon attracts parties of canoeists who normally get dropped by floatplane somewhere on its upper reaches. In late summer, with the fierce winds and shorter days, few chance paddling it.

As I finished rounding the bend I saw why the wolf had been keeping an eye out—down below on the willow-covered bank stood four little wolf pups, their mother a few feet away. They all had the same creamy-blond fur as the wolf up on the ridge. When the pups saw me they immediately scattered, diving into some willows. The pups' reaction had been so swift that it seemed rehearsed, as if their parents had trained them in exactly what to do on any hint of danger. Their mother, meanwhile, was very brave: she came right down to the shore and growled in my direction. I wish I could have told them they had nothing to fear from me. Then she tipped her head back and howled. This brought her mate down from the ridge. The whole performance filled me with awe: I admired how brave and devoted they seemed, putting themselves squarely between the hidden pups and me. As I continued drifting downstream on the current the female wolf actually followed me along the bank, keeping an eye on me, while the father remained with the pups. But then one of the pups squirmed out of the willows and came right out into the open on shore, looking at me curiously as I drifted away.

Whatever happened in the miles that still lay ahead—fierce winds that might strand me for weeks, swamping in frigid rapids, winter closing in before I could reach the finish line—seemed but a small matter to have seen wolves up close in the wild. Watching that family of wolves had felt almost magical, an experience I knew I would always cherish. It's the kind of thing that I hope remains possible in a world that leaves fewer and fewer wild places for wolves to roam.

At camp that night, I tallied up the day's sightings: a moose, a caribou, two eagles, six wolves, a red fox, a dozen tundra swans, and no humans. That's what I think anyone would agree is a successful day. To cap it off, I'd paddled for thirteen hours and slept on a beach overlooking the river.

✴

The nights were growing darker, with the sun completely disappearing for four or five hours below the horizon. Signs of the changing season were now everywhere. As I paddled my lonely way downriver, flocks of snow geese passed overhead heading south. The scenery had continued to change, too, with great hills splashed with red, gold, and green as the autumn transformed the land into a colourful quilt.

But by afternoon the skies had turned dark and dismal, altering the mood of the landscape; with its high ridges and rocky shores, it now seemed a dreary place. The river here was only about three hundred metres wide and enclosed by high gravel banks. Ahead I could hear the roar of whitewater.

Paddling through the rain, I approached the start of the whitewater in my canoe. They were deep rapids, free of visible rocks, but with big standing waves that could easily swamp a canoe. Naturally I decided to canoe right through them. By this point I had a pretty fair idea of what the boat and I could handle.

I allowed the main current to suck us down the centre toward the towering whitecapped waves. With my paddle I steered into them. The canoe rode over the crest of the first wave, becoming almost vertical as the bow soared into the open air. Then we plunged into the next wave, throwing frigid water in my face. I exhaled at the shock—there's nothing like a bucket of ice-cold water smack in the face to wake you up.

It was an exhilarating roller-coaster ride through these big rapids, the canoe flying up and down as I steered and paddled, with one eye on what lay immediately in front of me and the other on the best course farther ahead.

When I'd passed through the last of the big waves, I glanced down and saw that my knees were submerged; a considerable amount of water had accumulated inside the canoe from the wild run. A pack of matches sat bobbing in the canoe. Fortunately, I had extras.

I pivoted toward shore and paddled into a rocky area to unpack everything. Canoes can hold quite a lot of water before they sink, as I knew from past experience fooling around with them in rapids or big waves. Still, I figured it was prudent to dump out the water before continuing, especially since I knew I was nearing the Thelon's dreaded giant lakes.

These windswept lakes form a chain more than two hundred kilometres long. They're known for their treacherous winds and waves. Most parties of canoeists who descend the Thelon opt to arrange a pickup at the start of the lakes by floatplane or even motorboat shuttle, in order to avoid crossing them. Crossing them solo, late in the season with cold temperatures, shorter days, and violent winds, is one of those things in life that many people will tell you are best avoided.

That 1970s era report I'd photocopied had warned about the dangers of these lakes, noting that even in mid-summer gale-force winds were common. Of course, it was now well beyond mid-summer, so I didn't have to worry about those mid-summer gales. Instead, I could look forward to the larger gales of September. The report had also warned about the complex web of islands and channels that connects each of the big lakes, and how easy it is to get turned around in these mazes.

I reached the first of the lakes shortly after passing through the big rapids. This part of my route was also the one I'd studied the least beforehand, devoting most of my memory space to the labyrinthine complexity of the many dozens of lakes in the central portion of my journey. Plus, I figured, if I did make it this far, the thousands of kilometres of travelling up to this point would have prepared me to work things out once I got here.

As it happened, at the point where I thought I was almost at the first of the big lakes, known as Beverly Lake, the maps on the GPS indicated that the channel I intended to follow was a dead end. This gave me a moment's pause as I drifted on the current, seated in my canoe, staring at the map. Somehow I thought the map looked wrong: although it claimed this was a dead end, the perceptible current suggested otherwise. I took the shoreline to be not a peninsula but rather a large sandy island. I decided to stick with my gut rather than the maps, and chose to paddle down the allegedly dead-end bay. Four kilometres of paddling later, it was with relief that I came round a bend and saw a vast expanse of frigid water riddled with whitecaps stretching off to the horizon. (Well, relative relief.)

It had been the correct channel after all: the map was wrong. (It might seem surprising that twenty-first-century maps can still have errors on them, but it's more common than supposed. Not only do sandy channels appear and disappear with the shifting currents and ice melts, but even today human error and educated guesses remain part of the mapmaking process—especially in a place as immense as Canada's North.)

Now all I had to do was get across the lake. The wind was blowing hard to the north, so I decided to follow the lake's rock-strewn south shore. It didn't offer much protection from the wind, but it was a shorter overall distance, and with dark skies above, I wasn't sure how far I could make it before conditions ruled out further travel on safety grounds. Given the weather, it was critical that I stay close to shore now; risking any kind of big water crossing was dangerous.

About twenty kilometres of hard paddling brought me to a great peninsula, beyond which lay a collection of windswept islands. The winds had shifted as I neared the peninsula. To round it promised to be tricky, as I'd have to paddle broadside to the large waves that were crashing into its shore. I debated whether to attempt it now or gamble on better winds come morning.

What swayed my decision was the sight of thunderclouds massing on the horizon. The high winds would move those clouds quickly in my direction. With the fierce winds and coming storm, I needed to make camp—the peninsula would have to wait for morning.

The land sloped up from the lake to level tundra, which seemed aflame with bright red colours that had transformed the leaves of the arctic berries. Among these were dashes of orange and yellow scattered about where the little clumps of dwarf birch had turned out their fall suits. It was all wonderfully beautiful, although the massive storm gathering on the horizon somewhat diverted me from pausing too long to admire it. The good news was the presence of some rocky hills nearby; any bolts of lightning, I hoped, would strike these and not my tent poles.

However, for once the billowing winds turned out to be friendly, and to my great relief they blew the thunderstorm right past my tent, narrowly missing me. I watched it drift rapidly by over the lake. Rain and winds remained, but these I could handle as I huddled inside my tent for the night, warm and dry.

✳

I woke to the tent shaking in high winds and heavy rain. I shivered in the cold as I sat up. I'd taken to sleeping in my warm jacket again, with the hood zipped up. I peeked out through the door: the lake looked angry, with whitecaps ravaging it.

"Well," I said to the tent, "I guess we'll just sleep a bit longer until this blows over."

That didn't pan out the way I'd hoped. An hour later the rain had only turned heavier, and the winds stronger. The combination of the two allowed water to start pooling inside my tent. So I packed everything up, and just crouched near the door, staring at the storm, waiting for any break. I grew anxious about my prospects; I thought of those accounts of canoeists stranded for weeks.

Time was critical. But there was no way the peninsula could be rounded in such fierce winds and stormy weather. So I decided to set off on foot and scout things out, to see if I could formulate some alternate plan. A kilometre hike brought me across the hilly peninsula to the far side: the wind was still fierce here, but the lake wasn't nearly as exposed and so the waves weren't as much of a factor. I concluded that if I could portage everything here I'd be able to continue paddling into the narrow maze leading to the next body of water, Aberdeen Lake. At this point, I'd hoped that all my portaging would be behind me, but with fall canoeing in the arctic I had to accept such unconventional approaches to things as the only way I was ever going to reach Baker Lake before winter.

Back at camp my tent was getting drenched; I packed it up in the rain and wind. There was no denying how miserable it was trekking with my first load for nearly a kilometre across steep, hilly terrain, and then down into a swampy valley. My hiking boots were quickly soaked right through. With cold, wet feet, I returned to fetch my next load. (Fortunately, on the way back I did find some cloudberries.)

Transporting all the loads up the steep hills and across willow thickets and swampy lowlands to the lakeshore was a little exhausting. But I felt confident my plan would work—fierce as the gusts were, bypassing the open part of the lake should enable me to continue.

When I had everything across I ate two energy bars, switched out of my drenched boots and socks into some dry ones and my waders, then set off paddling hard.

The wind was brutally fierce, but if I could overcome it for just a short distance I'd be able to escape into the maze of islands, which would shelter me from the waves. That island maze snaked for over forty-two kilometres before reaching Aberdeen Lake.

Finally, once inside the islands, I found I could mostly paddle— except in those places where the twisting, confusing channels faced into the wind. Here the powerful gusts proved too much. Then I had no choice but to set my paddle aside, step overboard into the shallows near shore, and drag the canoe with rope.

The navigating here was among the most challenging I'd encoun-tered anywhere on my journey. The islands all kind of blended into each other, concealing passageways between them; to find my way I relied as much on detecting the current as I did on reading my maps. Yet when the wind gusted, the current could be hard to detect. I once found myself heading down a side channel only to discover that the headwinds had hidden the flow's real direction. I'd almost gone up a false passage— one that would have taken me into the mouth of an altogether different river, the Dubawnt. However, when I saw the current clearly, I realized my mistake, and paddled back to the far shore, finding the right passage.

In the midst of all this wading and dragging I felt my left wader suddenly filling with freezing water. The spruce-gum patch had punc-tured. There wasn't anything I could do about it at the moment; no spruce trees were anywhere near here—so I ignored it and kept going. At least my other foot was still dry.

That lasted about twenty minutes. Then my right wader sprang a leak and flooded. This was harder to ignore, but I chalked it up to one of those days we all sometimes suffer. You know the sort, when noth-ing seems to go in your favour. It was just one of those days.

My progress against the bitter winds was painfully slow, and by the time I set up camp that evening I'd made it only about halfway through the island maze. I had to stop a bit early in order to take care of my gear. With both sets of my footwear, the hiking boots and waders, now soaked, I was in a dreaded predicament I'd so far avoided on my journey. My cargo pants and tent were also wet from wading and the rain. Further complicating matters were the nightly temperatures that were starting to drop down to freezing.

To take care of things, I pitched my drenched tent without the fly, letting the wind rush through it to dry it out. My pants I strung up on a paddle and my hiking boots I placed on the overturned canoe to dry as best they could. I also had, as a sort of backup measure, baby powder in my first aid kit; I sprinkled it in my hiking boots to help absorb the moisture. Whether it'd work or not I didn't know, but just now I wanted to believe it might.

The more difficult question was how to get the waders dry. The best I could do was prop them up with rocks and let the wind inflate them. This worked tolerably well. Fortunately, stashed away in my backpack was a secret weapon I'd been saving: a pair of *eighty-dollar* waterproof Gore-Tex socks. These magical things I'd owned for years and had never used—judging it wise to save them for when it really counted.

The rough days ahead, I had a strong feeling, were going to be that time.

× 20 ×

THE STORMS OF SEPTEMBER

Frost blanketing my tent greeted me the next morning. Those terrible words—*winter is coming*—were in my head again. Ahead of me, beyond the island maze, lay the frightening expanse of Aberdeen Lake: over seventy kilometres of open water to paddle across in what were likely to be big waves and fierce winds.

I began by pulling on dry wool socks, then putting the Gore-Tex socks over them as an outer layer to keep them dry. Next I strapped on my hip waders, which were still damp in the boots, although with my magic socks that didn't matter. I wore three layers to protect me from the cold winds: my warm wool-blend base layer, my fleece sweater and cargo pants, and finally my outer rain pants, warm waterproof jacket, toque, and gloves.

With the canoe repacked, I pushed off. Stiff headwinds slowed me through the remainder of the maze; it took me four hours to reach the vast expanse of Aberdeen Lake. I found it a rather bleak and desolate-looking place, with stony shores filled with dark grey boulders and smaller rocks. It reminded me of the islands in the High Arctic where my friend Travis and I had canoed together. Looking out across the waves, I sure wished I could've had Travis with me now. Facing these waves, a strong paddler in the bow would make all the difference. (I made a mental note of this for the purpose of future trips.)

My plan was to hug the north shore: this might possibly expose me to more winds and waves, as well many bays, but the south shore had its own share of bays, and more critically, two gigantic peninsulas jutting far into the lake. Taking the south shore would therefore demand a lot more paddling just to get around those great peninsulas. So, for better or worse, I chose the north shore.

With the wind chill it was below freezing. I kept warm by paddling hard, riding over whitecaps, following the bleak shore. Some ways up lay a chain of islands; I drove myself on with the thought that they'd at least offer some respite from the wrath of the open lake. Wave after wave my canoe glided over, rising and crashing. In the fierce winds, my canoe at times seemed to barely move forward at all. I'd have to pick a point on shore—a jagged boulder, or pile of rocks—and keep my eyes on it to reassure myself that I was still moving forward.

By early evening I'd reached the islands. Things here weren't much easier, since the winds were still howling, but at least within their sheltered reaches the waves weren't dangerous. I camped on shore near the end of the island chain and at the start of a wide estuary. Some river I didn't know was draining into the lake here, creating mud flats extending far out into the water. Crossing seemed difficult, but that was a problem for the morning. In the meantime I made camp as the sun sank below the horizon. With the nights growing steadily longer, I no longer had the tactic in my arsenal that I'd used on Great Bear of paddling by night and sleeping during the day to avoid the winds.

✳

To cross the estuary a strenuous portage was necessary, as I couldn't drag my heavily loaded canoe across it, nor could I avoid it without paddling back some ways around islands. It was a slow start to the day, sweating as I sunk into the wet clay, hauling everything a kilometre to water deep enough to paddle. On the bright side, it let me stretch my legs before getting into the canoe.

Once I was across it, I was back on the lake facing waves. For safety I kept as close to shore as I could, but too close and the surf was a little much. Frequently there were considerable bays along the north shore; some of these I chanced cutting across. It was a little bit dicey, given the waves were generally massive; I rode over whitecaps while paddling as fast as my arms would allow. What gave me the most worry was that a sudden uptick in the winds might catch me far offshore in the middle of a bay. The hardest parts were rounding rocky points, where I was most exposed to the wind.

I managed to cover fifty kilometres over thirteen hours of paddling; when I finally stopped for the night I felt grateful to be back on dry land, even that desolate shoreline. After months of daylight it was a little strange to see sunsets and real darkness again. The night seemed darker than ever as I sat alone on the stony shore, watching the last glow of red dip below the horizon. Without the midnight sun and the singing and chirping of the little shorebirds, things felt pretty lonely.

The following morning dawned almost calm, allowing me to escape from Aberdeen Lake. I soon passed into the smaller narrows leading to the third and final expanse of big water. Navigating these relative narrows could be difficult, given the low shorelines of gravel and rock that blended into the hills and high ridges lying back from the water. They'd be even more difficult to navigate for the majority of the year when everything was blanketed under snow and ice—the time when traditionally most arctic travelling was done. But what told me I was on the right track was the sight of ghostly rock cairns overlooking the far shore— these were inuksuks, *real* inuksuks, ancient stone pillars pointing the way. I knew they were centuries old at least. Unlike the stereotypical southern "inuksuk" that has proliferated beyond all bounds over recent decades, these real ones didn't have arms and were composed of hundreds of small, carefully stacked rocks, as opposed to giant boulders. It was obvious that considerable labour had been required to create them.

It was another forty-one kilometres of paddling through smaller lakes and channels before I reached that last big expanse of water.

Halfway through, though, a gale rapidly materialized and pinned me on shore. These were the strongest winds I'd seen yet, rendering any kind of travelling impossible. It forced me to make camp early above a pebbly beach. My tent I carefully angled into the wind, securing it with extra guy lines and rocks piled on top of the pegs. The fierce winds did let me dry out some gear that had become wet from waves splashing into me. My clothing I spread out on the ground and pinned down with rocks. While letting everything dry, I found some crowberries to snack on.

Since there was little else I could do, I decided to call it an early night. But just as I was about to crawl into my tent, which was shaking rather violently in the wind, I spotted in the far distance specks moving inland along the horizon. Climbing a small hill for a better view, I saw it was a muskox herd. I counted about twenty of them, moving at a surprisingly fast pace. This made me a little anxious; I hoped they didn't come in my direction. If I could, I would have repacked my canoe and moved on to get away, but the gale kept me trapped where I was. On the other hand, there wasn't anywhere I could go that muskox couldn't go too. I watched the herd until it disappeared among the hills, reassuring myself that the muskox had been heading away from me. The only other wildlife about were flocks of snow geese that seemed to congregate in the narrows, but these didn't frighten me all that much.

The next day I was up at four a.m. to take advantage of whatever morning calm I could. Three hours of hard paddling brought me through some smaller lakes and then to a swift-flowing channel where a great bald eagle was perched on a boulder hunting fish. I zoomed along as rapidly as I could, admiring the eagle's enormous wingspan as it took off toward the penultimate lake of my journey—a frightful expanse of frigid water that stretched beyond the horizon under grey skies.

I took the north shore again; it had served me well across Aberdeen Lake, and I hoped for a repeat of that success. Across these new dark waters rose a mountain shaped like a giant tidal wave, a tsunami frozen in stone. High slate grey ridges and stupendous rock outcrops, ancient beyond conception, marked the distant shore of a bay I'd have to round. Closer in, lining the near shore I intended to follow, were dark cliffs, boulders, and stony beaches.

A mere seven thousand years ago, none of this land would have been visible—it was all at the bottom of the ocean, aside from the mountain summits, which just crested the saltwater as bleak little islands. Melting glaciers had at that time caused sea levels to rise, creating a vastly enlarged Hudson Bay, known as the Tyrell Sea. As I paddled under the unbroken grey skies through the remnants of this lost world, it looked like a desolate moonscape of rock and gravel, with hardly any hint of living things, no grasses, willows, or other vegetation.

In places my curiosity about the rocks was such that I couldn't resist going ashore to inspect them. Some were hundreds of millions of years old: ancient Precambrian rocks blasted by unknown eons and exposed in their present state during the last ice age. A little farther along a flock of snow geese passed in front of some grey mountains. Against the cliffs in the haze they looked almost like something prehistoric.

I couldn't see across the lake, the distance was too far, but large swells were rolling in from the south; fortunately my canoe rode over these without trouble. I kept paddling steadily, keeping my eyes fixed on the barren ridges towering in the distance.

Some hours later, I was surprised at the sight of a deserted fishing camp. Beneath grey cliffs stood a handful of ramshackle, collapsing structures of rotting plywood and weathered timbers. The wind had largely died, leaving a strange calm hanging over the land; the only sounds were the lapping of swells coming in from across the lake. Amid the desolation of the gravel and rocks the decaying structures assumed a rather eerie air.

By the close of the day I'd reached midway down a giant, rocky head-land nearly cutting the lake in two. The skies had stayed overcast all day, and now they looked increasingly stormy. The stony shoreline offered few appealing places to sleep, and the sight of three muskox grazing higher up on some grassy hills induced me to push on a little farther. At last, under a light rain, I halted to make camp on a decent enough spit of sand and gravel. I had to haul my gear a ways inland to reach it, but once everything was set up, it felt comfortable enough for one night.

✳

Cracks of thunder jarred me awake. A lightning flash illuminated the inside of my tent. I counted the seconds until the next burst: the storm was somewhere to the north, but a little too close for comfort. Another flash of lightning lit up the sky; it seemed the mountains north of me had been struck. I crouched to minimize the amount of my body touching the ground, which I always did when camped in lightning storms—that way, if you do get struck, less of your body will be grounded and your survival chances will be better.

Eventually the sky's fury passed away, and I lay back down to sleep.

By four a.m. I was awake again; my internal clock telling me it was time I was paddling. The morning calm was when I made my best distances, and I needed to take full advantage of it. It was September now, so I couldn't afford to miss it.

My task was to round the remainder of the giant headland I'd camped on. The end of this point, jutting far into the lake, promised to be a stormy, dangerous place. Paddling up the rest of the headland I sometimes cut across smaller bays, saving me time from hugging the shoreline. Crossing one of these bays I saw specks in the distance moving along the opposite shore. As I neared I began counting them— over thirty muskox.

I gave myself a break on the relative calm to drift in and watch the herd. At one point a big bull, with giant horns, galloped at a smaller one, driving it off. This performance the large bull repeated several times, giving me unpleasant sensations about what it might be like to be on receiving end of one those charges. As I drifted a little closer the bull came toward the water and snorted at me, though I was in too deep water to having anything to fear—well, anything to fear from muskox.

An hour of hard paddling later and I'd made it around the point. The winds had increased steadily, which made paddling exhausting, but fortunately the waves weren't too big. Still, once I rounded the point, I had no choice but to make a long detour back up along its opposite side to a place where I could safely cross over to the lake's eastern shores. In perfectly calm weather I'd have chanced crossing the open water to where I needed to get to, but not in the high winds of September.

The detour was a long one, but I was rewarded by the sight of some graceful long-tailed jaegers flying by. They're striking white and black seabirds with long tail feathers that dangle behind them like streamers on a kite as they soar across the water, hunting fish.

The jaegers weren't the only animals moving over the windswept shores. With excitement I spotted a family of three caribou, two adults and a young calf, trotting along on a ridge. On those rocks grow hardy lichens that the caribou feed on.

The wind had continued to increase, but once I'd traced the headland up to a point where it was only a kilometre across to the lake's eastern shore, I figured I could safely manage the crossing. The wind was blowing from the east, which meant I'd have to paddle into a headwind the whole way, so I rested awhile to gather up my energy. In the middle of the crossing I'd be about a half-kilometre from the nearest land. This wasn't much compared to the bigger crossings I'd done earlier, but in the stiff winds it sure felt like more.

Hard strokes brought me across the bay to the far shore, where I found the most chaotic jumble of boulders I'd ever seen. Boulders and rocks beyond counting smothered every inch of shoreline, extending up a low ridge far inland—leaving not a speck of soil anywhere for so much as an arctic willow to grow on. This went on for kilometres, a wasteland of rocks that looked impossible to even walk across without twisting both ankles. But nearly everything has an upside, and the raised, rocky shore helped shelter me from the increasing winds.

When I reached the end of the bay I had to turn into the headwinds, which had grown almost impossibly strong; at times my furious paddling did nothing but hold me in a standstill, like a hamster on a treadmill. I would have camped, but the shoreline remained an endless rocky waste, with nowhere to stake down a tent.

So I pushed on, using up the last of my strength to cross another, mercifully smaller bay. The winds were howling now—I needed to find somewhere soon to put in before conditions turned any worse. A little farther on was a small bit of tundra grass amid the boulders. I headed for it.

Under ordinary circumstances, it probably wasn't what most people would call an enticing campsite, but after kilometres of exposed rocks, to me it looked like a patch of paradise. I made camp quickly, securing my tent with extra guy lines to hold it against the gales. Across the lake were beautiful mountains sloping up gracefully to exposed summits, their lower flanks a blaze of fall colours.

With the tent up and time on my hands, I decided to hike inland to scout things out. There turned out to be nothing but ancient wind-swept rocks, so I figured I'd better head back before the weather turned any more severe. My ultimate fear was a wind gust would catch my canoe and carry it into the lake while I was gone, or waking up in the morning to discover that it had vanished in the night on a gust. I'd heard of this happening once to an unfortunate party of campers, though there were eight of them, so they could divide the two who'd lost their canoe between the three other boats.

Fortunately my canoe sat overturned just where I'd left it—but the sight of the damage to its hull, especially a big patch wearing alarmingly thin, wasn't very comforting. Ahead of me still lay dangerous rapids where hitting a rock could puncture the canoe and spill me into the icy, turbulent water. I knew that these very rapids had drowned past travellers. I piled some rocks on my canoe to help secure it in the winds and stashed my other gear underneath it. Meanwhile my tent was shaking, the poles nearly buckling from the force of the winds pounding down on the tent's sides. The gusts were freezing, and to keep my gloved hands warm I waved them about. I felt better after I'd boiled water in the shelter of some boulders, making hot tea and a freeze-dried meal. Tea really can make any scenario better.

The winds remained fierce all night, and this time the dawn brought no relief. With dismay, I stood on the rocky point and looked across the stormy waters at the whitecaps. A flock of snow geese passed overhead, apparently heading south for warmer climes.

All day the wind raged, fierce and cold, without a single break. Unlike earlier, here, given the rough shorelines and the strength of the winds, it wasn't possible for me to press on by wading and dragging the canoe with rope. All I could do was wait.

Lying in my tent that night, I thought I heard sandhill cranes making their eerie calls in the dark. Of all birds, it's the cranes' strange-sounding calls that have the greatest documented range, remaining audible for miles away. The sound of these calls echoing across the windy and forlorn, darkened landscape was really quite something. But I couldn't be sure if I heard them at all, or if it was merely some trick of the wind.

× 21 ×

JOURNEY'S END

Come morning, the wind still wasn't any better—indeed, it seemed worse. I'd been stranded for two days now on that rocky point, with no apparent escape. After hours of idleness, I decided to set out on another hike. Only a calm spell could help me now, but anything was better than sitting idle.

I promised my canoe and tent I'd be back in a few hours, then set off northeast to see whether I could spot where the Thelon River re-emerges from the lake. As I strode on I admired, in spite of the wind and desolate rocks, the beauty of the Arctic in fall. Across the water were alluring mountains composed of white sandstone, which reminded me of the quartzite mountains of Killarney on Lake Huron's north shore.

Eventually, the rocks I was hiking across gave way to more soil, where tundra grasses, bearberries, and little clumps of dwarf birches reappeared, adding colour to the land. As I moved through the birches, flocks of rock ptarmigans would suddenly flutter up from their hiding places. In summer, these ptarmigans have brown plumages to camouflage with their surroundings; in winter, they turn white. All of the ones I startled were white, which I didn't find at all comforting.

After I'd hiked about four kilometres, I spotted ahead, near where the lake narrowed back into a waterway with a perceptible current, a couple of small plywood cabins. They were perched overlooking a little cove and appeared deserted. As I neared I saw strewn outside each one considerable rubbish, with empty fuel cans, gasoline jerry-cans, plastic bottles, and odd scraps of plywood. The only inhabitants were mice that had torn up the place. Evidently, though, canoeists in the past had stayed in these cabins, as they were dirty and full of garbage, with graffiti on the walls. One comment written in pen noted that the winds were fierce. No kidding, I thought.

A little farther along, opposite the cove from these dilapidated cabins, was a third structure made of plywood. I scrambled across some boulders to take a look at this smaller hut. Coming up to it, I noticed a pile of rocks with a crooked, weathered cross sticking out of them. The permafrost makes digging graves difficult, so, traditionally in the arctic regions of the world, bodies are piled over with rocks. This one had been disturbed, and the skeleton was plainly visible, with lichens growing on its skull. It looked old. The empty eye-sockets were left gazing straight up at the sky.

Suddenly, I felt a little lonely. I realized my canoe and tent were probably beginning to worry where I'd gone off to, so I decided to turn round and head back. As I retraced my steps, trying not to twist an ankle, I hoped for an evening calm that might allow me to paddle again. Back near my tent I spotted some little brown birds: Lapland longspurs. They fluttered off, but it felt nice to have some brief company.

✳

September 4 dawned with winds that were slightly less fierce. That was all I needed. As fast as I could move I had my tent down, rolled up, and everything else hauled down to the rocky lakeshore. The waves might pick up at any time, so I intended to make a dash for it. Ahead were the closed-in waters of the Thelon's final stretch—if I could get there, I'd be free of the big waters of the lake.

My canoe I packed quickly yet carefully, knowing we'd likely be running through waves or rapids before touching dry land again. With my waders on I pushed the canoe out into the water and then jumped in, paddling hard. The wind gusted, pushing me back toward shore, but I shoved off the shallows and drove on. Strong strokes brought me to where the current became perceptible; I raced along, passing ancient mountains as I went.

Several hours of steady paddling carried me down the river's snaking course, through some rapids, then across a wide-open stretch where the winds were fierce. Once I'd crossed this windswept expanse I could hear the frightening roar of much bigger rapids. I paddled into a rocky cove above them and went ashore. I needed to go ahead on foot and take a good look at what this thundering stretch of river contained.

They were the dreaded Aleksektok Rapids, which extend for nearly a kilometre. As far back as the 1920s they'd been credited with drowning local hunters and trappers, and in more recent decades, when travel by motorboats from Baker Lake had become the norm, even those much larger boats had swamped in them with lives lost.

The morning clouds had dissipated, leaving the skies blue and the sun glaring off the torrent of rushing water. Despite my polarized sunglasses the glare made scouting difficult, it was hard to read the rocks and currents. I could certainly see that these were dangerous rapids, with a stretch of massive waves in their centre perhaps ten or more feet high. Nevertheless, it seemed that I could safely paddle through them if I stuck close to shore and avoided the violent water in the centre.

I returned to the canoe and informed it of my decision. I explained that the gouged-up, threadbare hull need only last us through this final rapid and then another eighty kilometres more of easy paddling and our journey would be at an end.

I'd run more challenging rapids before, but this was the Arctic in September, with steady winds and a bad noonday glare. Still, having come so far, it'd seem a shame for things to end badly here. So I left nothing to chance. I fetched my helmet, which I hadn't worn on the journey aside from during the arctic terns' air raid, and now buckled it up. It was actually an old skateboarding helmet, which I recommend over any other kind of helmet for this sort of thing.

With my worn, chipped paddle I shoved off from shore, paddling a short way toward the sound of thunder. Then I let the rip-roaring current suck us in.

"Here we go!" I shouted to the canoe, angling us as I did toward the right shore.

The fearsome waves roaring in the centre made my palms sweaty, or else that was merely from the thick rawhide winter gloves I was wearing. Some turbulent water smacked the canoe, but I kept us going steady downstream.

Then *boom*—a rock smashed the canoe's hull on the right while my eyes were foolishly transfixed looking left at the danger in the centre, quite oblivious to the swift shallows near shore. This rock tipped my canoe vertically on its side—cold water splashed in, soaking my right glove that grasped that gunwale to balance it. A centimetre more and I'd be swimming, but I leaned to the opposite side, righting the canoe just in the nick of time. Not for nothing do I practise that kind of balancing stuff on little ponds.

The plummet through this long, roaring rapid was like a blur; we flew through more swifts, passing by low cliffs. There was some water in the canoe from my near spill—at least I thought it was from the near spill. But maybe that rock I'd struck had actually punctured the bottom—a final straw that broke the canoe's hull. If so, then my canoe was actually sinking.

I raced ahead paddling through the remaining rapid, in order to ascertain whether my canoe was in fact taking on water. A half-kilometre on there didn't seem to be any appreciable increase in water levels within the canoe, so I judged it undamaged (relatively speaking). A few hundred metres more and we were through the final stretch of the rapid, leaving its thunder and fury safely behind.

I steered into the rocky shore and halted on the bank. There was only one way to tell if my canoe had actually punctured: I emptied all my gear, flipped the vessel over to dump out the water, then repacked everything and set off once more. Paddling along, there didn't seem to be any more water coming in. Finally I was satisfied that the canoe hadn't punctured.

From there it was easy. I paddled on all day, zooming along on the swift current. On shore I passed flocks of white snow geese flying over blood-red hills and herds of muskox beneath rocks as old as time. Elsewhere caribou grazed on ridges that were brilliant tapestries of white, red, orange, green, and grey. In the distance loomed big and majestic hills. On and on I paddled, knowing but not really believing that my journey was nearly over.

By late evening I'd paddled down through the last of the Thelon and into the blue immensity of Baker Lake, an inland arm of Hudson Bay that three centuries ago had been mistaken by explorers for the Northwest Passage. The lake is freshwater, but the occasional seal and even beluga whale swims up into it from Hudson Bay—as well as the odd polar bear, which eats the seals (and hopefully nothing else). Three years earlier local hunters from the community of Baker Lake had killed a beluga whale in the lake, and I'd heard stories of wandering polar bears coming near town where they'd had to be shot. But such things were rare.

I pulled into shore on the tundra beyond the river's mouth and made camp for the last time. The town of Baker Lake, population about two thousand, was still another eight kilometres farther on, but it was getting late.

The date was September 4. It had taken me only twenty days to get here from Sifton Lake. My concerns about being unable to match the pace of the paddlers who'd done that stretch back in the 1970s over forty days, had proven unfounded. Likewise the more recent speedy duo from the late 1990s, who'd been dropped by a floatplane near where my last resupply was and had taken thirty-three days for their mid-summer run to get to this point. I'd relied on some unorthodox methods—wading, hauling, and dragging rather than sitting out the bad winds, making thirteen-hour days of travelling when conditions dictated. But really, above all, I'd simply tried to be like a tortoise, with the mindset of "slow and steady" beats the hare. As for my overall route from north of Eagle Plains in the Yukon, I wasn't sure how that stacked up, since no one else had thought to attempt such an unnatural route.

But I was getting ahead of myself. The journey wasn't quite over yet, and a lot can happen paddling eight kilometres alone on an arctic lake. I reminded myself that the dawn could still bring some crazy weather, a bear could still maul me in the night, a muskox could still plow into the side of my tent, or lightning could still strike me down. There was still eight kilometres to go.

It was with a strange pang of sadness that I set up my tent on the tundra for the last time. I'd come so far and, despite the hardships, had so loved the journey—the routine, the wildlife, the plants and rocks, the landscapes, the wildness, the glorious skies, even the storms a little (at least when I was warm and snug in some sheltered nook)—that a part of me didn't want it to end. No stormy, icy lake I'd ever crossed, roaring massive river I'd poled up, ice floes I'd pushed on through, or pathless portage over chaotic rocks seemed half so daunting and demoralizing as the thought of what my email inbox might look like upon my return.

I lingered that night, looking over the silent tundra and the glassy lake—it seemed ironic that it should be calm now when I least needed it to be, almost as if nature itself was willing me to stay. A nearly full moon rose above the placid lake, casting an enchanting glow across the water. A good hour I sat there in silence, soaking in the feel and atmosphere of it all.

✳

No bear came in the night and ate me. No lightning struck my tent. No storm whipped the lake into an unnavigable frenzy. Not even a muskox bothered to come trample me. Instead a peaceful night gave way to a tranquil dawn.

Still, my heart wouldn't let me leave yet. For so long I'd wanted to get to this point—the end in sight at last—and now I somehow didn't entirely want to get there. For a second or two (well, maybe an hour or two) a mad idea passed through my mind of avoiding that human settlement, and going on still farther, down the vastness of the lake and into the saltwater of Hudson Bay itself, the very heart of the domain of polar bears. But the gales wouldn't allow it: winter would be here in weeks and snow and ice would bury everything.

But after months alone, you might well ask, didn't I crave real food? A hot meal? A shower? A real bed to sleep in? Maybe a couch to watch a movie on? Or even to know what had "happened" in the world since I'd been away? Sure, some part of me did, but the other part didn't.

I decided not to paddle into town that day after all, but instead spend one last day and night alone on the tundra, lingering where I'd camped. So I stretched out comfortably on the lichens beside some rocks, writing in my journal and enjoying some tea. I even made a little campfire with some dried-up willows.

It wasn't long before a playful arctic fox came along, staring curiously at me and then running and dashing around between boulders. This fox still had his summer coat, as if to tell me that winter really wasn't so close after all. Three tundra swans flew overhead, making their trumpet calls as they passed, as if to say goodbye. Some snow geese also flew in close, landing by the shore.

An arctic ground squirrel scurried about among the willows and rocks a few feet away from me. The curious fellow climbed up on a rock, standing on its hind legs to look right at me. The squirrel then chattered cheerfully, as if to speak with me. All the wildlife, it seemed, had come to say goodbye. Even a lone muskox wandered by on the tundra, though he was nice enough to say goodbye from a distance and not give me a heart attack with a deafening bellow.

The following morning, September 6, marked the end. I slowly packed up my camp for the final time, folding everything with more than usual care. My canoe, scarred and gouged but never punctured, I packed quietly on the water's edge. Then I bid goodbye of my own and set off paddling, though not terribly hard.

As I paddled over that last stretch I reflected on how my journey had actually gone remarkably smoothly. I hadn't suffered any injury worth mentioning—just bruises, scrapes, a few lost toenails, and muscle soreness of the kind any contact sports athlete is accustomed to. I'd had no illness of any kind, as untreated water hadn't bothered me at all; I'd never once so much as used my bear spray; my canoe hadn't tipped or swamped (though maybe it came close a few times); I was never really lost or turned around for any significant stretch of time; and I didn't lose a single piece of equipment. I'd completed my journey ahead of schedule, or rather ahead of what I had been pre-pared to do if need be; and somehow I even managed to come in slightly under budget. Reflecting on it all like that, I wondered if I'd set the bar too low, and if my adventures would seem merely dull to everyone else.

Two hours later I crossed the final bay and glided toward a place that loomed on the horizon like a sort of mirage—concrete and metal buildings, trucks, motorboats, and, hovering offshore, a gigantic steel-hulled freighter ship. Beyond the ship towered eight or nine enormous steel vats for holding oil or diesel. Floatplanes were anchored nearby and a helicopter passed overhead, likely flying to the massive open-pit gold mine that had recently opened north of town and that had brought heavy machinery, transport trucks, regular flights, and hun-dreds of employees with it.

I paddled into shore, gliding into a gravelly beach beneath a hotel and some other modern buildings. It all looked very alien, very strange; I hadn't seen a town since Fort Good Hope nearly three months before. It seemed incredibly dense, closed in, and noisy, as transport trucks rumbled through the streets and pickup trucks and four-wheelers raced about. I stood up in the beached canoe, balanced with my paddle off the bottom, looked around, then stepped over my gear and onto dry land. My journey was over.

※

I lingered in town for several days. No one took much notice of me—it was a bustling place, with lots of people from all over coming and going on account of the booming gold mine north of town. I maybe looked a little thinner and more ragged than the average miner, but there was nothing about my beard or long hair to separate me from anyone else.

I did take a few hikes outside town with some locals, and even went on a motorboat up the lake some ways. I heard there was talk of opening a uranium mine nearby.

My most interesting conversations, however, were with an old-timer I met at the hotel restaurant. (If you're curious about what I ate, that was principally just yogurt, which I craved mainly.) He was old enough to remember the old days—when Baker Lake had been a trading post and he'd been in the fur trade. He even showed me some black-and-white photographs from his youth and of some adventures he'd had travelling the land. Chatting with him was like talking with a history book come to life. I asked what he thought of the extraordinary changes that had taken place over his lifetime, and whether he missed the old days at all. He did, it seemed, but he surprised me by saying he hoped to retire to Edmonton—at least for the winters.

Conversing with this wise personage reminded me of Betty, and her dogs, Winston and Vicki. I wondered how they'd been. She'd asked me to let her know how my journey went, so I figured I'd call her and tell her.

With my journey over, for the first time in a long time I wasn't sure where to go next. I didn't really have a home to go back to: the only place I ever thought of as home was the woods, particularly the ones that surrounded my parents' home. Those were the woods I'd fallen in love with as a child, where I'd first learned about plants, animals, and the wild—the place where I'd slept under the trees nights beyond counting. But that wasn't my home anymore; it hadn't been for years. Since I'd left I'd drifted, renting temporary places in seven different towns in as many years, trying to find a place I could feel at home in. My current address was Sudbury, another mining town, and that's where I'd be heading back to, after a stop in Rankin Inlet then Yellowknife.

I wasn't looking forward to the long flights on my way back. I'd never much liked flying; it makes me a little nervous (I'm not much of a risk-taker). Worse yet, my canoe and I were to be separated, as I couldn't afford to ship it home. It'd be a very sad goodbye. But then the airline people, after hearing of my journey, offered to ship my canoe at no cost to Winnipeg, where, they said, I could make arrangements to retrieve it.

And that settled things. Four months since I'd met Betty in Old Crow and nearly four thousand kilometres of trekking and paddling later, my adventures were over.

I was headed home—wherever that might be. Ideally, I thought to myself, near a lake somewhere, with some forest, and birds, and wild animals.

AFTERWORD

Nowhere makes you feel as small and insignificant as wandering alone across ancient lava flows that were already a billion years old before the first dinosaurs ever walked the earth. Nowhere makes you feel so alive as on a pristine lake, the spray of cold water in your face and an impossible horizon to be reached with your paddle strokes. Nowhere I know conjures up so much enchantment and wonder as an ancient forest, with fragrant spruces and tamaracks, birdsong, and wolves that look you in the eye. There's a kind of magic to these wild places; the kind of thing that can't be captured in words.

It's a magic that's becoming rarer in our fast-developing world, which pushes back the wild a little more, year by year, including here in Canada. But it's still there, if you trouble yourself to look for it— you don't necessarily have to wander for months alone in the wild to find it. Look at that great old tree, that field, that bird, that squirrel, and you might just catch a glimpse of it.

I think everyone can benefit by becoming a little more attuned to wild places—even if it's just for a day, or merely an hour to "unplug." I'm asked how I deal with the stress of my journeys, but in reality that's easy. What's hard is dealing with the stress of a modern, hyper-connected world—traffic, emails, texts, social media, 24/7 connectivity, paperwork, asphalt, concrete, noise. That's stressful. But there's a tonic to it—take a stroll in a nature park, or sit and watch some birds, or if you really want, try plowing a canoe through ice. If you let it, it will work its magic on you: that's the beauty and charm of nature. It can help us de-stress, rejuvenate, and reawaken our sense of awe.

But that's also why it's crucial we find ways to preserve and restore wild places in Canada and beyond—from the vast areas of the North, to the very fringes of our sprawling cities and even within them, to the countryside and small towns, and everywhere in between. When we lose these things, we lose something of irreplaceable value and something indispensable to our physical and mental well-being; we lose the biodiversity of the planet—the magic of our world.

The solutions to prevent that are pretty much known, it's just a matter of will. And the first part of that is to care enough to want to change things. If this book helps anyone care a little more, or to look upon wild nature with fresh eyes, my journey will have achieved its purpose.

ACKNOWLEDGMENTS

It's perhaps ironic that for a solo journey, I incurred debts to a great many people for their kind help, support, and encouragement, without which my journey wouldn't have happened. I must thank everyone who donated to my GoFundMe page, or otherwise made contributions to my fundraising campaign. This includes Theresa F., Mallory Sheldon, Meg Sanderson, Cody Hancock, Kim Yallup, Barbara Davies, Michael Reaume, David Shoalts, Craig den Ouden, Shyrill Españo, Steve Chapman, Jason Garner, Barb Dyker, Steve Fechner, Louise R. Smith, Anthony Podell, Brian Costello, Alex Letkemann, Daniel Turko, Ed Anderson, Elaine Anderson, Larry Stern, Carl Cencig, Allyson Rowley, Kathleen Connors, Buddy Andres, Keleigh Goodfellow, Minor Fisheries, Bill Van Vliet, Laurie McNamee, Bill Guerin, Trevor Milne, AB Charty, Mary Pennington, Sheri Roy, Allan Schmidt, Barbara, Sylvia, Ingrid Kern, Stephen Black, Marilyn, Pierre Gould, Katie, Melissa Ruf, John Locke, Michael Stinson, the GoFundMe Team, Andrew Zyp, Curtis McEwan, Linda Ploen, Mark Mcnulty, Todd Shoalts, and John Davies. I also thank for their generous support Kekoo Gatta, Phil Ritchie, Rick Taylor, Clayton Smith, Todd Barber, Carolyn Botari, Connie Shoalts, and Paxton and Peggy Allewell. I regret if I've overlooked some people who supported me; if so, please forgive me and know that I thank you. I must also extend a very special and heartfelt thanks to Elizabeth, whose support and encouragement was very generous and deeply touching.

Without the support of these individuals and others, my expedition wouldn't have been successful—and instead, I might have a written a book on moss.

I thank also the Royal Canadian Geographical Society for their support, especially John Geiger and Wendy Cecil. Their support, encouragement, and wise words before my journey were much appreciated. I also thank MEC for their support and the expertise of their always knowledgeable staff. I'm indebted further to the amazing Nova Craft Canoe—especially Tim and John—who build the toughest, best canoes a paddler could wish to own. I can't recommend their canoes enough. I thank also Rocky Mountain Barber for their support and encouragement; if you have a beard, they're the ones to see about it. Outdoors Oriented in St. Catharines, Ontario, was also supportive of me, and their staff are likewise very insightful when you have to make important life decisions about which brand of tent or socks to choose. Alpacka Rafts provided me with one of their ingenious inflatable rafts, which I used when crossing rivers around Old Crow. I thank also McMaster University's alumni association for their generous support and encouragement, especially Karen McQuigge, Kris Gadjanski, and Allyson Rowley. And I thank Brock University for their support as well, especially Kevin Cavanagh and Maryanne Firth. I thank also my doctoral supervisory committee, particularly Dr. Ken Cruikshank, who were understanding of my leave of absence from research. I thank Calm Air for seeing my canoe's return south, and Steve at Ahmic Air for his expertise and the professionalism and excellence of his pilots, as well as Chuk at Plummer's Lodge for his kind support.

I thank also Barclay Maude, Marty Wojtunik, Francis Luta, and Patrick Cameron for their support and encouragement, particularly at the start of my journey, and Mike Reid at the end, as well as Francis throughout. Chuck Brill and Mark Richard were also superb. Chuck has been an outstanding partner on many adventures, and his wisdom and encouragement at the start of my journey were very much appreciated. Mark, too, I owe a debt of gratitude; he also helped and encouraged me at the beginning of my journey, which meant a lot, and his generosity extended even to giving me his own hiking boots, which I wore throughout my journey. Alas, I'd return them now, but fear that would be a very inadequate thanks for what I owe him. I thank also my friends Wes Crowe, Travis Hill, and Chad Rumsby for their encouragement. Chad, especially, I thank for his kind gift of goose jerky. I further thank my family for their support and encouragement; especially my brother, Ben, and my father, for helping ship my things to Yellowknife. There were many others who assisted or encouraged me with kind messages or emails; I thank everyone who wished me well.

On the book side of things, I was fortunate to benefit from the expertise and professionalism of a great team at Penguin Random House. Nick Garrison has now edited three of my books, and as always, his keen insights and clear vision has greatly helped to improve things. More than that, it was actually Nick who, years ago, made a gift of a fine paddle to me—the paddle I ended up using on my journey, so that makes me indebted to him twice over. Samantha Church handled the book's publicity, while David Ross, the managing editor, kept everything on schedule and running smoothly. Jennifer Griffiths did a superb job designing the book's cover, layout, and maps. I'm thankful to each of them for all their hard work. I also thank Nicole Winstanley, the publisher, for believing in this story, and Scott Loomer, the sales director who helped it find its way to readers. The copyeditor, Karen Alliston, carefully scrutinized the manuscript and helped correct errors. I'm much in her debt for her keen insights and careful attention to detail. Justin Stoller, the assistant editor, helped on a number of fronts and his attention to detail was also very much appreciated. I'm also lucky to have a great literary agent, Rick Broadhead, whose excellence and encouragement has been indispensable to me.

Above all, I must thank Aleksia for her invaluable assistance in all manner of things, from educating me about electronic equipment, to the use of satellite phones, to logistical support, to insightful editing, and much else. So highly do I esteem her that I asked her to marry me. But that's a story for another time.

© Aleksia Wiatr

ADAM SHOALTS has been called one of Canada's greatest living explorers. He is also an historian, archaeologist, and geographer, and in 2018 was named Explorer-in-Residence of the Royal Canadian Geographical Society. Shoalts holds a Ph.D. from McMaster University where his research examined the influence Indigenous oral traditions had on fur traders in the subarctic and Pacific Northwest. He has done archaeology in four countries and enjoys long walks in the woods.